Alison Sehmi

Glad to Be Me
A journey into Life

Glad To Be Me
A journey into Life
Copyright © 2014 Alison Sehmi
The right of Alison Sehmi to be identified as the author of this work
has been asserted by her in accordance with the
Copyright Designs and Patent Act 1988

Published by Alison Sehmi
ISBN 978-0-9930799-0-0

All Rights Reserved.
No part of this publication may be reproduced or
transmitted in any form or by any means,
electronic or mechanical including photocopying,
recording, or any information storage and retrieval system,
without permission in writing from the author/publisher.

Scripture quotations taken from the HOLY BIBLE.
NEW INTERNATIONAL VERSION.
Copyright © 1973, 1978, 1984 by International Bible Society.
Used by permission of Hodder and Stoughton,
a member of Hodder Headline Ltd.
All rights reserved.

Printed by Verité CM Ltd
West Sussex, UK

Cover Photo Copyright © Pritt Sehmi 2014

**This book is dedicated to all those friends over the years who said
"~ You should write a book! ~"
Thanks...I did!**

Thanks also go to the many people who have been part of my life and part of my journey, especially:

My husband, Pritt who is by far my biggest encourager to do and be all that I can and all that I am, and without whom I never would have discovered my hidden potential.

I love you.

Reverend Kenn Baird who helped me to 'think outside of the box'. My 'Timothy Course' certificates still hold pride of place in my office.

My son Aaron, for being a huge part of my life: may God swiftly restore the years the locusts have eaten.

My parents, for without them I would not have been born and this story would never have been written:

- Mum, for your love and always doing what you thought was right.

-Dad, for your thoughtfulness, support and acceptance of me.

My sister who introduced me to Jesus my Saviour and sang Keith Green songs (loudly) to get me out of bed for Church on Sunday mornings!

The Sehmi clan, scattered far and wide, who all came together to be part of our Wedding Day and in doing so made it even more special. My acceptance into the family will not ever be forgotten.

Kay and Salomon Joubert, for being spiritual parents to Aaron and myself and for your support at crucial times… but most of all for just being my friends (and my 'sister').

Verité CM for helping me realise my dream.

But mostly to Jesus, my Saviour without whom this story would have had a very different, and darker ending.
May His story of love, grace and redemption shine through these pages.

All events depicted in this book are true to the best of my memory.
However, some names have been changed to protect the individuals concerned.

Contents

Chapter 1	Early Years	7
Chapter 2	The Dump	15
Chapter 3	My Family	24
Chapter 4	Adolescence and Anguish	34
Chapter 5	Working Girl	45
Chapter 6	Pony Passion	52
Chapter 7	On The Up	69
Chapter 8	'Pilgies'	78
Chapter 9	Rollercoaster Ride	85
Chapter 10	Animal Antics	94
Chapter 11	Unexpected Turns	103
Chapter 12	Old Ladies and Cheeky Squirrels	113
Chapter 13	Biker Chick	125
Chapter 14	Where Past and Present Meet	134
Chapter 15	Parenthood	143
Chapter 16	Learning Through Life	151
Chapter 17	Water Company	159
Chapter 18	A New Direction	165
Chapter 19	The Promised Land	175
Chapter 20	Liberty and Theology	185
Chapter 21	Christmas Blessings	197
Chapter 22	Ruth	205
Chapter 23	Friends In Low Places	210
Chapter 24	Run A Straight Race	220
Chapter 25	And God Was In The Whirlwind	233
Chapter 26	A Fair Swap	244
Chapter 27	Guernsey Weetabix	254
Chapter 28	Footprints In The Sand	266

Chapter 1
EARLY YEARS

Picture the Scene:
The High Street, Guernsey: It's the late 1960's, and people are bustling about on the picturesque cobbled street, flanked by shops of the likes of Woolworths, Liptons and Boots. A middle-aged upper class woman approaches a pushchair being steered by a young mum, and looks down into the upturned cherubic face of its small passenger.
"Helleow," she croons haughtily, her accent denoting a silver spoon at birth. Surprised, but unperturbed, the little angel looks up at her and answers back with an endearing smile – and a perfect echo...
"Helleow."
Time stands still.
The poor woman turns puce and after exclaiming, "Well!" in utter disbelief and disgust, marches briskly away, her back ramrod straight in disapproval. Meanwhile the child's mother attempts to apologise, but is unable to disguise her humorous view of the situation due to the tears of laughter running down her face. Welcome to my world.

I loudly announced my arrival on planet Earth very early on November 23rd 1966 at the Amherst Maternity Hospital on the beautiful Island of Guernsey: a paradise of golden sandy beaches, stunning cliff walks and quiet lanes where daffodils, snowdrops, buttercups and a whole host of other sweet smelling flowers arrest your senses; where fluorescent mesembryanthemums' vibrant colours glow in the sun; an island where time stands still and the air is fresh; an ideal place for a child to explore life and grow.

The youngest of two girls by three years, I was everything my sister wasn't: cheeky and mischievous and an insecure extrovert with a touch of lazy-itis. We were both blonde haired and blue-eyed, but that is where the similarities stopped. As a baby she would stay where she was put, sitting prettily in her pram for all to admire when Mum took her out, while I, to my mother's dismay a few years later, managed to end up upside down, with my blanket on the floor, my shoes off and my hat strewn diagonally over my face before we had crossed the threshold of the front door. She, a china doll with delicate features, pirouetted through childhood, apparently sailing though life's problems as on eagles' wings. Petite and pretty, she danced daintily at ballet classes and charmed everyone she met with her shy smile. I, on the other hand was a chubby child with two left feet and a lisp, who ricocheted through life like a pinball, never quite understanding why and unable to stop. I lived from one hug to the next and was eager to please to the point of desperation. In contrast, my favourite word was 'NO' and I could muster up a bottom lip you could perch a pterodactyl on. I was exasperating and lovable at the same time, a complex bundle of affection and wilfulness that clashed constantly. It was only as we became older that I realised that my sister and I weren't that dissimilar – we just dealt with life differently.

Nevertheless, I had a happy early childhood, with many fond memories. My father was a good provider, often working many long hours to care materially for his family, although this meant that he wasn't home much during my earliest years; often leaving in the mornings before my sister or I were awake and returning after we had gone to bed. The only regret I have is that it took until I was in my 20s before I really appreciated my dad and understood what sacrifices he had made for the sake of his family. My mother was a stay-at-home mum, as many were in the Sixties, and nurtured her little family with love and wisdom, becoming a valued friend for both my sister and I over the years.

My first school, Vauvert Infant School, was situated a

mere ten minute walk from our house, and herein lies my first recollection of the aforementioned lazy streak. Not only did I dislike walking, I was very adept at vocalising the fact. My mum called it 'whining'. I prefer to call it 'gently advocating my aversion'. I was excited about starting 'big school' until I found out that I had to walk there and back. I was horrified! There and back? Well, as far as I was concerned nothing was going to make me go. I was adamant about that fact and thought up every excuse to stay at home.

"I don't feel well...."

"I'm tired..."

"I've got leg ache..."

"I've got ear ache..."

"You'll get a bum ache in a minute..." would come the exasperated warning.

At an impasse with my stubbornness, Mum strived for a solution. Eventually, as I was too big to carry and too heavy to drag along the road, she had a brainwave and allowed me to stand on the back of my old pushchair while she wheeled me to school on my first day. It was a success. I wouldn't sit in it – that was for babies - but I was quite happy to be chauffeured around like a princess!

However, once we rounded the corner at the top of the hill and were in sight of the school, I got cold feet and decided that actually, I really didn't want to go after all. Jumping off the back of the pushchair and mutinously standing my ground, I put on my most defiant face and threw the biggest tantrum I could muster. Finally, after all forms of bribery and threats had been exhausted, my sister was sent down to the school on a rescue mission. She returned with my new form teacher (much to my mother's embarrassment) who bodily picked me up and carried me down the hill, still shrieking, through the school gates and into my first experience of education. I would love to say that things improved from then on – but, alas, they didn't. At home time we had the whole commotion again, but this time in reverse – with me screaming and hollering, as Mum bodily carried me out of the school gates: I had loved my first day at school so much I did not want to go home. This became a pattern for the next year.

As a younger sister, everywhere I went my older sister had gone before – if you are a younger sibling, you will know what I mean. What a shock it must have been for her previous teachers to be faced with me! My first teacher, Mrs Gradwell, was an amazing influence on my young mind. During that year I developed a love for learning that I have never really lost - despite my best efforts. She was my hero and I followed her around like a little puppy, which usually meant I was often getting in her way. The day I took it into my head to 'help' her shut her car door swiftly deteriorated from very good to extremely bad, culminating in one very black thumbnail, squashed fingers, an inconsolable child and an absolutely mortified teacher. But days when you are young seem to wander endlessly, and those early school years were no exception. I spent many hours under the enormous sycamore tree in the school playground throwing 'helicopters' up above my head and watching them fall dizzily onto the pile at my feet. Fond memories of my first pancake throw (and subsequent rescue of the mess from the floor); playing 'tig' and 'kiss chase' in the playground; winning a race at the school sports to the amazement of all and guzzling the tube of Smarties 'prize' in one mouthful; drawing people with wonky shoulders and banana fingers and forming first friendships - are all etched forever in my mind.

Unfortunately, it was also at this time that I was introduced to the 'Monday Diary'.

Some person, somewhere, undoubtedly with no thought whatsoever, decided that for the first lesson every Monday morning each child was to write a diary describing what he or she had done over the weekend. That sounds like fun – but my sister and I spent every Saturday night and all of Sunday with our grandparents. We absolutely loved going and we adored our grandparents but you can only write about watching 'The Golden Shot' and 'Mr and Mrs' on TV with Granddad on Saturday night, and taking the same dog to the same common for the same walk every Sunday so many times. Obviously, it was time to initiate Mrs Gradwell into the delights of my very fertile imagination – and I did so with extravagant abandon. One week my father would be a policeman and the next he would be a fireman. I wrote all about his adventures and spared no details. Thankfully, Mrs Gradwell recognised that I had a very active imagination and never chastised me for making up so much in my diary. Maybe she enjoyed the change from the usual "we went to the beach" or "we went to the park", which just about summed up what you could do in Guernsey when I was young! Interestingly enough though, sometimes fact proved to be stranger than fiction...

Situated in the English Channel between England and France, Guernsey is the second largest of the Channel Islands, Jersey being her big sister. Alderney, Sark and Herm, her smaller siblings dotted along her east coast, have a charm of their own: all similar but unique in their own way. My father owned a small (16ft) speedboat, red and white with all the creature comforts of a skip, and sometimes on a Saturday we, as a family, would travel at the speed of light (or so it seemed) to Herm, the closest island. We would cover the 3-mile distance in a matter of minutes, although having sea spray constantly lashing one's face meant that the entire trip was made with eyes screwed tightly shut and the view was never really appreciated! The weather always factored strongly in our trips out; as calm water meant that I ended up with only a mildly numb bottom when we reached the island. However, choppy water and medium winds would fill me with dread as experience had told me to expect to be unable to sit comfortably on the wooden school chairs for a few days afterwards, as I knew I would have to perch on the edge of the seat leaning slightly forward to rest my poor bruises.

It wasn't all bruises and bumps though, and the positive memories far outweigh the negative. The taste of salt on my lips, and the force of the wind blowing my hair into impossible tangles were par for the course, and 'racing the dark in' as we strove to get back before the sun set completely (due to having no lights) were exhilarating times: I still remember the thrill of seeing the pale blue sky ahead of us as the sun began to sink slowly behind the island, then looking over my shoulder to see the inky blackness of night creeping up behind us and feeling a wave of apprehension that maybe we wouldn't make it this time. But my fears were always groundless and we would make it into the mouth of the harbour with seconds to spare, waving to the Harbourmaster in his office as we slowed down to the accepted speed, although this usually meant that by the time we moored up we were in pitch darkness! Sometimes we would go a little further to Sark, 9 miles away and slightly larger than Herm, and my dad would invite a friend to spend the day with us. Often this would be one of the taxi-drivers he employed. Unfortunately I only ever knew these men by their taxi call signs, resulting in my Monday Diary stating, "We went to Sark with 'Whiskey!'" I dread to think what went through my teacher's mind as she read this, but I do know that my mum always had a lot of explaining to do on parent-teacher nights!

"What are you playing at? You could have killed us!"

We were returning home from Herm one afternoon and my mother was staring incredulously at my father, as he steered the little boat towards the slipway, where the Landrover was parked, trailer attached, ready to transport us home. She was a strange shade of white, while he seemed oblivious to her obvious distress and kept grinning at her in a triumphant way. You ask me why? I will explain:

Guernsey operated two ferry services to Herm, which were very popular with tourists. 'Herm Seaway' used ferries that looked like empty fishing boats, and which would roll slightly sideways, even in the calmest water. They could accommodate about thirty seated passengers and were extremely slow, usually managing to be overtaken by just about everything else on the water, (apart from dinghies and marker buoys!) as they chugged lazily across the three-mile distance. Admittedly, this meant that the view could be appreciated and there was plenty of time to study the puffins that colonised one of the tiny rocky outcrops on the way. They loved the attention and would put on a show for the tourists, flying at low altitude around the boat and skimming the surface of the water like flying torpedoes.

'Travel Trident' on the other hand, had Catamarans (twin hulls joined together lengthways), which could hold 150 people. These would travel a lot faster and there was room to walk around on board. Parties called 'Booze and Cruise' were often held on board at night, consisting of a crossing to Herm at normal speed, then a disco and 'booze-up' while out of the jurisdiction of Guernsey's strict 'Methodist' liquor licensing laws, while travelling at a snail's pace back to Guernsey. These started out fun, but gradually degenerated and were eventually stopped when people, under the influence of much too much alcohol, started falling off the ferry, or performing jumping off 'dares'.

This particular day, while slowing up to enter the harbour, Dad had spotted the 'Trident' loading up passengers, ready for another crossing and thought it would be a great idea to see if he could get his little speedboat to go underneath, between the two hulls. Unfortunately, he never mentioned his intentions to the rest of us so we were totally unprepared when, instead of steering past the 'Trident' so my sister and I could wave at the passengers as we usually did, he just yelled "Duck!" and aimed at the bow of the ferry. We disappeared from sight, ducking hastily to keep our heads intact and emerged unscathed from the stern, much to the amusement of the ferry passengers ...and the wrath of my mother. Looking sideways at her, Dad shrugged his shoulders.

"It was only a bit of fun" he commented, as if that explained everything and made it all right. My sister and I looked at each other, eyes shining with excitement then back towards the ferry moored behind us, and waved at the gathering crowd, our faces wreathed in huge smiles: we had thought it was fun too!

Chapter 2
THE DUMP

Our little family at this time lived in a bungalow affectionately known as "The Dump", the reasons for which will become clear. My father was in the throes of starting up a taxi business, which went on to become very successful, and had rented a bungalow which had garages - complete with electricity and a mechanic's 'pit' at the rear, and an office on the other side of the drive. The positive side to this was obvious. Everything was on hand, from the office where the firm was run to the garages where, being a qualified mechanic, he could work on the cars at any hour of the day or night if needed. Often he would work overnight on a taxi that had developed problems during the day to ensure it was roadworthy by the time the driver arrived for work the next morning. Once he spent all night knocking out a dent in the side of the car and re-spraying it, only to have the driver radio in after an hour on the road with bad news.

"I don't believe it! Some idiot has just ploughed into the car. It's a mess!"

Oh well, back to the drawing board!

However, being constantly in greasy overalls meant that he would often be mistaken for the 'grease monkey' by inspectors, who would condescendingly ignore his greeting and offered hand, asking him to fetch the 'boss'. He would come inside the house, wash his hands, take off his overalls and return, introducing himself and smiling at their reddening faces. One inspector actually took it upon himself, while my dad was making himself presentable, to inspect the garage unaccompanied: a place he had no business being. My father found him; a little worse for wear, at the bottom of the pit, having slid between the planks that loosely covered the hole. Physically, he had a lucky escape with the damage being limited to his pride becoming severely dented. He was lucky he didn't lose his job.

The negative side was not so obvious... unless you lived in the bungalow. It was draughty (our budgie died of pneumonia) due to ill-fitting sash windows, and the only form of heating was one lonely coal fire situated in the front room. Apart from in the heat of summer the house was never warm. It was like camping, but without the adventure trails and the singsong around the fire. It even had the big spiders to keep us company on cold winter nights. Nothing in the house worked as it should have done. The plumbing in the bathroom was from a different planet and the paraphernalia that we went through at bath times was a sight to behold. Close your eyes and picture this ...

Turn on the bath taps...no hot water. Leave these taps on while turning on the sink taps...ah, no water there either. Ok, now close the bath taps...Aaah, now the sink taps work. We now have hot water, but unfortunately, not in the bath. Now, turn the bath taps back on and close the sink taps...and Voila! Water... every time we wanted a bath! And I won't even mention the little wriggly things that sometimes dropped into the bath with the water and had to be fished out with an old sieve! The big white geyser for heating the water was no better as it had a fault and would never light with the switch. Situated on the wall above the bath it had to be lit with a match while the gas hissed out at face level. At the time, I never gave it a moment's thought, as it was normal daily life, but now I am amazed we survived long enough to grow up.

"BOOOOM!"

Mum looked up at my sister and I in horror and ran for the bathroom, just in time to meet one of the taxi drivers exiting the room with no eyebrows and smoke pouring from his singed fringe. The toilet in the taxi office was out of order and so, by default, the toilet in the bungalow was the obvious substitute. However, the toilet room didn't have a wash hand basin, so not only did we have strange men traipsing in and out of the back of the house all day, but they also wandered up the hall into the main bathroom afterwards to wash their hands. This driver was just one in a long line of drivers that day who had made the journey, but he had not been warned about our temperamental boiler. When it hadn't lit the first time, he had peered into the opening to check the pilot light was lit…and tried again. The explosion that caught him head-on gave him a lovely shiny appearance and unique eyebrows, but we were all aware that he'd had a very lucky escape. My father thought it was hilarious and I don't think he stopped laughing for weeks. Even now that poor driver is mentioned at family barbeques amidst many tears of laughter.

The front door was never used so access was through the old back door situated in a recess with three steps leading down to it. The wood was old, and when wet the door would swell until it became almost impossible to fully open. This, coupled with broken guttering just above the door, resulted in us running the gauntlet whenever it rained. Many times we would be struggling to unlock the door and force it open as the water cascaded down our necks and filled our shoes: my sister and I would joke that we had the only 'moated' house in Guernsey! But children always find ways of having fun, and this house was a playground for us. Because it was so awful, nobody minded what we did to it. The bathroom door had a really old fashioned hook on the back, to hang dressing gowns on, but we discovered it was much more fun to stand on the side of the bath, hold onto the hook and swing with the door as it shut, dropping to the floor as it came to a stop. This continued until the day we dropped through the floorboards. We concealed the hole well with the loose flap of linoleum, but this only fixed the problem until the next person ventured through the doorway (including taxi drivers!) The hidey-hole we had created later became a favourite place for our cousin to 'park' his Matchbox cars in when he visited.

Knock! Knock!

We didn't have many visitors so a knock at the door usually sent me and my sister racing into our parent's bedroom where we would conceal ourselves behind the curtains and spy out the callers: friend or foe.

Knock! Knock!

Jostling for the best position and subsequently the best view, we peered out between the curtains to see who could be calling, only to quickly draw back and look at each other in dismay, as the awful truth dawned.

"Oh no! It's —" groaned my sister, yanking the curtain back across the window lest we should be seen and acknowledged.

"Let's hide!" My suggestion was greeted, as usual, with a withering look, and we both sat down on the floor in despair. My parents had friends, acquaintances and relatives that had an uncanny knack of making us feel like the 'poor relations'. With hindsight, when I look at the conditions we lived in, I can see they probably thought we were! They would look disdainfully around as they sat down, as if they were afraid of being bitten by some unsavoury insect.... or my sister and I: we could never gauge which. And it was one of 'them' which we now faced spending an unthinkable afternoon with. Suddenly, the same thought crossed our minds and we giggled conspiratorially.

"We'll get it!" we shouted, running down the hallway towards the back door.

KNOCK! KNOCK!

"I'll open the door, you stand on the mat" whispered my 'commander in chief' sister. Obediently, I stood next to the doormat in readiness, as she turned the doorknob. Slowly the door opened.

"Now!" came the urgent whisper, and I stepped neatly onto the corner of the wooden surround that loosely framed the mat recess. As expected, the opposite corner began to rise, and as our visitor stepped forward and pushed against the door it stopped abruptly, rendered immovable by the risen woodwork.

The resounding 'THUD' that followed, as wood and forehead connected, sent us into peals of giggles hastily stifled by our palms. It was a favourite game of ours, one we never tired of, and it worked like a dream every time. Still giggling, we left the door stuck fast and ran back up the hallway into our playroom, pushing the door almost shut and listening breathlessly.

"Hello?" came our mother's voice, 'Oh! The door seems to be stuck, hold on a minute."

Fresh giggles emitted from the playroom as we heard the sounds of the door being opened, alerting her to our mischief. Unable to keep the smile from her eyes, but determined nevertheless, to let us know that we were in trouble, she continued, "Oh hello, do come in. Girls! Come and say hello to —"

Although our victim...er... visitor would look suspiciously at our angelic smiles while crossing the threshold, turning to inspect the door which now moved with ease, nobody ever cottoned on to our little 'joke' made at their expense, but would continue, with a bewildered air, past us up the hallway and into the front room.

Later on however, came the warning of what was in store. "Alison Jane! Come Here!" Uh oh, we knew we were in BIG trouble when we were summoned by our full names. But it was worth every moment!

The Bungalow had originally been a double fronted shop with accommodation behind and this whole shop area became one massive playroom for my sister and I. We initially slept in bunk beds situated in the corner of our parent's room, which was great, as their double bed made a fantastic landing platform when we launched ourselves from the top bunk yelling "Geronimo!"

"Are you jumping on the beds?" we would hear from the kitchen.

"No, Mum!" we would chorus. Well we were, strictly speaking, jumping from one bed to another, not actually jumping on the bed itself. But she wasn't fooled, and after the headboard had bounced against the wall after we had dive-bombed our platform…um… our parent's bed, from the top bunk once too often, we were exiled and the playroom then had to double-up as our bedroom.

The bunks were separated and I chose the east side of the playroom to sleep in. My sister preferred to sleep against the front door of the house as it had an 'alcove' feel (which upgraded the need to use the back door to permanent and compulsory), a choice made more interesting when the postman called. My father decided to put up studwork walls so our 'bedrooms' could be separated, but working the long hours he did, he never got further than the wooden framework. Again, this provided opportunities for new games and we learned to roller-skate through stud framework very rapidly – not to mention very precisely to avoid the splinters!

Growing up next door to a cab office was interesting, made more so by my father's sideline – that of hearse driving. He kept a large black hearse at the back of the garage, in the far corner, and it would peek eerily like a shrouded ghoulish vulture out of the inky blackness, casting spooky shadows all around it. I was petrified of it and would never venture anywhere near it. One of the taxi drivers was also terrified of it, along with anything connected with death, and wisely steered clear. However, sometimes Dad had more than one funeral to attend and so he needed somewhere to store the second coffin. Naturally, he couldn't collect the deceased from the morgue and then pick up the mourning family members with a spare coffin in the hearse, and he obviously couldn't leave it in the taxi office: it needed to be somewhere safe, somewhere out of the way and protected from the elements. The taxi drivers' toilet was housed in a separate building to the rear of the office: a single room attached to the main building but accessed from outside by a narrow, dingy, dark, unlit alleyway that ran parallel to the side and back of the office…an obvious place to store an empty coffin.

Nobody minded much and Dad only left it out during daylight

hours, as he could store more than one coffin in the hearse overnight. Well, almost nobody minded. One morning Dad had an early funeral to attend and so he had placed the second coffin in the alley, standing it upright so that it fitted into the corner and took up as least space as possible, then he drove away sedately to collect his 'passenger', blissfully unaware of the chaos that he was about to unleash. The drivers began arriving for the early morning shift, and as was usual, most of them decided to 'spend a penny' before setting out on the road. Suddenly the tranquillity of the morning was shattered as a bloodcurdling scream rent the air. Wondering who had been murdered, everybody rushed out of the office as this poor aforementioned driver shot past them like someone possessed. The unearthly sound of his horrified screams continued as he bolted blindly down the road, finally fading as he turned the corner and disappeared from sight. No one coming off the night shift had thought to warn him about the coffin propped up in the corner of the alleyway, and unfortunately, no one knew the lid had come open either. Therefore when nature called, he had wandered, totally unprepared and unsuspecting, straight into the open satin-lined coffin, in semi darkness.

I am not sure he ever recovered.

Mind you, having the hearse was very handy the day the link operator double-booked a customer who needed to be at the docks for the ferry home, and no taxi was available. Dad telephoned the customers, an American couple, with an original but remarkably simple solution. They were intrigued by the idea put to them and agreed. Therefore, half an hour later, they arrived at the harbour in style. The crowd parted, giving preference to the slow moving hearse, then stared open-mouthed as two American holidaymakers alighted, with their luggage, and began taking photographs of each other next to the hearse. Dad lost a fare that day: he couldn't accept payment, as the vehicle was not a licensed taxi, but he knew something they didn't. As the booking error lay firmly with the taxi company, had they missed their ferry, Dad would have had to pay for them to stay somewhere overnight, something he couldn't afford to do. Besides, seeing the incredulous looks on the faces of the other passengers as they watched the events unfold was well worth the lost fare!

Being situated only one road away from the Fire Station also had its benefits. The link operator would often call out to all the drivers when a fire engine was being sent, sirens blaring, on its way to a fire. One afternoon, the call came over the radio:

"Hey! An engine has just left the station! Some poor soul's got a fire." The radio fell silent for a couple of seconds. Then, a little louder,

"Uh, a second engine is on its way out..." And a little louder, " no, a third...wow! Some poor unlucky so-and-so is in for a bad time."

As the link operator clicked off the microphone the telephone rang.

"Hello" he answered.

"You'd better come home," said his wife, "The house is on fire..."

Meanwhile the next stage in our lives was gradually fitting in place. My dad had started building a bungalow next door to his parents and I remember standing on the foundations, excitedly making notes of where my 'bedroom' was going to be. It was fun to visit the site periodically and watch the walls gradually becoming higher, the windows appearing, and the roof being put on. Friends and acquaintances (and taxi drivers) with experience in the building trade gladly shared their knowledge with him enabling him to do most of the work himself. His father, who was a qualified plumber, also helped by installing the heating and all the plumbing. In all, it took six years to build, and when I was nine years old we moved from the draughty old 'Dump' to our brand new, double glazed, centrally heated bungalow on a hill with a view – and a proper bedroom.

It felt like a palace. No coal fire, no draughty old sash windows, and no lino on the floor. No water cascading down our necks at the door – now we had a porch where we could stand in the dry whilst fumbling for the key; a tiled bathroom; a fitted kitchen; a garden (ok, so it was full of building rubble, nails and weeds that grew higher than the washing line, but it was a garden nonetheless!). But the best bit for me was that I had my very own bedroom for the first time ever, with built in cupboards and wallpaper that I had chosen. The colour scheme was white with orange and yellow, so it always felt like summer when the sun shone through the window. However, the sliding doors took a little while to get used to, causing a few bruises on more than one occasion.

I loved my room. It was my special place where I could close the door and retreat into my own world, with my imagination or a good book. Well, unless my sister wanted to practice her scales, that is. Having a bedroom that was twice the size of my sister's did have one major drawback. The piano had to live somewhere, away from a heat source, and the most obvious place was… yes, you've guessed it…my room! And my sister made sure she practised her scales at the most inopportune times – like when I was about to go to sleep, or on a Sunday morning – early. Housing the piano also had other drawbacks – I was expected to keep it dusted, and I couldn't use the excuse "I forgot" when asked why I had not practiced my piano playing. How can you forget when it takes up an entire wall in your bedroom and you have to dust it everyday? Mind you, I rather think I had the better end of the deal, as my sister was an avid fan of Donny Osmond when we moved in, and she had also chosen the décor of her room.

The result? She had to live with a purple bedroom dedicated to Donny for years to come. I call it poetic justice, actually!

Chapter 3
MY FAMILY

My father is the oldest of three brothers, and as such, was brought up to be responsible and to continue his father's good name in the Island community. He matured from a young "Rocker" with a "DA" hairstyle and a powerful motorbike into a respected member of the community, but with a few hair-raising feats along the way, although he never lost the love for the powerful motorbikes! He loved anything mechanical and motorised, especially if it involved speed, and realised very early on the necessity to harness this need for speed if he was to survive longer than his teens; so he looked for avenues to live out his passion in relative safety.

On Guernsey's West Coast is a beach called Vazon, a long (by Guernsey standards) sandy beach, relatively free of rocks, and ideal for 'sand racing'. It was here that he discovered his hidden talent. Being an amateur sport, many of the cars that raced were hand-built by the drivers, and Dad managed to put together a car that would leave his competitors standing at the start-line with sand in their faces, which were green with envy. Some of his more outspoken critics were convinced that he had somehow broken the rules to make his car go faster, but there was never any proof to corroborate their jealous outbursts. One even went so far as to buy the car from him; take it apart, piece-by-piece; scrutinize each part; then reassemble it. It never went properly again. He progressed from sand racing cars to racing a motorbike and sidecar at the "Sprint": an individual race against the clock along the relatively straight mile-long stretch of the Vazon Coast Road, and the Hill Climb at Les Valles de Terres, St Peter Port, where racers would again compete against the clock one at a time, but this time up a winding snaking steep road bordered by high banks and granite walls, which demanded the utmost concentration if one intended to reach the top in one piece.

"...And here he comes now...banking sharply into the first bend... he's going great guns...and he's faster than his record-breaking first run this morning!"

George Torode, commentator extraordinaire, was whipping up the crowd as my father and his passenger raced at breakneck speed up the hill-climb. Slightly stretching the truth, he added, his voice rising in the excitement of the moment "...And as he takes the third corner, I can almost see the whites of his eyes...!" Then, without so much as taking a breath, he continued, "... aaaand he's coming back down the hill..."

Breaking down whilst racing for the title of record holder was not good, but after an hour of welding, fixing, and replacing, Dad was back in the game, and walked away with a new record. I loved to go and watch, holding my nose as the smell of hot oil and burning rubber emitted from the "pits" and clamping my hands over my ears as each competitor showed off, revved his engine and shot away to the roar of the crowd. Sometimes I would wait at the top of the hill behind the barrier by the finish line, so I could see the final burst of speed as Dad came around the last bend and entered the final straight. It was often the most exciting part of the 'climb'. Indeed, one race meet was more exciting than most as I stood with my mother at the barrier, waiting with bated breath for the first sight of the nose of the sidecar as it hurtled around that last bend.

We had been listening to George Torode shouting himself hoarse, his excitement becoming caught by the crowd as Dad gave the performance of a lifetime and we knew he was really pushing for another record. Finally he appeared, like a blur shimmering in the summer heat amid the cheers and shouts of his loyal followers, and we saw him change gear and really open up the throttle for the final straight.

"He's really moving it!" shouted Mum in my ear. I nodded and turned back as he hit the finish line, full throttle open. But instead of slowing down his speed continued to increase. Instinctively we both screamed and moved away from the barrier, which had suddenly become a target.

"What is he doing?" I yelled to Mum, as we saw him quickly look back at his passenger whilst seeming to struggle with the machine. She just froze and looked horrified as he plunged towards us and it seemed as if he was about to run us down, but at the last moment we heard an audible 'click!' and he suddenly swerved violently and screeched to a sideways halt amid burning tyres...just a few feet away from us. After what seemed like hours, (but was probably only seconds) I exhaled slowly, suddenly aware that I had been holding my breath, and watched Dad's passenger dismount shakily from the sidecar. Dad took off his helmet and came over to us.

"The throttle stuck," he explained, " and I was so busy trying to sort it out, I didn't realise how close I was to the barrier." He took one look at my mother, who had turned a strange shade of pale and grinned.

"A miss is as good as a mile, eh!"

He managed to acquire sponsorship from a local retailer and so, for a while, he raced in the colours and advertising of "Just Jeans", even making a commercial which was shown on local TV. Somewhere, someone probably has a copy stuck on an old VCR. I know my dad has! But, being a man who did everything to his utmost, it wasn't long before he was beating his previous records every single time he 'climbed the hill'. This stopped it being exciting for me, as it became a foregone conclusion at each race meeting that he would walk away with the first prize and another record. Finally he realised that he was missing the thrill of the race as no one was able to challenge him and so he decided it was time to spread his wings farther, and launched out into circuit racing in the UK. He raced at Brands Hatch, Snetterton, Donington Park and other venues in the UK, with the professionals – but always as an amateur – and usually finished in the first three over the line. He would have gone far with national sponsorship, but he was an unknown playing with the 'big boys' and sponsorship wasn't forthcoming. He also hill-climbed in France, narrowly escaping with his life after his passenger lost his grip on a sharp bend, launching himself into the space – and my dad into the French countryside via a hedge at 120 mph. He refused to retire, though, until he had completed the Isle of Man TT race, which he did a few years later.

Never one to shy away from a challenge, he started Judo lessons in his thirties and became the first Guernseyman to train and acquire his 1st Dan black belt in Guernsey – instead of training in the UK. And he did so simply because he was told that he was too old to do it. He was, and still is, a man known to be true to his word, honest and reliable, always ready to protect those in society who are vulnerable: women, children and animals.

My mother was the younger of two children, and rather a handful for her mother who was striving to bring up her two children alone in a time when divorce was frowned upon. Her passion was skating, usually in the road, as there were not many cars about in the mid to late fifties. Often the other girls would ask her to teach them how to skate, and here begins my mother's rather mischievous streak.

"Just watch what I do and copy" she instructed her friend one day. She skated effortlessly out of her gate and down the footpath that bordered the entrance to the housing estate, picking up a little speed as the path began its gentle downhill incline. Reaching the corner, she neatly stepped off the footpath, rolled smoothly across the road and came to a controlled stop at the waist high wall on the opposite side.

"Now your turn!" she called to her friend, beckoning her on with her hand after checking for traffic. Her friend launched herself unsteadily from the gateway and, with arms akimbo, made it to the corner of the footpath at the bottom of the incline. But as she stepped off the path, she was moving too fast and lost her balance, screaming as she shot across the road, arms and legs doing the "windmill of death" until she came to an undignified stop by hitting the wall at full pelt and toppling headfirst into the large clump of stinging nettles on the other side. My mother would have helped her if she hadn't been laughing so hard she couldn't stand. Later on a skating rink was opened at the St George's Hall on the seafront and she learned to speed skate and dance on skates, being taught by one of the ushers by the name of Cliff. Incidentally, many years later he also taught my sister and myself to skate and then went on to court my mum's mother, finally marrying her and becoming a wonderful granddad. Isn't it amazing how a chance meeting can change lives?

As you can guess, my mother was rather a rebel: that is until she met her dashing knight in shining armour and fell head over heels at first sight...well, almost...

" Who on earth is THAT?" the young blonde teenager incredulously asked her friend as a stranger appeared at the doorway and was greeted heartily by all in the room – all but the two girls, that is. They were at the "Bunker Club" so named because it was held within a discarded German bunker, left over from the Island's Occupation. The object of her derision? A handsome young man sporting a "DA" hairstyle, wearing a fluorescent shirt, jeans, winkle pickers and fluorescent socks... and carrying an umbrella. She thought he looked ridiculous and disliked him on sight.

They were married two years later, had two children, acquired a dog, and settled down to family life.

My sister was my best friend, my nemesis, my accomplice, my telltale and all that older sisters are, everything from 'bossy' to 'encourager". From a very early age I could not pronounce her name, and so she became known as 'Gaggy', within our family circle. She still is. We played together, laughed together, cried, schemed and plotted together. We fought over toys, we fought over dolls, we fought over skates ~ and we fought over the Wendy House.

Ah... the Wendy House. It stood in the playroom, proudly rising out of the floorboards like a fairytale house. It was made out of fabric, with a plastic tubular frame: rather like a tent, but less stable, and had little strings to tie shut the door and windows. There were window boxes filled with brightly coloured flowers painted under each window and a doorway set in a fabric frame approximately six inches off the ground, no doubt to create a kind of doorstep.

One day my sister and I were playing together when my mother was startled by a load wail.

"Whatever is the matter, Alison!" cried Mum, running into the playroom, to find me standing outside the Wendy House, teddy in hand and a lungful of air ready to emit the second wail.

"Gaggy won't let me in!" I howled, gulping back a hiccup.

"Let her in, it belongs to both of you" commanded Mum, sternly. She was met with a stubborn silence from within the House. Upon further investigation, however, she agreed with my sister that I should, in fact, not be allowed into the Wendy House.

I was blessed with short legs, which never really left the ground when I walked. This, coupled with a tendency towards approaching everything like a bull in a china shop, was a dangerous combination. I could not, however hard I tried, step over the fabric door step without tripping, a manoeuver made more disastrous by the grabbing of the door frame as I crashed to the floor, bringing the house down on top of me.

Therefore I was hereby banned from the Wendy House... and I resented it for years.

As we grew older, we competed in other ways. We both played piano, (often playing duets) went horse riding, and roller-skated and were often compared with each other by our family and friends alike. For me, this added to my need to be liked and accepted, and I was devastated if she was thought to be better than I at any of them. One thing we never competed in, however, was dancing. She loved it, and still does. I hated it, and still do! We both developed our individuality in our own ways, and matured at very different times in our lives. She was always levelheaded, cool, calm and collected, even as a teenager. I was impetuous, immature, easily worried, and too easily influenced well into my twenties, and I was often jealous of her ability to simply enjoy life, without finding herself a victim of her circumstances. However, time can be a great healer, especially with Divine help, and we are now good friends, able to recall shared memories of our childhood with many tears of laughter (including the Wendy House!)

I was blessed to have grandparents who were very hands-on. My mum's mother was a slim lady who always dressed smartly. She never learned to drive so her mode of transport was bicycle or feet, although she did progress to a moped in her later years, and she was very fit and healthy. Often she would come and take my sister and I out for pushbike rides around the north end of the island; sometimes to the beach and occasionally to the park. My sister quickly grew tired of this, but I never did and adored my little gran with her soft Southern Irish accent, her ability to make up silly rhymes at will (a gift which I inherited), and the table tennis lessons in her garage. She was as hopeless at table tennis as I was and we would spend most of the time ducking as the balls ricocheted off the garage walls and disappeared under the door into the outside world, crying with laughter until we couldn't stand and had to dash for the toilet.

But best of all was my Nan's specialty: hot water with cider vinegar and honey.

"Could I have a drink please?" I usually asked within minutes of being in her house and then I would wait expectantly as she nodded and reached for the cider vinegar bottle on the shelf and put the kettle on to boil.

"Oh goody", I thought, anticipating the tingle of the hot honey and vinegar drink on my taste buds. Days spent with my Nan were magical, with countless hours spent looking at the many souvenirs she had brought home from her travels around Eastern Europe. She had Russian dolls that all fitted inside each other; a large wooden windmill that, at the turn of a key, played "Tulips from Amsterdam" while the wooden sails spun slowly round; a lovely black jewellery box with a glass front, displaying two elegant dancers inside who spun round in each others' arms in front of mirrors to the beautiful tune of "Waves of the Danube" by the Romanian composer Ion Ivanovici. She knew how much I loved that music box as a child, and years later when she moved into a nursing home, she insisted I have it. It still sits on my dressing table in perfect working order and is played regularly.

We ate homemade lentil soup, or homemade stews; so amazing I can still remember the taste of them after many years. She only ate health foods and always baked her own Irish soda bread (in a tiny Baby Belling Oven that regularly burnt everything to a crisp!) that we would eat warm, and which crumbled so much that that we had to smother it with honey to keep it together. Every year for my birthday, she would make me a homemade fruitcake with icing dripping down the sides and cherries on the top. It never looked professional, but it was made with so much love, and so full of taste, that no matter how nice the birthday cake was that my mum bought from the local baker, it was my Nan's homemade one that I really looked forward to.

An independent lady with a "can do" attitude, she organised sports days for the bored kids in the local housing estates and lobbied the Guernsey government for changes that the island needed, never giving up until she succeeded. Guernsey can be very 'behind the times' in a lot of things and Nan was incensed that the 'Gent's' public toilets in the Town were open evenings and Sundays, whilst the 'Ladies" were firmly shut. She hounded the States of Guernsey for years, organising protests and writing to the local papers, and it was only because of her persistence that they were finally opened, originally only on Sundays, but then also in the evenings. The world, especially Guernsey, lost a one-of-a-kind lady when she finally passed away in 2011, at the ripe old age of 93.

My father's parents, on the other hand, never went near a health food shop.

Nan was a gentle, plump motherly figure who was a hug waiting to happen. Nothing was too much trouble and there was always a warm welcome in her house. Pop kept himself much to himself, spending his time in the garden caring for his apple trees, his bushes of delicate red and pink fushias that hung and gyrated in the wind like dancing dollies, and his huge purple, pink and blue hydrangeas. A Second World War veteran, he could be a little unpredictable, and would bellow "Ruddy Kids!" when my sister and I got under his feet. Nan often said that the man who went away to war wasn't the man who came back, and it saddened her. Sleepovers at their house always started with a hot mug of Ovaltine before bedtime and then being tucked up in bed. My sister and I were supposed to share a double bed in the spare room, but I was a fidget who kept her awake all night, so it was decided that she would have the luxury of a double bed all to herself, while I slept in the 'Zedbed' in my grandparent's room. Usually within an hour however, by hook or by crook, I had managed to contrive some reason to vacate the old hammock type wire sprung based instrument of torture, and was snuggled in their bed, in-between them. I slept like a log, fidgety, warm and cosy, although I vaguely remember hearing someone muttering "Ruddy Kids" during the night.

"Come on you two, time to get up. Breakfast is ready!" These words were music to my ears, as breakfast at Nan and Pop's house consisted of toast, smothered with a pool of melted Guernsey butter, which was then soaked up with spoonfuls of soft brown sugar. Having lived through a World War they had experienced lack, and now they made up for it. The cupboards were always bursting with food and they generously gave what they had. I missed those breakfasts when we finally moved into our house next door, as we no longer stayed overnight, but living where I could see them everyday more than made up for it. Their house was square and detached, surrounded by a narrow gravel path... a perfect circuit for bicycle riding, but it was a work of art to ride my pushbike around it without knocking over the tubs of strawberries that grew along the back wall, and without scraping the skin off my knuckles as I turned the corners. Many times I caught my handlebars on the corners of the house, resulting in grazed knees, bruised knuckles, a dented bike ... and many missing strawberries as consolation. But these were times of youth and laughter and life was an adventure to be explored. The driveway was an unmade dirt track, which shook the bolts of my bike loose as I careened down it at full speed, usually losing control on the bottom corner whilst navigating the end of the greenhouse and landing in the patch of nettles.

Mum and Dad would arrive in time for Sunday tea unaware that I had, once again, narrowly escaped killing myself, and stay to eat with us: salad, cold roast meat and ham, pickles, bread, trifle, and very sweet sickly processed cakes (the favourite being French Fancies) before taking us back home to our lovely draughty 'dump,' with it's cold lino and temperamental gutters. Looking back, it amazes me now to see how insecure I was, when I was surrounded by so much love and acceptance from my family, but sometimes these things are hardwired into our psyche, and it takes effort and a lot of reprogramming to pull negative beliefs out of our system and to begin realising how precious each one of us is. And often it needs God to give us the strength to believe it. Me included.

Chapter 4
ADOLESCENCE AND ANGUISH

"Help!" I thought nervously, seeing the large building out of the window, as our car cruised to a stop next to the playground. Settling in at our new house had also involved moving schools: my sister had started at the local secondary school while I had left Mrs Gradwell and my friends behind at Vauvert and entered life at Castel Primary School. I had always been an "A" stream student, so I was surprised to find myself placed in the "B" stream for the first year. I found out later that my new Headmaster and my new form teacher had decided between them that I would benefit from being in a class where I would be encouraged to grow socially and build self-confidence rather than academically as they recognised my potential, but they were not blinded to my immaturity and insecurity. Although I was well able to keep up academically with the rest of the class and could have been in the "A" stream, they could see that emotionally I was not ready, and my form teacher, Mrs Holmes, took me under her wing and nurtured me, enabling me to find my feet. It was a wise decision.

My first friend was a small quiet girl called Joanne who lived just five minutes away from my house. We played 'horses', 'Bionic Woman' and 'Charlie's Angels' together in the school playground, it being the mid 70's when Jamie Summers and Steve Austin were all the rage. Every little boy ran around in slow motion being 'bionic' with all the sound effects, while all the girls wanted to be Farrah Fawcett and tried to run gracefully, flicking their hair and talking into imaginary 'handsets' to 'Charlie'. They were good days full of fun and innocence. I, however, preferred to play 'horses' and would often gallop around the playground pretending to be Black Beauty with a classmate riding piggyback. One break time as I was being a 'horse' while one of my classmates, a rather chubby girl, was being the rider, I ran across the part of the playground that I usually avoided while playing this game as it inclined downwards towards the school building. I realised that I was running too fast and let go of her, begging her to get off. She wouldn't, so to stop myself being throttled as she hung on tighter, my hands resumed their original position behind my back to hold her weight as I tried desperately to remain upright.

But I stumbled, and as I felt myself fall forward I realised with horror that my hands were clasped behind me and that my face was going to hit the ground at running pace. I closed my eyes and waited for the impact. I didn't have long to wait as I landed with a thud and skidded, face first, another three feet or so, before grinding to a halt with my 'rider' still in situ. I heard faint screaming then realised it was me, as I lifted my face out of the bits of tar and gravel so prevalent in school playgrounds and the sound grew louder. Blinded with pain I ran, unaware of where I was going, and somehow managed to find my way to the doorway, where I was met by the teacher on first aid duty who, alerted by my screams, had rushed out to intercept the banshee. I was ushered, dripping blood from the many lacerations on my face, into the first aid room where she proceeded to bathe my torn flesh with almost neat Dettol. I am sure my fresh screams were heard the other side of the island. However, when my mother collected me at 3:30 I realised that they couldn't have been, as judging by the utter shock on her face at the sight of my injuries, I knew she hadn't heard me. Unfortunately the school had failed to inform her of my accident and so her horror at what had befallen her child was raw, and indeed painful to behold. I knew I looked hideous and avoided mirrors for quite a while. And it was a long time before I had the confidence to walk with my head up again.

Saturdays were my favourite days, when I would make my way to Joanne's house ready to embark on our weekly pilgrimage to the Saturday Morning Pictures at the Odeon Cinema. I would get there really early so we had time to play before we went, and we would play tennis using the garden hedge as the net and then play with her tortoise before visiting my paternal great grandmother, who lived just a few doors further along the road. She was a tiny, dainty little lady with sparkling eyes, and Joanne and I really looked forward to our visits. Although I did not know her very well, I knew she loved Canon Hall grapes, so we would go armed with a large bagful and sit with her while she fed us homemade Guernsey Gâche (a delicious spicy fruity tea bread) and reminisced. I was rather shocked to discover, many years later, that she had been rather buxom in her youth; well built and tall, as I only ever knew her as a rather frail elderly lady who stood only four foot high, and that never without help. But at nine years of age, life is thought of as endless and so we happily sat and ate and chatted as little girls do, never dreaming that she would close her eyes to this world and open them in the next in the not too distant future.

I loved Castel School and thrived under the care and wisdom that was practised there. I found my talent for writing stories and poetry, quickly becoming known as the 'class poet', and spent many hours in the Headmaster's study reading my latest piece of work to him, earning myself a choice of one of the many sweets he kept in a big tin. Many times I would emerge from his study and smirk at the scruffy boy who was waiting to go in. He was the school trouble maker and I knew whatever the headmaster had in store for him wasn't going to be found in a tin of sweets. I learnt to swim, something I had struggled with for years, and gradually became a good diver. I began to make friends although, always a bit of a loner, I often preferred my own company where I could be alone with my thoughts. I still am and still do. I discovered I could run relays and jump hurdles although I never made the grade to compete in the School sports day, as I always ran faster in bare feet, which wasn't allowed when trying our for the sports day teams.

Year 3 found me still held back in the "B" stream, much to

my delight, as Mr Le Page was a handsome young teacher who all the mums swooned over, and all the girls had a crush on! By contrast, the teacher for the "A" stream was about a hundred years old! I became part of the Netball team, able to score goals with an accuracy that was uncanny – unless I was playing in an actual match, that is, when my self-consciousness would get the better of me and my feeble attempts at goal scoring ended up anywhere but near the net. I was disappointed when I was placed firmly in reserve, but at least I still got to travel to the other schools for matches. My dad's taxi firm had the contract for driving us to the matches and, as it was usually him who covered those shifts, I spent many journeys ducked down behind the seat in front of me as we all sang 'tame' (ish) rugby songs at the tops of our voices. I never told anyone he was my dad and he never said a word either.

"Y… M… R… E… H… T… O… R… B…"

"What are you doing?" whispered Joanne.

"Shhh!" I giggled, still scribbling in my notebook, hoping the teacher in charge of the school choir couldn't see me. Joanne leaned over my shoulder to get a glimpse of what I was doing but, judging by her confused expression, I knew I'd have to explain.

"The words of the new song we've got to learn don't make any sense," I whispered, still giggling and scribbling, "So I thought I'd make them a little more exciting!"

"Oh!" Joanne exclaimed as the penny dropped, "You've written the words backwards!"

I hurriedly motioned her to keep her voice down, and showed her the finished piece. We practiced it during the week and at the next choir practice we both thought it hilarious when, while the rest of the choir were singing the calypso melody, " My brother did-a -tell me that you go Mango Walk…" we began to sing

"Ym rehtorb did a let em that ouy og ognam klaw" and nobody, not even the choir leader, noticed! "Yellow Bird", another Calypso song, (I think the teacher who picked the songs was dreaming of her summer holidays,) suffered the same treatment and became "Wolley Drib". Amazingly, nearly forty years later I can still sing them backwards, as my husband will testify (probably with a grimace!) but I am not sure if this is something to be proud of, or whether I need counselling!

By the time I was finally moved up to the "A" stream in the 4th year, I was champing at the bit, and more than ready emotionally to cope with the extra pressures. I will be eternally grateful for those positive early years and the space to settle in. I learned to play badminton in the 'after school club' and was entered in the school tournament. I was amazed when I made it through to the finals, but was beaten into second place by my new friend Beth. Beth and I both loved horses and one day she invited me to go with her while she exercised a friend's elderly horse. We spent many Saturday afternoons wandering about the field astride this old lollopy gentleman of a horse, having girly chats. But the highlight of the day was always going to her house afterwards, as her family were very different to mine, with an easygoing relaxed feel that reminded me of the 'Waltons', although it was a scaled down version!

The youngest child and the only daughter, she had two older brothers, one of which was her twin. Subsequently it was a very male-orientated household. The huge Hornby train-set that took over the attic room was accessed only by the loft ladder and was out of bounds to her, something she felt aggrieved over, being quite a tomboy. Consequently, if we were in and everyone else was out, we would make a beeline for the attic, climbing the ladder to stand surrounded by scenery, tracks, trains and signals, very aware we were in forbidden territory and keeping an ear out for the returning car. Thankfully the driveway was gravel so although we had a few close shaves, we never actually got caught, although I am sure we often looked guilty when we were asked, in all innocence, what we had been doing all afternoon and we had to think something up on the spot!

Unfortunately, life can deal unexpected nasty blows and events began to conspire to undo all the positive input I had experienced over the past three years, and to destroy my newfound confidence.

"You cheated!"

"Didn't, you did!"

"Didn't!"

Another break time and once again Beth and I were arguing. We had started attending the chess club run by our form teacher and we loved it, playing not only during the club times, but also during every break and lunchtime. However, we were not gracious losers and so every time we played, accusations of cheating inevitably followed, and the sessions ended in warfare.

"Right, outside now!"

And off we would go, to 'fight it out' behind the bike sheds, much to the delight of the other kids. I would arrive home covered with bruises on a regular basis, but was too embarrassed to admit that I had beaten up by my mate! Unlike me, she was very competitive and treated the fight as a badge of honour, whereas I just wanted it to be over so we could be friends again.

By the end of the school year, however, things had begun to turn really nasty and I began to be genuinely afraid to go to school. We had stopped playing chess and were no longer friends, but the negative atmosphere continued to make my life a misery. However, Someone was on my side and I could not conceal my delight and relief when, at the end of the term, I passed the 11-plus exam and she didn't, for I now saw a light at the end of a very dark tunnel that had threatened to spoil what had been a very positive experience of schooling. I felt so much a part of Castel Primary School that when the last day of the last term arrived, and I walked out of the school gates for the last time, I wept– but not in front of anyone. Peer pressure was starting to show it's ugly head, and I was still desperate to be liked.

The end of the summer holidays saw me, kitted out in my new Girls Grammar School uniform of Navy blue, joining all the other new kids at roll-call, waiting to be processed and sent off to our new form rooms and meet our new form teachers. It was all very daunting, as we were suddenly the 'little kids' again, after being the 'big kids' for the last year. The sixth formers were eyed with awe; they were, to us anyway, so grown up.

"Hello, I'm Maria. You're Alison, aren't you?" a brown haired girl asked me during French in our first week. "Yes", I smiled, wondering if I had a new friend.

"I remember you at Vauvert," she continued, "you beat me in a Sports Day race in the first year, in front of all my family. I was so humiliated; I never forgave you."

Hmm, not quite the good start I had envisioned! First year infants at Vauvert? That long ago? However, after I had delved deep into the recesses of my memory, it became clear. Every time we had PE, Maria had always been the fastest runner, and I could never beat her: until that fateful Sports Day when I won and guzzled the whole tube of Smarties in one go. Ah yes... now I remember! Maybe I should offer to buy her a tube of Smarties in compensation, as she was obviously still very traumatised by the event!

My first year there was pretty uneventful and I was a good student, but only when pushed, due to my ever-present lazy streak. Monday evenings after school were dull, as I endured a half hour weekly piano lesson with a lovely elderly spinster who did her best to encourage me to allow my natural talent out, something I didn't do until I was much older. It wasn't that I didn't like playing the piano: it just wasn't exciting like the weekends, which were full of skating at the local leisure centre, flirting with the boys, going to discos and horse riding. Then in the second year I acquired a new friend and things started to change. Nicole and I were like two peas in a pod. We liked the same clothes, the same boys, and had the same sense of humour, but unfortunately we were two bad peas in a pod and subsequently not very good for each other.

Back home things were changing, as my sister had become a 'born-again Christian'. She became a model student at school, changed her friends, and stopped hanging around with the 'old crowd', which included the boys. At sixteen, this was unusual behaviour, but I didn't take much notice. She and I lived in two totally different worlds whilst living in the same house, and I was too caught up in my own life, thoughts and fears to worry about her. Then one Friday she invited me to a youth meeting held by a missionary group from 'Youth with a Mission' (YWAM) who were visiting the Island from Spain. Curious, I went along and by the end of the evening I found myself raising my hand to accept Jesus into my life and become a Christian. I didn't really understand why, but I could see that my sister had stability in her life that was lacking in mine and that she was happier than I was, and I thought this 'Christian' thing could be why. I became part of my sister's youth group and church, who all accepted me with open arms but I was conscious that, as with school, she had gone before me and paved the way. Again I was known as the 'little sister' and it wasn't long before I felt the need to belong somewhere and be accepted in my own right. Although I continued to attend Church on Sundays I began to distance myself from the good influences in my life, and as I began to take my life in my own hands I found myself changing direction once more and knocking very loudly on the many doors of opportunities that presented themselves to encourage me to go my own way.

'Can you come to my house for tea on Thursday?' asked Nicole a few months later at school. Mum agreed and Thursday evening saw me at my friend's house, on my best behaviour, meeting her family. Tea over, we headed out for a walk through the lanes by her house, and this is where the real reason for my visit came to light. Nicole had a new boyfriend, a 17 year old with a 'bad boy' reputation. Her parents were immensely unhappy about it and had refused to let her date him, forbidding her to go out alone in case she met up with him behind their backs. Solution? Take a friend...

Robert was tall, dark and handsome – and he knew it. An arrogant flirt, he had a smile that melted hearts – and mine was no exception. However, he had no concept of what the words 'truth' 'honesty' or 'faithfulness' meant, and he left a trail of broken hearts wherever he went. I was obsessed with him from the first moment I laid eyes on him, and when he and Nicole broke up, I unwisely jumped straight in with both feet. We dated on and off over the next three years and the pattern never changed. I was addicted to him and worshipped him... and he never failed to tear my heart to shreds. No one person has ever, before or since, managed to wound me to my very core, whilst at the same time sink my heart to the very depths of despair at the thought of losing him. It was an unnaturally destructive time and the wounds from this injurious relationship went deep and influenced many decisions all through my adolescence and well into adult life.

At this time Mum and Dad were also going through changes, and were in the embryonic stages of separating. I was still insecure and my whole world fell apart. Although I still called myself a Christian, I felt totally out of my depth and began smoking and drinking, and searching for someone to love me. I knew I was going against all that I professed to believe in, but I felt powerless to stop my destructive behaviour. And then things became decidedly worse. Beth, my nemesis from primary school sat an entrance exam and passed, thus ushering her, like a Gorgon from mythology, into the Grammar School and my new life. She quickly became popular with some of the girls who I didn't really know and so the old pattern resurfaced, only now she had back up. It was an extremely dark time for me.

'Don't turn around...keep walking...don't let her know you're scared...' I kept talking to myself as I walked up the hill from school toward the shop owned by my parents. Unfortunately for me, Beth knew this was a regular trek and she would wait with her friends at the junction ready to intimidate me. As usual I fixed my eyes on the pavement and kept walking, never answering the accusations flying around, and breathed a sigh of relief when I was finally past them. Suddenly I realised that things would never change unless I changed them and I knew I could do this no longer. I turned around, looked her straight in the eye and, taking a deep breath, said "Beth, I am not running from you ever again. I am not scared of you anymore."

Then, with my head held high and my heart light and pounding, I turned and continued up the hill, leaving Beth and her little group speechless in the middle of the road. I honestly don't know who was the more shocked!

Amazingly, within a week, Beth began to talk to me and asked me about my 'faith'. I still considered myself to be a Christian, albeit a very mixed up, confused one, so I invited her to church that Sunday. To my utmost surprise she came, and not only did she come, but she invited Jesus into her life and changed overnight. I was excited for her, but mixed with that was jealousy, for she now had what I still didn't, and I didn't know how to move forward from that. I had never really grasped the meaning of being a Christian, although I attended church. I tried to live the right way, but it was hard work as I was striving to do that which only God can do – change the very heart of me, and I was very easily distracted and influenced. I struggled daily in my inner turmoil, as I desperately wanted to be all the things I knew were good and right, but I seemed unable to make them a reality. I decided to be baptised, along with most of the church's youth group hoping that it would somehow make everything right. It was a memorable day, but not for the reason you think it was...

"Wow!" gasped the Pastor, as he gingerly made his way

down the steps of the baptismal pool at the front of the church into thigh-high water. Having reached the bottom, he turned towards his congregation and his eyes rested on the thirty young people, (Beth included) clad in their white baptismal robes, waiting nervously. He took a deep breath, one that shuddered and shivered out of him, and as he began to turn blue my suspicions were aroused that maybe the water wasn't as warm as I had hoped. Then he confessed. Yes, the heater used to bring the temperature in the pool up to a respectable level had decided to break down and we were going to be fully immersed in ice-cold water in front of all and sundry...in November. After the usual jokes about looking for the Titanic, and corresponding iceberg, we bravely (foolishly?) took it in turns to give our testimonies, have a verse of scripture given to us and finally make our way into the watery grave (with audible gasps!) that signified that we had 'died with Christ and risen again with Him'.

The Scripture given to me was Isaiah 12 verse 2, which read

"Surely God is my salvation; I will trust and not be afraid. The LORD, the Lord, is my strength and my song; he has become my salvation."

I didn't know it then, but God was giving me a promise that was to become prophetic.

However, in the here and now, it made no sense to me, and so I continued to go to church on Sundays and live my life in opposition to the church from Monday to Saturday...and gradually, as I continued to make bad decisions, I couldn't cope with the guilt of having a double life, and so stopped attending church and continued living the same destructive way as I always had done. But God didn't give up.

Incidentally Beth and I met up again many years later and the only thing she remembered from those days was that I was the one who had introduced her to Jesus. What amazing Grace!

Chapter 5
WORKING GIRL

I had never been a saint, but as my parent's troubles spilled over into my life and all I held dear began crashing down around me, my insecurity was pushed to the fore and I coped in the only way I knew how... badly.

By now, Nicole and I were inseparable. Weekends were spent alternatively at each other's houses. We shared boyfriends, (but not at the same time!) the contents of her dad's alcohol cupboard (and what a disgusting mix that was), thoughts, secrets and attitudes, our behaviour often portraying us in ways that gained us unenviable, although unfounded, reputations. During this time an event happened that would shape my self-image for many years to come. Nicole's latest boyfriend lived across the road from me, and alternate Sunday afternoons would find us wandering about the lanes – the two of them joined at the hip and me tagging along. One particular Sunday we were joined by a rough looking lad who I vaguely remembered seeing, and smirking at, outside the headmaster's study at Castel Primary School as he awaited punishment. We nodded 'hello' and as I walked off with Nicole and her boyfriend he caught up with me and we began to chat. He was not the kind of boy to take home to meet the parents, so the four of us walked around the little back lanes to make sure I wasn't seen with him.

He was older than I, and very streetwise. I was a little uncomfortable in his presence, but foolishly ignored my misgivings although I was careful to make sure we kept up with the others. When he made a pass at me, I refused, but carried on walking and chatting with him. He continued to make unwanted advances and I continued to reject them but I was unaware that we had begun to slow down. Too late I realised that Nicole and her boyfriend had kept walking and were almost out of sight, and I became alarmed when I realised that this boy was showing no signs of heeding my rejections. The atmosphere grew tense as I continued to refuse him and then before I knew it I was being propelled into the nearest field where he forced himself upon me. The others were now so far ahead they knew nothing of what was happening. There was no violence, no bruises, nothing to show the violation that had taken place, just the feeling of utter helplessness as he took what was not his to take.

It was the longest few minutes of my life.

I ran home and spent an hour in the shower, but no matter how hard I scrubbed I could not clean off the feeling of being soiled. There are no words to describe the depth of self-loathing that was birthed in my spirit that day. I was soiled goods and I was convinced that no decent person would ever want anything to do with me. I told no one, but my shame was ever before me condemning me constantly and convincing me of my worthlessness as a human being. If my behaviour had been rebellious up to that day, from that point onwards it began to spiral out of control, as did my emotions. I discovered heavy metal music, with all its anger, and spent hours feeding my rebellious heart with lyrics filled with defiance. I was a time bomb, and it was only to be a matter of time before I went into self-destruct.

By now I was fifteen and my parents were on the brink of divorce. School was somewhere that I went but I learned nothing. Exam results were averaging in the single figures, as I struggled to cope with the fall-out from dissolving family life, teenage pressures, boyfriends and the guilty knowledge that there was a God somewhere who I was pretending didn't exist. Eventually I was called into the Headmistress's office and it was gently suggested that I would be better off not returning to school after the Summer Holidays. I agreed wholeheartedly.

The last day of term saw me strutting out of the school gates, regulation low-heeled shoes in my bag, stilettos on my feet, cigarette in my hand, and chip on my shoulder. What a difference from the last day at my previous school. In just a few short years I had come a long way – mostly downhill, and it was to be a long time before I would begin the slow climb back up.

I started my first job two weeks before the end of the summer holidays, on the cake counter at the local bakers. Unfortunately I was still very unsure of myself and this made me nervous, anxious to please and a little accident-prone. The routine at close of business was to transfer all the cakes into the huge chillers in the storage area overnight. One evening I had a large tray (about 3' by 2') of "Coconut Snowballs" stacked about three high, to store away.

'Hmmm, I'm not sure I can get this tray through those doors' I thought to myself, eyeing up the double doors to the storeroom and the tray, which I held lengthways. Inspiration dawned and I set the tray down on the floor, swivelled it round so I could carry it, smaller end first, through the doorway, and began to pick it up.

"Oh uh..." flashed through my brain, as the cakes shifted slightly ...and rolled slowly, like an avalanche, across the storeroom and under the chiller... all of them.

Time stood still....

I heard footsteps behind me, and the Boss' voice. "What on earth are you doing girl? Don't just stand there, stop them!" I looked helplessly at the last snowball as it disappeared under the huge metal fridge, then at the now empty tray in my hands, one end on the floor and the other just below my knee and suddenly saw the funny side. My Boss didn't. Surprisingly, he gave me another chance and moved me, even more surprisingly, to the cream cake counter. However, after I had dropped yet another cream cake in transit to the paper bag for a customer (why did they always separate and land sticky side down?) I was demoted to 'jam doughnut filler', which I did with great relish. Obviously I did it with too much relish (well, jam) and, although they sold like wildfire, I was deemed to be over-enthusiastic and was sent to work in the café upstairs.

At last I had found my vocation. I was let loose in the back room, where I was set to work buttering the huge slices of Guernsey Gâche to sell. Unfortunately it was still warm and smelt heavenly, and so I think I ate more than I put out! The warm scones were even more fun. They were served with jam and Guernsey cream and I was sent on many trips down the two flights of stairs into the kitchens to collect the fresh cream in massive icing bags. The kitchens were in the basement of the building: humid dungeons with low ceilings and inadequate ventilation. In consequence, the floor constantly had a greasy feel and many a Birthday Cake collected from there in perfect condition would mysteriously acquire fingerprints in the icing by the time the bottom stair was reached. The cream machine was mounted on a wall at the far end of the room and I would walk gingerly there and back whilst trying to look nonchalant. Once out of the kitchen however, the return journey was always like running the gauntlet: navigating two flights of stairs with no grab rails and 90° corners whilst wearing slippery shoes. In addition I had to dodge ascending and descending customers, and I find it astonishing that, of all people, I was the one who was sent on this trip daily.

It was inevitable. Armageddon. In a bakery. Maybe I shouldn't have been wearing clogs. Maybe I shouldn't have been in a hurry. But I was - and as I slipped on the fourth stair up with a bag of cream in each hand, my life flashed before my eyes. It was cream coloured. Having no hands free to stop my fall, I cannoned into the unyielding right hand corner; arms flailing, and winced as both bags hit the wall at full speed, nozzles pointing upward. The resulting white volcano that erupted was most spectacular. It reached the ceiling in no time, which was no mean feat. Again my heart sank as I heard the Boss.

"What the...!" then a deep sigh. "...Aaah, I might have known it was you."

Shaking his head, he turned and walked slowly back down

the stairs, leaving me in a sea of cream, with bruised shins and a very red face.

By now I was beginning to realise that maybe this wasn't the best job for me and began searching for another. But in the meanwhile, I was still at the bakery, and making a real effort to keep my days accident free. It worked for a while. Then I was asked to clean the windows. The bakery was a large old-fashioned corner building set in a pedestrianised area of the Town Centre, with two floors above ground level. The windows were extremely tall and the outside windowsills were wide enough to stand on. Guess how I knew that? Every Monday morning now found me balanced precariously over 20 feet above the precinct with cleaning rag in one hand and bare feet (remember the clogs!): the bucket of hot soapy water I sensibly left on the inside window ledge. I enjoyed this job immensely, and would sing to myself while I rubbed and scrubbed and made the glass sparkle, although I would often drop the rag, just missing the pedestrians, and would have to run quickly downstairs barefoot, past the enquiring raised eyebrow of the Boss, to retrieve it. However, I am not sure that I should have been left to my own devices for so long, as I began to think of ways to do my cleaning faster.

"I'll just pop the bucket out here for a moment," I thought to myself, after leaning in through the open window yet again to rinse my cloth. I was beginning to feel like an inverted cuckoo clock, poking my head inside the window instead of outside the door, and I was growing weary of it. I grabbed the bucket and lifted it out through the window, placing it gently on the window ledge beside me. Feeling very smug at my cleverness, I set to work with renewed vigour...and kicked the bucket. Thankfully, although I was above the shop's main doorway, nobody was drenched in the downpour that ensued, and the bucket itself miraculously missed all the busy shoppers, although some were splashed with the filthy water that exploded out as the bucket hit the paving slabs below, bouncing only once before rolling around in circles, and dribbling out the final drips over the feet of the stunned onlookers. One look at the face of my Boss and I knew my days were numbered. I needed another job – quick. I had worked there three months.

My parents were, by now, deep in the throes of divorce proceedings and Mum was working at Creaseys, Guernsey's answer to a department store. Because of her excellent work record, I was offered a position in the Toy department, which I accepted without any hesitation. This new job couldn't have been more different from the last. I had to dress smart and wear a uniform – and tights. I felt really grown-up and enjoyed being treated like an adult, although I was still only just sixteen. I had not been there long, however, when I began to feel unusually tired. I put this down to the fact that I was walking to and from work (an hour each way), as well as working an 8-hour day, so I thought it would pass. Then one day I became light-headed and almost passed out as I walked down the stairs at the end of my shift. One visit to the doctor later and I was in bed, sleeping. I had Glandular Fever, and the doctor was under the impression that I had been suffering with it, on and off, for about a year.

For my mother, the penny suddenly dropped. While still at the Grammar School, I would often feel so tired that I would fall asleep on my desk during lessons (usually German). I would also fall asleep at the drop of a hat in the most unlikeliest of places – the strangest being over an open chest freezer in a shop whilst looking for something for tea. The school, assuming I was out partying on school nights, had called my mother in on more than one occasion to admonish her on my nightly misdemeanours, but would not listen when she told them that I went to bed early and slept like the 'undead' until morning. Now it made sense. I had been unwell. As it happens I had a particularly bad case of Glandular fever, with a throat that felt like it had been sandpapered on the inside and flu-like tiredness and limb heaviness. I was sent to bed to rest... and slept for three months. I remember nothing from this time apart from waking periodically to find that two or three days had passed: it was a strange feeling, as I also couldn't tell whether it was am or pm when I looked at the clock and I found that extremely disorientating. Eventually I began the slow road to recovery but I had a tiredness and a weakness in my joints for a long period after all the other symptoms had gone and was left with a sense of loss over the three months of my life that had flown by without me, and that I would never get back.

My parent's divorce was proceeding slowly and Mum decided to move out of the family home, renting a house closer to the Town. Our family began to fragment as I moved in with her, while my sister chose to stay with Dad. I had lost my job at the toyshop due to my illness and knew I needed to look for work again, but it was to be another three months before I was fit enough to contemplate returning to work. It was like learning to live again: a short walk to the shop on the corner left me exhausted for hours and needing a sleep, but gradually I began to build up some stamina and started scouring the local paper's Situations Vacant column.

Then one day I saw it: my dream job in a Livery Stable! Excitedly I applied, and to my amazement I was accepted. I couldn't wait to start, although it meant that I had to walk a couple of miles to get there every morning by eight and then back again when I finished at six. But I didn't care. This was the job of my dreams and I wasn't going to let a small detail like exhaustion put me off!

Chapter 6
PONY PASSION

"Bye mum!" I called out as I left for work on my first day. I was finally starting at the Livery Stable and I was so excited at landing a job doing something that I had a real passion for. I had been horse and pony mad from a very early age and had learned to ride while at junior school. I had ridden, and fallen off, nearly every riding school pony in the island. Maybe I hold the record! And now I was going to work in a livery stable. Heaven!

My pony riding adventures had begun when I was nine, at a riding school in the north of the island called Baubigny (pronounced Bo-bin-ee) when, after school one afternoon, Mum took me on a mystery drive. My curiosity was piqued when we pulled into what I thought was a livery stable and I was left in the car while she went to talk to someone in the office. After what seemed a lifetime of staring out of the car windows at horses and ponies being led back and forth, but still unaware of what was going on, I was totally unprepared when Mum suddenly reappeared and beckoned me into the office. Puzzled, I followed her and stood dazed and bewildered when she smiled at the lady dressed in riding gear behind the desk, then beamed at me and said

"Do you want to come here on Wednesdays after school, or continue going to 'Brownies'?"

As the question sank in I could not keep the smile off my face! My love of all things equestrian had been growing over the years until by now it was a fully-fledged passion, so there was no doubt what my answer was going to be, but what Mum didn't know was that after enduring "Brownies" for years, which I hated with a passion (but had never told her), I had, in fact, been playing truant for at least twelve months and spending Wednesday afternoons at my friend's house, playing on her brother's bicycle! I suddenly realised though, to my mortification, that had I been truthful and told her earlier, I might have been riding for that year!

However, steadfastly leaving all things remotely associated with 'Brownies' behind, I turned up on my first Wednesday, nervous but excited by the sights and smells of a working stable and was taken to the tack room to be kitted out in a riding hat before being given a guided tour of the stables. The ponies seemed huge and I stared, wide-eyed with wonder, at these beautiful foot-stamping, mane-tossing creatures with soft velvety noses and warm brown eyes. Riding stables have a smell all of their own: hay, oats, tack, leather, manure, sawdust and mud all come together to make that unique aroma that distinguishes the horsey stable from any other farmyard smell. To this day, I cannot help but breathe in deeply when I catch even a small whiff of it, as it brings back so many lovely memories, much to the consternation of my friends!

My first lesson was fun. I sat astride a little roan coloured pony called Tango, who was more nervous than I was and jumped at every sudden movement or sound. Probably not the best pony to teach beginners on! But he was very sweet and as someone was leading him around while I gained confidence, I felt safe. The second lesson was as uneventful as the first, although I was beginning to feel nervous about his jumpiness. By the time my third lesson was due, it was deemed that I was competent enough to handle this little bundle of nerves without a leading rein, and I was sent off into the paddock with the other learners to begin my lesson. No one told me that the nervousness of the rider would always affect the pony. Believe me, this pony did not need any help, and as the lesson progressed we grew tenser and more nervous together until we were both as taut as a coiled spring.

Then it happened. What idiot would start up a pneumatic drill just as the most nervous pony on the planet was the other side of the wall? Tango, terrified out of his mind, bolted for the safety of his stable. I had never been so fast in my life! I held on as best I could, but everything was a blur of scenery, as trees, bushes and other ponies flashed by me at an alarming rate. I closed my eyes in terror, but opened them just in time to see the gate to the paddock looming up before us – as Tango came to an abrupt halt. Suddenly I was no longer sat in the saddle, but having my first jumping lesson – minus my pony.

I don't remember the landing, only opening my eyes to find myself looking up into my mother's worried face. By all accounts, my flying antics were rather spectacular, as I conducted a perfect front somersault in mid air, finishing my acrobatics with a resounding thud at my mother's feet! My instructor insisted it was important that I remount Tango in order that I would not lose my nerve, but it was a futile exercise to attempt to convince me to get back on, as I was hysterical. Eventually he took matters into his own hands, and as I whimpered in terror he picked me up and bodily plonked me in the saddle, holding me there while I desperately fought to get off again. With hindsight, I am glad he didn't give in, as I know I would never have voluntarily mounted a horse ever again if he had. And so, the next Wednesday found me back at the stables, giving Tango an extremely wide berth, anxiously anticipating a quiet ride on a quiet pony. However, as I was so young, there were only two choices of pony for me: Tango and Minstrel. Minstrel was a beautiful grey pony with a very long mane, which made him resemble a Pegasus, a fairytale pony. He was beautifully behaved but, still scared and sore from my recent flying lesson, I couldn't overcome my panic when his natural exuberance made him a little bouncy and I knew by the end of my lesson that I if I could find another riding school with quieter ponies I wouldn't be returning to Baubigny.

West Riding School was situated in St Saviours, one of the rural southern parishes of Guernsey, in a beautiful valley with lots of quiet lanes to wander through and dirt tracks just begging to be galloped along. The owner, Ray, was a big-hearted man, with a soft spot for nervous pupils and abused horses, and no time for ignorance. I liked him. Under his watchful eye I began to gain confidence and competence, even to the point of being comfortable with riding the more challenging ponies: these were days sweet with the smell of fresh hay, where the ponies were my friends and I felt safe. Well, almost.

Again I was the smallest person within my group, so naturally that meant I had the 'privilege' of riding the smallest ponies. Ponies tend to be more sedate the larger they are. Small ones tend to be a little aggressive and mouthy – like small dogs and people: as if they feel they have something to prove. Lizzie was a lovely tall piebald with the sweetest nature; Sugar was a steady reliable grey pony who put her riders at ease; Goldie was a roan who was a devil in the stable and an angel out of it; Pepsi was a strawberry roan with a mischievous side to his nature, but not a bad bone in his body. Patch was a skewbald who was the laziest, most conniving animal I ever met; Sunshine was a honey coloured dun, sweet natured, but with a stubborn tendency to do as she wanted, regardless of her rider; Merrylegs was a dapple grey Shetland pony, a small bouncing bundle of pure energy and strength, who needed brakes. He should have been called Tigger. And I got to ride... Patch, Sunshine and Merrylegs.

Did you know that a pony can be quite a spectacular springboard? Sunshine will always be remembered in my family as the pony who proved it and became a catapult. I should have known that it was going to be one of those days from the outset. It was a lovely sunny Saturday and the riding instructor decided that it would be a wonderful idea to take the group of six of us for a ride through the country lanes down towards the beach at Vazon, where those who wanted to could take a long gallop across the beach. As I was booked to ride Sunshine, who could be a madam at the best of times, I opted for the safer option of a canter on the Common opposite the beach with the riding instructor, Mandy. As we were getting the ponies ready and began assembling in the yard, Mandy went to tack up Sugar but then remembered that her saddle was in for repairs – so she decided to borrow Ray's 17hh chestnut hunter, Sceptre.

The ride down to the coast was uneventful: lovely scenery, happy ponies, and sun shining with just a slight breeze - just the perfect day for riding. As we neared the beach the ponies could smell the salt in the air and realised where they were going. Seven pairs of ears pricked up along with the pace as one very large horse and six small ponies broke into a gentle trot, nostrils quivering with excitement. Sceptre began to dance a little and I wondered how Mandy was handling him: she didn't look as if she was coping very well and had a rather worried look on her face. As Mandy and I parted company from the rest of the ride and watched them make their way down the cobbled slipway onto the long stretch of sand, she turned to me and confided that she was glad I had opted for the safety of the common as Sceptre could be very headstrong and she wasn't sure if she was capable of keeping him in check on the beach. Oh boy, thanks for telling me!

"I think it would be safer to just keep to a trot, if you don't mind." She apologised, knowing that I had been looking forward to a canter along the Common. I nodded and we started off at a lovely brisk trot. Before long however, Sceptre's pace changed into a canter and I smiled.

'Great!' I thought, 'obviously Mandy's feeling more confident.'

Urging Sunshine on into a canter, I began to sing as the wind blew through my hair. I felt on top of the world at one with my pony: and I loved the feeling of freedom I always experienced while riding, like the soaring of an eagle in the mountain skies. Noticing that Sceptre was picking up the pace a little and the gap between us was getting wider and wider, I pushed Sunshine faster so we could keep up.

Suddenly without warning Mandy parted company with Sceptre and I stared in utter disbelief as I watched her land with a thud on the ground, almost on her feet. I struggled in vain to rein in Sunshine, who was enjoying herself immensely as she continued in her quest to catch Sceptre and before I knew it we were in an uncontrolled gallop careering all over the common in Sceptres' wake as he, now riderless, just ran at random in whatever direction he wanted. Panic hit as I saw that we were heading for a tarmac road that cut across the common and as he veered right and headed inland up the road, followed by Sunshine and myself, my life began to flash before me.

"'Don't fall off, don't fall off" I repeated to myself, as I gripped the front of my saddle to keep myself steady. I knew that I would be seriously hurt if I fell onto tarmac at the speed we were going and was determined at all costs not to leave that saddle.

Meanwhile, further up the lane, a figure dressed in riding gear quietly stepped out of a concealed gateway and stood, like a barrier with her arms outstretched, in the centre of the road. She had been grooming her horse when, alerted by the sound of the clattering hooves on tarmac, she had quickly come to our aid. Sceptre saw her and swerved, wavered a little and then slowed to a canter and Sunshine and I began to gain ground. The young lady didn't move a muscle and I closed my eyes. Sceptre, his mane blowing in the wind, continued towards her at the same pace and then, at the last minute, he decided that she was an immovable object and skidded to a halt, his haunches almost touching the ground.

Sunshine, taken by surprise, also skidded to a halt as Sceptre stood catching his breath, but not soon enough as she had still been increasing her pace to catch him up, and as her head connected with his backside, I found myself being catapulted straight up her neck and over her ears. I landed neatly splayed out face down just behind his saddle with my feet dangling in mid air, and as Sunshine shook her head and backed off, I slid backwards with great embarrassment and landed in a crumpled heap at his feet, unscathed but a little shaken.

Eventually Mandy re-appeared on the scene, apologising profusely for jumping off (JUMPING OFF???) when she realised that she had lost control, and took Sceptre's reins from my young lifesaver as she thanked the girl for her help. We both remounted and made our way back to the beach to meet up with the rest of the ride to find that they had also had some hairy moments when my sister, who had been riding Patch, found out too late that the saddle's girth hadn't been tightened enough causing the saddle to swing around underneath him while he was cantering across the beach. She ended up being dragged across the sand on her back between his forelegs (at a canter) whilst looking up his nostrils and being choked by the strap of her hat, but she still managed a smile when he finally stopped and she was able to extricate herself from the tangle of reins that she had clung to like superglue and stand up – to be greeted by loud cheers and whistles by a crowd of teenage boys sitting on the beach wall!

It wasn't the best day's riding for either of us, but she gave up riding not long afterwards, probably because she decided that she liked her bones in one piece. Mandy, in the meantime, was roasted over hot coals on our return to the stables by Ray who was absolutely furious that she had 'borrowed' Sceptre without checking with him first. If she had done so, he said, she would have known that the 'bit' in his bridle was a new one: an experiment to see if he could be easier to control, as he was headstrong with a hard mouth. And the short answer to that question was ...er, no.

A few weeks later Mandy was again riding Sceptre, but this time with permission and an effective 'bit'. There were seven of us on the ride and as we assembled at the entrance to a rough-looking track, the ponies began fidgeting. We were at the start of a cantering track that was a favourite for the ponies (and riders alike) and they always grew restless and excited when they realised where we were headed. It was a steep uphill dirt-track about half a mile long with many corners, flanked either side by tall hedges, and it was fun to give your horse his head and fly like the wind. This time I was riding Merrylegs and I was told to stay behind on the road until the other ponies had got a head start. I couldn't understand why, as I was riding the smallest pony in the group.

"Just count to a hundred and give us a chance to get far enough up the track before you let him go," smiled Mandy as Sceptre danced around little Merrylegs and me, looking down on us like we were ants.

"How am I going to hold him back?" I asked incredulously, as we jigged in circles up and down the narrow lane. He was eager to be off and was shaking his head and snorting, backing into the hedges and bouncing on the spot. He was so short my feet almost touched each other around his belly, and it was strange to bounce around so close to the ground!

"You'll be fine!" she called back, "just count to a hundred, then come."

She, along with the rest of the ride, disappeared in a flurry of dust and thundering hooves into the entrance of the track and Merrylegs went wild. He was indignant at being left behind and neighed frantically, while trying to climb the hedges. I had the reins so short that I was fast running out of leather to hold on to, but still I could not hold him. I began to turn him in circles, which became smaller and smaller, until his nose was touching my leg and I could have used my fingers as the 'bit' - and he was still bouncing! I struggled to concentrate on counting but only managed to reach seventy - when he took off after his friends.

A large pony at a full gallop is exhilarating. A smaller pony is less so. A Shetland? I can only compare it to a piston engine at double speed; like the legs of a small child on a first bike trying to keep up with dad on a big bike with large wheels and gears. I thought my arms were going to be pulled from their sockets and my insides were going to be shaken loose. But it was FUN! We shot, like a bullet from a gun, up the track in a blur overtaking everyone on the way, and arrived at the top breathless and shaken, but oh so alive - and in front!

I loved this riding school from the word 'go'. The lanes and tracks became so familiar to me and as I grew, so did my choice of ponies. I got to ride beautiful Sugar, (who is the only pony to unseat me with a real 'bronco buck') temperamental Goldie, who loved sand and would sink to his knees ready for a good roll whenever he came across it – regardless of whether he was on the beach or the school paddock and oblivious to the fact that his rider was frantically trying to dismount before they were flattened! I rode the lovely Pepsi, who just bounced through life with a happy disposition and did whatever you asked of him with no complaints, and I rode Lizzie bareback: she was the widest pony I have ever sat on, with the highest backbone, and covered with the silkiest horse hair I have ever seen, and every muscle below my waist ached considerably for days afterwards from gripping hard with my thighs and knees just to stay on – resulting in me finding it extremely difficult to walk for a week after! I was now able to ride all the ponies - all but Merrylegs, for I had finally outgrown him – a fact realised when my feet almost reached around him when I sat astride him and almost dragged along the ground when he moved! Unfortunately, though, I still occasionally had to endure an hour's torture on Patch.

Patch really was the most infuriating pony I ever met. He would not do anything that was asked of him – ever. If everyone else walked, he trotted. If they trotted, he walked. If they cantered, he yawned and ...walked. If they went up a cantering track, he yawned and ...wandered. If we had a jumping lesson, he would walk sideways over to the jump, stare at it, then walk through it. On one noteworthy jumping lesson, when he wouldn't move, let alone get up enough speed to actually tackle the eighteen inch high jump, I was told to use my whip on him, which I hated doing. So I begrudgingly tapped him behind the saddle. "DON'T TICKLE HIM, GIRL!" bellowed Ray, at the end of his tether with this antagonistic lump of laziness, (Patch, not me!) "WHACK HIM!"

So I did. My whip snapped neatly in half, leaving me with the handle firmly gripped in my hand, the wrist- strap loosely around my wrist, and the other end somewhere in the bushes… and Patch…not moving an inch. He turned his head around so his nose was touching my knee and SMIRKED! I have never seen a pony do this before or since, but I kid ye not, he had such a smug look on his face that I wanted to shove the remains of my whip up his irksome nostrils. Suddenly there was a loud 'CRACK!' as the instructor flicked his lunge whip close to Patch's backside, and he took off with a start, nearly unseating me…. for ten paces. Ah well, back to the old drawing board!

Incidentally, Ray finally came to the conclusion that Patch couldn't jump. Then, a couple of months later, returning from a relaxing ride in the countryside, he spotted a certain skewbald pony alone in the field on his rest day, gaily pinging over all the jumps that were arranged in the centre of the field, while he thought no-one was looking. When he heard the sound of the hooves on the road, however, he stopped, put his head down and continued innocently eating grass. Who says they are 'dumb' animals?

Although I was seen as being popular, I was still very uncomfortable around many people and when the new generation of riders began to encroach on my comfort zone and my circle of friends I had made at West Riding I began to withdraw into myself. I was probably thought of as a 'horsey snob' as I began to spend most of my time with the ponies or alone with my own company, and after a couple of years I moved again to another riding school. This one was in St. Martins parish, across the road from Senner's Bakery and a chip shop. I found that some of the girls who rode there were in my class at Grammar School and we came to a 'casual friend' agreement that was only acknowledged at the riding school, and never at school, where we ignored each other with great skill.

Now in my early teens, I no longer relied on mum for a lift and would ride my battered Raleigh Shopper bike the three or so miles from my house to the riding school early in the morning so I could meet with my new friend, Chantal. We would help out with the little kids' rides then rush over to the chip shop across the road to buy our fish and chips, which we would eat with great relish sitting in the centre of the hay bales. One February, however, we were so cold that we couldn't feel our toes, so after buying our chips as usual, we stood firmly entrenched up to our calves in the steaming dung-heap instead and munched on our chips as our feet thawed out!

The lessons there were always fun as the instructor tried to keep his gaggle of teenage girls from chatting, giggling, fidgeting and falling off (that was usually me!). Chantal was the worst for losing concentration and wandering around with her head in the clouds and many a lesson was interrupted as the instructor bellowed,

"Get those toes IN and those heels DOWN Chantal, you are not a ballet dancer!" and she would come back to earth for a while, but not for long. We both had favourite ponies that, unfortunately, hated the sight of each other, resulting in many an interesting ride as we desperately tried to make them walk side by side on the road without biting and kicking each other so we could chat. We usually ended up by just blocking the road though, as they often ended up having a 'head to head'.

One of the most interesting lessons comprised of having a go at being jockeys. We shortened our stirrups to 'jockey' length and raced each other around the field. I am not sure whether it was because we were laughing so much or not but none of us stayed on for long, spending more time sliding down our ponies necks and then looking up their noses as we landed right in front of them. Unfortunately for us, we were not in the regular field, but in one recently vacated by some cows. I will leave the imagery to your imagination; suffice it to say that we were rather more at home in the dung-heap that afternoon!

But despite these good times I never really connected with the people there, apart from Chantal, and experienced my first brush with the real 'snobby pony club' set, which I didn't handle too well. So when Chantal stopped coming to the riding school, I found myself alone once again and it wasn't long before I began to look for somewhere else to indulge my passion. Finally I found a brand new stable that was opening up – The Guernsey Equestrian Centre, and booked my first lesson. It was a modern riding school and I settled in very quickly. Everything was new and spacious and each Sunday would find me on my bicycle, heading down to spend all day there.

I was so desperate by this time for a pony of my own that I turned my bike into one. I tied roller skating bootlaces (reins) to the brake levers and, as I still had my Raleigh Shopper, I found that I could sit on the empty basket holder behind the seat – thus I could ride my bike, steer it and stop it using only the 'reins'. Mum was very impressed with the level of control I had doing this...but she thought I only played this way in the driveway, never realising I was also 'riding' my pony on the main roads. I did stop though, the day I rode around a blind corner, hit a drain, lost control and landed on my bottom, causing a loud screech of brakes from the BUS that was driving behind me!

The Equestrian Centre, I soon found out, was the new venture for the previous owner of Baubigny Stables something I realised when I walked into the stable yard on my first day and came face to face with ...Tango. Thankfully, I had become quite a competent rider by this time and I didn't stand for his nonsense, although I was amazed that he was still the same bundle of nerves – and surprisingly, he was also still the favourite for teaching young beginners to ride.

It was at this stable that I got to ride a professional show-jumping pony while he was in transit between homes. It was here that I met the lovely Red Rum, the retired steeplechaser, when he was the Guest of Honour at the Guernsey Horse of the Year Show. It was here I learned how to get a terrified pony past rustling black plastic; past a noisy lawnmower; past a barking dog; past that juicy mouthful of grass growing on the hedge – at the bottom! It was here that I learned to land on my feet, reins firmly gripped in my hands, after some tiresome pony had tried, and succeeded, to unseat me - twice. It was here.... Well, you get the idea. So many memories and now, four years later, I was to realise my dream and actually work with 17 horses in a livery stable.

I eagerly set to work on my first day, but it quickly became painfully apparent that the yard owner was totally incompetent. During my first week, the food ran out because he had forgotten to order it, one pony went lame because he had forgotten to call the farrier when she lost a shoe, one young stallion escaped from the field and had to be prised off another pony in season... and I got stuck in the hayloft. I have never been entirely happy with heights and one lunchtime I was required to go into the hayloft above the stables to replenish a couple of the loose boxes. There was no ladder for access but apparently getting up there was no problem: all I needed to do was to climb onto the stable door on my right, then straddle the gap and place my other foot on the stable door on my left, thus bringing me into the perfect position to pop my head into the square loft opening. This done, I just needed to lift myself up into the loft. Sorted.

Only it didn't quite happen that way. Well, getting in was fine but when it was time to lower myself down feet first, I felt the first signs of panic hit. Dangling out of a hole in the ceiling with my feet scrabbling to find a foothold on two stable doors that were three feet apart, I began to lose my grip, both on the loft floor and my sanity. I managed to pull myself back into the loft, where I sat for the best part of the afternoon shakily hugging my knees and moaning with fear, resolutely ignoring all pleas from the supervisor to come to the loft hatch. Finally someone fetched a ladder and I was able to vacate my prison, although it was a good hour before I could stop shaking. They never asked me again.

It's amazing how different two horses can be in their stables. I could spend five minutes cleaning out Misty, who did her toilet all in one corner. Two shovels later, I was done and moving onto the next stable. Then I got to Nutmeg, who seemed to delight in kicking hers all over the stable, resulting in me 'panning for gold': it took me over an hour every morning to sift through her sawdust and replace her bedding. One morning the yard owner made a rare visit to the stables and shouted at me for taking so long with Nutmeg. I tried to explain why, but he shouted me down each time I opened my mouth, finally making me retreat into the shell that was always waiting in the wings of my life to be my refuge. However, he became so verbally abusive that anger eventually rose up in me and I stopped being scared. This was a dangerous place for him to be in, because unfortunately for him, my boss had a speech impediment: he stammered, and the more he shouted, the more he stammered.

When it first happened, I stared at him in amazement, but as he turned puce in frustration and began to get stuck on the first letter of each word, I began to see the funny side. Now, I had had a stammer when I was a toddler, as well as a lisp, and because of it I became extremely self-conscious and hated people watching me when I spoke, so I knew how humiliated he must have been feeling, especially as all this was happening in front of all the other staff members who worked at the stable, and had come over to watch the 'new girl' get a 'roasting'. But he was totally out of order to be attempting to make a spectacle of me for the amusement of his staff, and so instead of feeling empathy towards him, I began to lose respect.

Too late I realised that I was smiling. Horrified, I tried so desperately not to, but the damage had been done. He turned and left the yard, leaving me standing alone holding my shovel, surrounded by accusing glances from the other girls. I was shaken from the confrontation but I could not, try as I might, feel sorry for him. After all, this situation was of his own making and could have easily been avoided, if he hadn't been trying to impress the other girls, especially the head groom who was later to become his wife.

And finally, just when I thought I had suffered all the horrors of this livery stable… I experienced the terrifying phenomenon of being kicked by metal shoes on hooves attached to powerfully muscular back legs. Nobody saw it happen because I was taking 'Fred' out to the field by myself just after my lunch-hour; a journey that would normally take 10 minutes each way. Although an absolutely adorable pony that looked like Black Beauty, Fred, being a youngster, was very excitable and this day he was in higher spirits than usual, bouncing along the track and tugging at his leading rein. As we neared the field, the other horses called to him causing him to toss his head and dance with excitement. He pulled the rope from my hands and just as he got directly in front of me, he gaily kicked out in glee and ran to meet his friends. My feet left the ground and I flew backwards, landing only when I hit a large log used as a jump in Cross Country Eventing, which knocked all the breath out of my body.

Then the pain in my chest hit. It was unbearable. I could not breathe, move, or call for help. I coughed and spat out blood. Fear, pain and panic hit me in waves as I sat against that log for over an hour. Eventually, I was able to make my way slowly back to the stables, every breath invoking a sharp pain in my chest, to find that I had not even been missed. The incident was passed over and my request to be checked over at the local A&E

at the top of the road was refused. But I was still in pain and occasionally I would check the dark bruising that was spreading from shoulder to shoulder as the day wore on.

It was six o'clock in the evening, at the end of my working day, before I was able to get to the A&E department. Thankfully, an old friend of my parents had begun to give me a lift home, as I both worked and lived within his own homeward journey, and he very kindly detoured to the hospital so I could be seen. They were very busy that day and when the doctor finally came to me he sharply tapped my chest in the middle (right where the impact had been) and then just to the left and the right. I gritted my teeth and gripped the sides of the bed so hard with the pain that my knuckles turned white. In fact, I believe that if I had been in a "Tom and Jerry" cartoon I would have been Tom, hanging upside down from the ceiling by my toes, looking like I had just stuck my finger in an electric socket.

And the verdict was...?

"Well, it could be broken. Or it could be fractured. Or it could be just bruised. I can't tell." And I was dismissed.

I arrived home rather worse for wear and told an increasingly outraged mother of my day's adventure, ending with the 'helpful' comments of the doctor.

"Didn't he even offer you an X-ray?" she demanded, incredulously. I shook my head miserably, beginning to feel very tired, battered and bruised, and wandered off to bed. The next morning I walked slowly to work and continued to muck out seventeen horses, gritting my teeth every time I had to lift the dustbin of soiled bedding shoulder high to empty it into the trailer. And the next day I did the same... and the next.

Saturday finally dawned. It was my day off, so I slept a little longer, then decided to get up, but I couldn't move. Not an inch. Eventually mum came into my bedroom and had to bodily lift me into the sitting position by putting her arm around me and bearing all my weight while I sagged against her like a soggy hammock. Once I was up, she telephoned the surgery and booked an emergency appointment with the family doctor. He took one look at my bruises and winced, then proceeded to ... oh, ever so gently... feel his way around the bruised areas as I explained what had happened. Finally he sat back in his chair, his face growing darker with anger and informed me that my breastbone and ribs were fractured, a condition made worse by the fact that I had continued to work for the rest of the week. I was signed off work for three months and told, in no uncertain terms, to hand in my notice immediately.

My dream was over. I had worked at the stables for a week and a half.

Chapter 7
ON THE UP

By now you must be thinking that my life was just one long list of alternating disasters and slapstick moments, and looking back over the last six chapters, I can see why. The truth was that I had always had a rebellious spirit, a stubborn streak and a strong self-will. Unfortunately I was also very good at making extremely bad decisions, due to my aforementioned character traits, which resulted in spending the next period of my life reaping the consequences, without actually learning from my mistakes.

One Easter when my sister and I were small, we had received seven Easter Eggs each but we left them unopened, preferring to eat Mum's small box of chocolates that we had bought her instead. This is the only time my father ever threatened to use his belt on us – and it put the fear of God into us. However, when our Easter Eggs were also confiscated as punishment, (un)-righteous indignation rose to the fore and revenge was plotted. We packed up our favourite toys and were all set to run away in high dudgeon, to our Grandmother's house (during the worst storm that year), in the smug knowledge that we would never be found...(?), when my sister had an attack of conscience and tearfully confessed all. Was I repentant? No, I was incensed.

A few years later, I stole a bar of chocolate from the local Health Food shop, whilst out for a bike ride with my little Irish Nan. She was so disappointed in me when she realised what I had done that it saddened my selfish heart, as I truly loved her and was devastated when I realised I had hurt her. A very sore bottom followed, courtesy of my father, and a return trip to the shop to pay for the stolen goods, but still I did not learn and, in true fashion, returned to my thieving ways as a young teenager.

Now, as a parent myself, I see what a nightmare it must have been for my parents. No matter what was said, shown, encouraged or enforced, I paid only lip service to obedience and determined to go my own way, whatever hell that led me into. Which leads me into probably the darkest chapter in my life. By the time I was fit to return to work after my ribs were fractured, I was spending more and more time on the Citizen Band (CB) Radio, the latest craze that was sweeping Guernsey at that time. Although CB radio attracted all sorts of people from all walks of life, unfortunately, especially in Guernsey, it was mainly a craze amongst the unemployable, the strange and the downright weird – and, of course, stupidly irresponsible rebellious naive young girls like myself. As a result, my choice of friends was becoming an issue of alarm for my mother, and my prospective boyfriends even more so. The final straw came when I began secretly dating a 34-year-old man of dubious character when I was sixteen.

Secrets can never be kept for long in an island that measures approximately 24 square miles, where everybody knows everybody else and word spreads like wildfire. Subsequently, Mum eventually found out and tried everything to stop the relationship; after all he was only 3 years younger she. Eventually, out of sheer desperation to make me see sense during yet another row, she shouted the one sentence that was guaranteed to make me dig my heels in, whatever the consequences:

"You are not dating that man while you live in this house!"

There, it was said and she regretted it the moment those words were out of her mouth, but they, like every other word that we utter, were non-returnable. Within a few days I had packed my bags and moved into a squalid little flat with a man I hardly knew. Over the next six months I existed in a daze, as he stole from me, beat me, and paraded me in front of his friends, always wanting to show me off like an exhibit to make them envious then flying into a jealous rage when they admired a little too closely – resulting in yet more bruises for me and more confirmation that I was worth less than nothing. The police were constantly on our doorstep due to his illegal dealings and he was no stranger to the inside of a cell. Once again I was in a situation of my own making that I felt powerless to change. Anyone who has been in an abusive relationship will understand the utter hopelessness that is felt when the fear of leaving is greater than the fear of staying. Eventually he was arrested again and because of his existing criminal record we both knew that this time he would be returning to prison. Suddenly I saw an opportunity to get out of this trap I was in and I plucked up the courage to do the thing I should have done six months earlier: I called Mum.

"Hello, come in"

It was good to hear Mum's voice and see her face. After hearing that I was desperate to come home she had invited me around to her new house for supper and a 'heart to heart'. Over a plate of spicy Chilli con Carne, I chatted and waffled and poured out my heart, but by ten o'clock in the evening, I still had not said what I had come to say. Finally, as I was getting ready to leave I plucked up all the courage I could muster.

"Can I come home?" I blurted, looking down and expecting a rebuff. Instead I was hugged and gently told that the answer was yes if, and only if, I was coming home for good, not just until he came out of prison again. Was she kidding? Within days, while he was in the courtroom being sentenced, I frantically packed and mum took me home to clean sheets, clean clothes, peace and sanity. A week later my sister returned from Spain, where she had been taking part in a six month Discipleship Training School with the missionary training organisation YWAM (Youth with a Mission), and also moved back home, sharing my bedroom and bringing more normality into my life.

But I was still an angry young person: angry at the world and everyone in it for turning me into a victim… and angry with myself for allowing it. Still, God has ways of taking the pressure lid off to enable us to vent in safety, then waiting in the sidelines until we are ready to move forward, maybe years later. Then, and only then, will He lead us into our own wilderness experience, where we can begin to deal with the core issues that make up our psyche – in His timing and in His presence and under His protection. In this case the vent was a shed, a digital watch and a hammer…

"Oh the Yellow Rose of Texas is the only girl for me," I sang gaily, swishing my paintbrush up and down the wooden wall of the shed. I didn't particularly like the song, but it had been going around my head all day and I had finally succumbed to a sad desire to sing it. This was my therapy: me, a tin of whitewash, a selection of paintbrushes and time to myself in the shed. However, it was getting late and I was feeling hungry and tired.

"It must be time for tea soon," I thought as, true to form, the alarm on my digital watch suddenly sprang into life and massacred The Yellow Rose of Texas in its high pitched mechanical whine at double speed, reminding me why I didn't like the song, but also announcing that it was, indeed, teatime. I quickly washed my brush in the jar of turps, splashing a little on my watch as I did so.

"Ah, food" I thought with satisfaction, wiping my watch and finding the 'off' button that would herald peace. However, the song continued. I switched it off again. Again, the screeching pitch refused to abate. Frustrated, I tapped the watch – but to no avail. I shook it. No effect. I shook it harder…still no effect. Irrational anger surged through me at an alarming rate and although the intensity of it frightened me, I was powerless to control it.

"Shut Up!" I snarled, through gritted teeth, although why I thought it could hear me, I have no idea. Still the noise reverberated around my head and set my teeth on edge. Furiously I unhooked the offending article from my wrist and smacked it against the side of the shed. The glass cracked…and the song continued. Near to tears with frustration I threw the watch on the ground and jumped on it. The glass shattered all over the shed floor and the strap snapped off. And the remainder of the watch belted out "The Yellow Rose of Texas" albeit a little off-key now.

The whole situation had become surreal and all I could think of was silencing this torturous sound. I ran over to the toolkit and selected a heavy hammer, and standing over the watch I whacked it with everything I had. Bits of watch flew in all directions and I held my breath, listening for the silence… and heard, extremely quietly, like an old scratched vinyl record playing in a basement, the whisper of that dreaded song haunting me.

Flabbergasted, I stared in disbelief at the few bits of technology, now spread like a shipwreck around my feet – and finally found the funny side, realising that I had directed all the anger, frustration and helplessness that had been building within me at a poor inanimate object – and won! Why I didn't just take off the watch and leave it in the shed to let the battery run down while I had my tea, I will never know. Ah, but now I think about it…

The next couple of years were a time of restoration. I left behind the CB radio, the old lifestyle and the old friends and started a new job at Pete's Chip Shop in the Town Centre. I bought my first car, a blue Reliant Kitten (the same size as a Reliant Robin, but with four wheels!) and learned to drive. My driving instructor was called Peter and he had the most unusual method of driver training I have ever come across. If I did something wrong, he would punch my left shoulder, non too gently may I add, and bark,

"What did you do?" or "What didn't you do?" And he would continue to periodically punch my arm until I worked it out and gave him the correct answer. It was all done in jest, although I really looked forward to the time when I didn't have a 'dead' arm by the time the lesson was half over.

He was very thorough, but highly unorthodox, as you have probably guessed, and was happy to teach me in my own car, at my request, rather than his 'official' Learner car, although he teased me constantly about the fact that my 'Kitten' was made of fibreglass and riding in it was like sitting in a cardboard box – a small one. As my test approached, he decided that it was time teach me how to drive without being distracted by outside sources… so he brought his two children along on my lesson and told them to misbehave as much as they liked. This was before seatbelts were compulsory in Guernsey, so these two children jumped up and down, swapped seats, hung out of the windows, fought, screamed and shouted in the back of the car for my entire lesson, and it worked!

The day of my test dawned… but it was not bright and sunny. It was a wet windy January day, with a little slushy snow left on the roads from the flurries that had escaped over to the island from France. My hour-long pre-test lesson had gone horrendously. I had made every mistake I could think of and even some that I hadn't yet thought about and I hadn't known the answers to any of the ten Highway Code questions that my instructor had fired at me. We arrived early at the test centre next to the Fire Station and I waited in the car while he disappeared into the office to book me in. Fifteen nerve-wracking minutes later I spotted a man walking hurriedly towards me with a clipboard in his hand, while the rain soaked his papers and the wind tried to rip them off the board. After managing to get himself into the passenger seat without losing either the clipboard or my car door to the elements, he turned to me, soaked and windswept, smiled and introduced himself.

"So," he began, "This is your car, I presume. I can't say I've ever sat in a 'Kitten' before. Where do you park it overnight?" I told him that it was parked at the Leisure Centre car park opposite Mum's house.

"Oh," he grinned, "Does it not blow away when there is a high wind?"

Inwardly I groaned. 'Oh no, another comedian.' I thought.

We went through the checks. Lights working? Check. Horn working? Check.

"It doesn't meow then" he sniggered as my little horn gave out a mournful "paaarp." I smiled and shook my head. By this time my nerves were beginning to get the better of me and I was starting to get a little jittery. Finally, he settled himself back into his seat and asked me to start my engine: my driving test was well and truly underway.

I didn't get off to a good start. It was still raining but I drove 500yards to the junction at the end of the road before I remembered to put my windscreen wipers on. Moments later I joined a traffic-jam and sat unmoving for five minutes before realising that I was, in fact, in the school-run queue of parents who were parked waiting to collect their offspring from the local junior school. I swore quietly under my breath, pulled out and continued past them, while the test examiner chuckled gently as he looked nonchalantly out of the side window. Then as I approached a junction at the top of a steep hill (with a 60° incline) the engine stalled. Without a moment's hesitation or delay, while holding the car on the brow of the hill with clutch and brake control, I instantly switched the engine off and immediately back on again. As it fired into life I indicated left and moved slowly off the junction and up the hill.

Within seconds, the examiner had instructed me to find a safe place to stop and once we were safely parked up against the kerb he turned in his seat, fixed me with a 'look' and enquired,

"Do you know the procedure when a vehicle stalls?" I nodded. He waited.

"Handbrake on. Restart the car. Mirror, signal, into gear, check mirror again, then move slowly off." I quoted.

"So would you mind telling me what that was all about?" he demanded

"Well," I responded, "I know my car. If I stall it and don't start it within seconds, it won't start for at least half an hour. And I didn't fancy sitting on the brow of a hill at a junction for thirty minutes." I looked down, waiting to be told I had failed, but to my surprise I was just told to continue towards the Odeon car park for my reverse parking.

It has been said that Guernsey people abhor a vacuum – and will promptly park their car in it. This was never so true as on my test day. The single lane, one-way car park was shaped like a horseshoe and, as usual, the cars were parked nose to tail. I was asked to park on one of the corners in a space only 12 inches longer than my car and I smiled. The steering lock on my little Kitten was amazing and the car could turn on a sixpence, but even I was surprised at how smoothly I reversed and parked the car without any problem at all. However, I was so excited when I was instructed to return to the test centre around the corner that as I pulled out of the parking space I turned the wheel too far to the right, shot across the road and up the footpath the other side, before correcting myself and returning to the road. Again I swore under my breath, and although I thought I saw a smile hovering around his mouth, by now I was absolutely convinced that I had failed. But apparently not, for when we arrived back at the centre the examiner picked up his clipboard, which he had laid on his lap, and began to test my knowledge of the Highway Code. I was amazed as he asked the exact same questions as my instructor had earlier that morning – only now I knew the answers… and I passed!

Very proud of myself, I drove down to the Town Centre and parked my car in a thirty minute limited parking spot so I could rush into Mum's work to tell her. I got out of the car, pushed the lock toggle down and slammed the door shut…and then saw my car keys dangling in the ignition. Panic hit. This was in the days before mobile phones, and I had no money on me and no way of getting home to pick up my spare set of keys – and even if I did get home, I couldn't get into the house as my front door key was also laughing at me in the car. So I ran all the way to Mum's work, told her my news – including the car keys fiasco

- and she ran upstairs to the staff room to get her front door key for me. I then ran around the corner to the taxi rank, jumped into the first available car, explained the need for speed and was duly raced the mile to my home. The taxi waited outside while I grabbed my spare keys and my handbag, and then raced me back down to mum's work. I paid the taxi driver, rushed in to the shop to give mum her key back and then ran back to my car. I had been twenty- eight minutes. Exhausted, I went home too tired to celebrate.

Chapter 8
'PILGIES'

However, there is always a 'down side' to every good thing, and now I was 'with wheels', my sister enlisted me as her personal taxi driver, coercing me into driving her to all her church activities, then returning later to collect her and bring her home. I knew everyone, as they were the youth group I had previously belonged to and they were always pleased to see me although I would never stay for any of the meetings, preferring instead to continue to convince myself that I was all right without God. But eventually, as I'm sure she knew I would, I began to yearn for what I had lost. And on June 23rd 1985 opportunity knocked. As I dropped her off at the local Baptist Church Manse for a youth 'after-church' meeting, she hesitated before closing the car door.

"Why don't you come in and stay for the meeting, Alison? You know everyone there and they'd love to see you"

"And" she added with a cheeky smile, "There's food afterwards!"

I was torn. I had my stand that I had taken: that I didn't need God, and to back down would severely dent my pride, but inside me there was a yearning that was increasing. Finally I agreed and there was a cheer as I stepped in the hallway of the Manse to be greeted by smiling faces and hugs. Reverend William Fransch and his wife, Celia, were extremely hospitable and, despite my initial shyness, I found that before long I was feeling part of the group. As the evening drew on, however, I was aware that the longing within me was growing with an intensity that I couldn't shake. I wanted, really wanted, to belong: to be part of this group of people, who were warm and friendly, with a happiness that went beyond their smiles; to be loved; to be accepted. The longing grew stronger and stronger until I could no longer contain it. I tried to suppress the tears that were springing up – I hadn't wept for years and I was horrified that I was about to do so in front of people, but again, the emotion overwhelmed me. I needed to tell someone how I was feeling; it was too big to keep to myself. I had recently been listening to my sister's Keith Green albums on my car stereo when alone in the car and had been drawn time and time again to "The Prodigal Son Suite", a song written from the son's perspective. Suddenly I could see it clearly ...God was calling me back and I needed Him – and I knew it; it was time to stop running.

I spotted a friend of my sister's across the room that I got on well with and deliberately made my way towards him. His name was Peter, a man of Indian descent, who had a gentle way about him, soft spoken and warm. After the men I had been exposed to over the years, there were very few that I now trusted, but Peter was one of them. I was feeling vulnerable and needed to feel safe as I attempted to open my heart.

"Peter," I whispered, "Would you pray with me? I want to give my life back to Jesus."

His smile lit up his face as he began to pray and lead me along a path long forgotten, where I found hope and forgiveness, and a brand new start. I didn't know it then, but this precious man was to become like a brother to me over the next few years, and was destined to play an even bigger part in my life as I got older.

Life began in a new direction from that day onward. Mum was sceptical. 'I'll give it a few weeks', she thought, watching to see the old 'me' return. But it didn't. I began to spend more time at church and with my sister, and we became good friends. I began to change, although I struggled in vain with the addiction to cigarettes, the one battle it seemed I would never win. However, I stopped swearing which was a miracle, as I had a mouth that a navvy would have been proud of, and my sense of humour started to become innocent instead of crude. Life still consisted of struggles on a daily basis, but the lessons learned began to shape my character in a positive way, although it was hard to give up my old way of dealing with issues, as in order to do so, I had to admit I was wrong and that my ways had not worked. Pride has an amazing way of keeping one bound to ineffective thoughts and actions, even when logic and wisdom screams one's folly from the rooftops.

Friday nights became the highlight of my week, as my sister and I would pile into my car, now upgraded to a Mini Metro, and drive to the West coast, up a dirt track lane to Fort Richmond, an old fortification built on a cliff edge. Here, in the basement Pilgrims Temperance Bar had it's home, run by George Torode, an original Guernseyman, and Peter. George was later to become one of Guernsey's most beloved authors, writing a series of "Donkey Books' about Guernsey's eccentric characters, never realising that he would be remembered as one of them. He had an insatiable desire to see people find the love that only God can give and his whole life was devoted to showing them exactly where to look. Pilgrims was one of these places; somewhere for the lonely, displaced youth of the island to meet in safety and ask honest questions about life, death and all things in-between that matter. It was a place of acceptance, faith and practical love, and God bought many a hurting soul in through the doors to be nurtured back to spiritual health - sometimes gently, sometimes not quite so; but always as God led.

Pilgies, as it was affectionately called, was a unique experience. Soft drinks hung in optics around a 'bar' and we, the patrons of the establishment, were encouraged to pick out different flavours which George would mix together to make some foul smelling beverage that we then had the privilege to name. 'Aircraft Fuel' is the one that stands out for me, a dark evil looking liquid that only the bravest would venture to try out! The room was no more than twenty square feet, but it housed a bar, a couple of low coffee tables and seats - and a stage, on which stood an old piano. The walls and arched ceiling were painted black, with fluorescent planets and stars glowing from it that created a feeling of being outside on a clear night. There was a permanent musty smell which wasn't so bad after an entire can of air freshener had been sprayed around the room each week, while we sat in the car-park and waited for the fumes to settle, and it was so damp that every week the piano went more out of tune until it eventually gave up altogether.

George supplied Hot Cross Buns in summer and Crumpets in winter, and played extremely loud music on the record player, usually old '78' vinyls of really old gospel choirs. Later in the evening we would have a time of praise and worship, thanking God for his greatness and praying for any needs. Since the piano had sadly squeaked out its last note a drum kit had appeared in its stead, which George played loudly during these times, as he had been a drummer in a local group in his youth. Two or three guitars usually accompanied him, as there were many talented (and not so talented!) musicians who frequented Pilgies – and they were all encouraged to participate. And it didn't matter if you weren't musical as there were always a few tambourines supplied that could be whacked until your ears rang in time with the enthusiastic clamour!

It was an exciting time full of noise and busyness, and people from all walks of life, both churchgoers and teenagers just bored with nowhere to go, came to view Pilgies as a second home. Friendships were forged which would span decades, and most of the young people went on to join missionary organisations, to fulfil dreams that had been fuelled by the unselfish love and motivation that was shown and lived by George, and all that Pilgies stood for.

"Quiet please!" shouted George, above the chattering of noisy teenagers, "Tonight, we have a performance!" The crowd quietened as my sister and I took a deep breath and launched into our offering. We had written a song about Pilgies that afternoon on the spur of the moment, to the tune of the old hymn "To Be a Pilgrim" and that same night we sang it, amid lots of laughter, to our friends who were proud to be part of this small Friday night community:

"It is Friday night again; we're all on our way,
We've been waiting all the week, just for this day
We drive for miles and miles - from Town down to the sea
We drive through mud and slush
To be at Pilgrims

When we get there it's so cold, our toes are freezing,
So the heaters are turned on to stop us from sneezing,
Out comes the can of Haze to kill that musty smell
We choke to death as well
Oh who'd miss Pilgrims!

This is George, now he's a loon: he's the local nutter
He concocts these famous drinks to make you cough and splutter
Our throats are raw and sore: his music is so loud
We have to scream and shout
To talk at Pilgrims

Try the crumpets - they're a gem: oozing with butter
Guess who keeps forgetting them? Yes, it's that nutter!
When will he ever learn the 'till' works better here.
But still we come each year
Cause we love Pilgrims"

It was clear as we finished that we had captured the very essence of a typical Pilgies night, which everyone identified with and somewhere there is a video of George and I years later performing it again, to the delight of the reminiscing crowd. It was also during this time that I discovered that I could write songs. I had always had a flair for writing poetry but now I found that along with the lyrics, usually about my newfound faith and the goodness of God, there often came a tune. Sometimes I would sit by one of the coffee tables at Pilgrims and write a complete song, lyrics and music, while the noise level in the cramped space reached 'deafening': it was as though I could just retreat into another world and switch off the racket all around me.

However, even though I loved writing and singing the songs, I still had no self-confidence and was convinced that they weren't very good, so I wouldn't sing them to anybody: no audience allowed, just me and my keyboard, God and the wind. Later on though, I did share one song with Peter and was surprised by his reaction. He was in the throes, he said, of organising a set of studio sessions to professionally record some of his own compositions and had asked my sister to be his backing vocalist.

"But I only have two songs, and I wanted three" he finished telling me. "I'd like to add that song onto the tape, if that's alright with you? You can sing the main vocals and your sister and I can be your backing vocalists."

And that is what we did. We practised for weeks and weeks at a church which kindly lent us their building on Sunday afternoons, and had many fun times, the memories of which still make me chuckle today and then we recorded for weeks and weeks. The 'studio' was on the top floor of somebody's house with limited space and equipment, so when any of the musicians were recording and they needed to hear the song, my sister and I ended up on the landing outside the room singing into a microphone direct into their headphones. The exciting part was that due to severe lack of space on the landing, we had to share the microphone and face each other without giggling, which we didn't manage very often.

At one point Peter pulled out a flute and proceeded to lay down a flute soundtrack, much to the astonishment of all of us. Never, in all the weeks and months of rehearsing in the church, had we seen as much as a glimpse of a flute and none of us knew that Peter even played one! But as we listened in silence while he played a hauntingly beautiful melody that wove in and out of the main tune, I realised that he had a lovely sensitivity in his playing. I closed my eyes and felt all the tiredness drift away.

'Wow, I could listen to this all day' I thought dreamily. It was a very special moment.

Recording is a very intense business and takes a lot of concentration when the pressure is on to get it right. It was extremely hard work for me especially as I was working a six-day week at the time and all the recording was being done after work until ten o'clock in the evening and later- but I didn't mind as I was doing what I loved – singing. Eventually it was finished and we were all invited to sit in on a mixing session so we could all have a say in how the final product was put together and mixed down. The final result was called 'Footprints', and when my sister presented a photograph of a beautiful Guernsey sunset that she had taken, we knew that we had our cover design. The cassette tape that was finally produced was not for sale but was given to our friends and families, and even made its way to other parts of the world, including Australia and Spain.

Chapter 9
ROLLERCOASTER RIDE

"Are you coming on Saturday, Ali?" my sister asked one Friday. Nodding enthusiastically I grinned. "Yes, I wouldn't miss it for the world"

"Why, what's happening on Saturday?" queried Mum, coming into the lounge where we were sat like bookends on the sofa.

"I'm going to join Gaggy, George and Peter in Town," I answered, as mum's face dropped.

"Oh." She retreated back into the kitchen, unsure how to handle this latest development.

George, Peter and my sister had started to sing Gospel songs in the Town centre every Saturday afternoon accompanied by tambourines and a guitar, and Peter and George also preached the Gospel: something that embarrassed Mum so much that she took pains to steer well clear of it. Now, to her horror, I was going to join them – not every week, but when I could – and she was horrified! But I loved it. We sang some of our Pilgies 'Gospel' favourites, including "This Little Light of Mine", "Hand Me Down My Silver Trumpet, Gabriel" and "This World is Not My Home" along with a whole host of really ancient gospel songs, most of which I had never heard of! I learned them pretty quickly though, and before long I was belting them out and harmonising when I couldn't reach the high notes.

By this time I had grown tired of working at the Chip Shop and had started work at a dry cleaning outlet situated by the bus terminus on the seafront. I had a lovely view of Castle Cornet out of the window and listened out eagerly for the 'BOOM!' of the noonday gun, which was fired from the Castle every day for the benefit of the island's visitors, as it also signalled my lunch hour! I was promoted to Manageress after only two weeks, in charge of two other counter staff and second only to the Manager of the dry cleaning section, and I loved it. It was long hours, but I enjoyed rising to the challenge of the responsibility I had been given and always made it into work whatever the weather.

Guernsey is not known for having snow as it is in the warm gulf stream of the English Channel, nearer to France than England, but occasionally some manages to sneak past the warm air and blanket this tiny island, wreaking havoc with traffic on its narrow roads and steep hills. That winter we had snow; so much in fact, that I abandoned all hope of driving to work. It was only a five-minute drive, but it was all down steeply winding roads with hairpin bends thrown in for good measure and it wasn't worth risking the possibility of demolishing my car – especially when we only had snow for three days at most! The twenty-minute walk was almost as treacherous as driving, but at least I could hang onto gateposts and lampposts on my way down the almost vertically steep hills. The bottom of Candie Road was my greatest challenge, for just as I managed to slide to a halt at the corner I was faced with a 180° bend to the left as it joined up with the main hill on its way down to the new car park at the harbour.

Thankfully someone had installed a metal railing on the edge of the pavement, so instead of skating across the road, or slaloming down the hill, I managed to hang onto the railing and pull myself around while my feet went in every direction but the one I was aiming for, before running the gauntlet of trying to cross over this main road on the corner with the odd car careening downwards towards me with no control whatsoever. By the time I reached the relative flat just before the pedestrianised part of Town where the final hill dropped down between the shops toward the seafront, its cobbles hidden under ice, I was feeling a little shaken by the near-falls I had encountered. The wind was now whipping the new falling snow in my face and I bowed my head, dug my hands deeper into my pockets, hunched my shoulders and marched resolutely along the pavement, thankful that I was not sliding downhill for a few minutes and able to keep my balance. However, I knew once I got past the buildings on my left that I would again be running the gauntlet.

BANG! I was almost knocked out by the force of the metal pole that loomed up suddenly in front of me. I had walked into a scaffold pole outside one of Guernsey's most prestigious hotels. Keeping my head down, I stepped neatly to my right, secure in the knowledge that I would miss the next pole, and resumed my course, my head ringing from the contact with the unyielding metal.

BANG! My head felt like a battering ram as I marched straight into another pole. I shook my head and, muttering to myself, again took a step sideways to the right without looking up… and marched into a third pole. I heard a stifled laugh and looked up to see a man at an open window in line with one of the lower ledges of the scaffold in tears, unable to withhold his mirth one minute longer. I also saw that, had I looked up sooner I could have avoided nearly knocking my brains out. The scaffold had been set out parallel with the front of the hotel, diagonally across the pavement. Had I continued in a straight line, I would have missed the other two poles, but stepping to the right as I did, had put me in the direct path of the next pole: no wonder the man couldn't contain himself! Embarrassed as I was, there was nothing for it but to make light of it. I shrugged my shoulders.

"One of those days!" I acknowledged to my audience of one, and walked sedately on with as much dignity I could muster as his laughter, now unfettered, rang mockingly in my ears. A few days later, while the snow still lay thick on the ground, I began to walk across the zebra crossing in front of my house and felt my feet grow ominously cold. Looking down halfway across, I realised I still had my slippers on and had to turn back, to the amused smirks of the drivers waiting to continue on their journeys and I wondered, was I always destined to be the butt of some joke?

Meanwhile my sister joined a Spanish singing group called 'Exalto', who were part of YWAM, and went on tour with them for six months around the USA. The weekend before she left, she organised a 'Thank Offering' evening in our church, to publicly thank God for all that He had done for her. It was to be an evening of dance, sketches and songs and Mum was invited; I am not sure who was the most surprised when she accepted! That decision to go was to be a turning point in her own life, as that evening she too walked the road of repentance and forgiveness and began her new journey.

Mum, coming from a background without any form of Christianity, knew nothing about the Bible. Consequently, every night for the six months that my sister was enjoying herself in New York and Texas, I endured being woken on a regular basis as she discovered truths and promises that had filled her with delight as she read her Bible in bed. It was nice to share her excitement – I just wished it had been during daylight hours!

They say that the best way to learn is to teach and I suddenly found myself having to search my Bible for answers to the myriad of questions that Mum flung at me. It was good for me as it made me continually go to my Bible for these answers instead of seeking out my sister and asking her, which is what I would have normally done. Finally the six months passed and my sister returned home, becoming excited when I told her about mum's nightly question and answer sessions, and her exuberance and enthusiasm with her newfound faith.

"But" I warned her, "It plays havoc with your sleep!"

That night we had just settled nice and snuggled in our beds, drifting off to that semi-conscious state that dreams inhabit, when it started.

"Hey! Guess what?"

My sister and I sat up straight in our beds, awoken by the shout of triumph that had emitted from our mother's bedroom.

"What is it?" we chorused back, aware that it was nearly midnight.

"I've just found out where the rainbow came from!" came the excited reply. We groaned and pulled the duvets back over our heads.

"Go back to sleep, Mum."

Great – now she was waking us both up!

Mum and I had formed quite a close bond during the previous six months and we had shared many amazing moments together, some funny – like the church service on the Sunday morning after a wedding, when there had been an extra chair placed on the platform at the front of the church. The Pastor had made his entrance from the small door at the back of the platform, as he always did, during the first part of the worship and prayer whilst the congregation's eyes were closed, and sat, as he always did, on the end chair - only two of the chair legs were not quite on the platform and I looked up just in time to see an explosion of arms and legs as he disappeared from view behind the pulpit and his Bible went sailing over his head. By the shake of Mum's shoulders I knew I wasn't the only witness, but it took all my willpower to not laugh out loud, as everybody else had their eyes shut and the mood was very meditative. I daren't close my eyes for quite a while, as every time I did the scene replayed before me like a movie and most of the morning had passed before I could stop chuckling quietly to myself.

We also shared one of the most amazing spiritual moments I have ever encountered and I believe that, had she not been with me, I would have doubted to this day what I saw happen. We were on our way to church one Sunday evening. It had been a glorious summer: the sun was warm and the breezes light, and on this particular day we had decided that we would go for a drive before setting out for church. Although one of the downsides to living in a small island of only 24 square miles is the fact that it only takes twenty minutes to get anywhere, there are 400 miles of winding roads that can alternatively make the journey last hours! I was driving, and we took the main road that would lead to the 'top parishes' in the south of the island.

Although Guernsey is so small, there is tremendous diversity in the landscape of the parishes: the North of the island is low-lying, with long stretches of sandy beaches, a windswept 'common', and many rocky outcrops, perfect for mackerel fishing. The East is mainly built up with the main Town, consisting of narrow little cobbled streets in between squashed higgledy houses, some which date back many years, including the house where Victor Hugo, the exiled French author, wrote 'Les Misérables' and 'Toilers of the Sea'. A smaller shopping 'town' called The Bridge lies further along the East coast towards the North, where industrialism is the name of the game. Massive gas tanks, electricity power station and many welding and shipping companies make up the majority of buildings here, along with an old harbour. A sweeping look out to sea reveals the tiny islands of Herm, Jethou and Breqhou, with Sark lurking behind them just to the right and Jersey beyond them all on the horizon. A clear day will result in also being able to see Alderney to the far left, while occasionally the visibility is clear enough to spot a nuclear power station on the coast of France: indeed at night car headlights can often be seen moving along the French coast.

The West coast is picturesque, with sandy coves and eroded grassy headlands, where the sea walls built as a defence against the onslaught of the tide show many signs of rebuilding from when high winds and high water clash and waves crash onto the coast roads, depositing boulders and seaweed on cars and leaving all manner of debris in it's wake. Here is where you'll find rough unmade dirt tracks leading to car parks where locals and visitors alike sit and gaze in awe at the sunsets, which are like no others in this world, and which are never the same twice. Lihou, a tiny island with only one house and an old haunted priory, lies just off this side of Guernsey and is only accessible at low tide, when the cobbled causeway that joins the two islands is uncovered.

The South is by far the prettiest part of the island, with tall cliffs sheltering tiny pebbly coves that can only be accessed by steps built into, or against the rock. Cliff paths are in abundance, with wild flowers, panoramic views, many hidden beaches and gorse. Guernsey granite is used in building many of the traditional cottages, and these are in abundance here. Pleinmont Point, the south-westerly tip of the island, is a favourite place for walking and exploring in the ferns and the gorse; to stand on the rugged cliffs and watch the waves crash against the rocks below, while rabbits abound and children play in the 'Fairy Ring', a place that local folklore would have us believe the pagans of old (and not so old) would worship their deities.

We decided to drive through the southern parishes, where we could enjoy the scenery and maybe buy some flowers from one of the many hedgerow stalls set out at the end of immaculately kept driveways. Here, just past the Airport, there is a hotel along the main road which is unique: it has a scarecrow type 'witch' on her broomstick perched between the chimney and the roof, making it a very recognisable landmark, and immediately after the hotel is a small crossroads with an extremely narrow single track lane on the left of the main road and another one, almost as narrow and almost opposite, on the right. These lanes are very seldom used and so narrow that most people drive past them without noticing that they are even there.

We drove past the hotel commenting on the 'witch' and wondering what the story behind her was, and as we approached the crossroads a red car suddenly appeared at the left hand junction. It was going so fast that I could see that it was not going to be able to stop, and in that split second I braced myself for impact. It never came. What happened next was so inexplicable that I struggle to describe it. My car went into suspended animation – like 'warp speed' in reverse. I did not take my hands off the wheel nor my foot off the accelerator. We were driving at 35 mph (the Guernsey speed limit) and my speed dial still showed 35mph – but we were not going anywhere. We watched the red car as it overshot the junction, raced across the road in front of us and disappeared down the lane on our right. I blinked and we were driving again, as if nothing had happened. The whole thing had taken just a split second, but it had felt timeless and I still had not moved my hands or my feet.

"Did you see...?" Mum's voice trailed off as I turned my head towards her, unable to believe what I had seen. I nodded slowly. We continued in silence as the enormity of what had happened began to dawn on us both. To this day I firmly believe that God intervened that day and sent His angels to protect us, and it is an awesome feeling. The ironic thing is that when we got to church we were so excited that we told everybody... and no one believed us!

But soon the winds of change were blowing again. My sister seemed very unsettled, although she appeared to fit back into her old life: she attended the same church and returned to the same job but she was different, and within a short time her desire for space and city life won the day and she moved back to Spain. Then the winds of change became hurricane force as Mum's personal circumstances changed, resulting in her also deciding to move – to England. I was persuaded to choose to stay in Guernsey: after all it was my home. I was part of my church community, I had a good job and maybe I was now mature enough for independence, so I moved into a rented room in a boarding house with Shani my cat, confident that life was on the up.

However, I had not realised how much I had relied on others to keep me accountable, and now my entire support system was no longer in place life began to feel complicated and upright living again seemed to be beyond my grasp. I gradually stopped going to Pilgrims and began to withdraw a little into myself. I still attended the same church, but again I began to feel distanced from the people there. I was lonely and found that I had relied on my mum so much to be my friend that I did not really know anyone else. I had no one to be a 'spiritual parent' to me: no one who I could share my struggles with, and I began to fall back into the old routines and meet up with old friends from my old life.

When my Pastor told me that I was a role model to the younger members of the youth group and that I had to stop seeing my current boyfriend, who was not a Christian, instead of sharing how I was struggling I became angry. Amazingly enough I was still immature and unable to handle the responsibility of being an example to other kids, so I reacted in the time honoured traditional way that I knew. I rebelled and left the church – and married him.

Chapter 10
ANIMAL ANTICS

"Do you take this man…?"

It was 1989 and I was standing at the altar dressed in white. It wasn't a dream but it felt like one. It was my 'big day' and all my family were there. So were his, although I wasn't quite so pleased about that. My wedding present from my dad had been a pony and open trap to ferry himself and the Bride-to-be to the church and then the Newlyweds from the church to the reception. Almost everything had gone to plan but we hadn't counted on the weather. We had had a lovely dry summer and I had been looking forward to parading along Guernsey's west coast in bright sunshine like a princess in her carriage. The reality hit when I opened my eyes on the day to find the sky looking ominously overcast and a cool easterly wind whipping up the dust. Half way to the church the heavens opened and the wind blew the rain sideways. It was the only Saturday to have rain that summer. So, covered with blankets and a golfing umbrella we splashed our way around the coast to the church and nobody saw me decked out in all my finery (and blankets) as everyone who had been caught out in the rain had their heads down against the wind, or were hiding behind, and fighting with, umbrellas. I arrived at the church dry but my father was two-tone, as he had held the huge umbrella more over me than himself on our trip and it had not quite covered both of us, leaving him with a dry pale grey suit on one side and a wet dark grey suit on the other. Thankfully he was drying nicely now we were here and I was able to concentrate on what the vicar was saying.

"I now pronounce you husband and wife."

It was a fairytale wedding. As the first in my generation of the family to wed, I had wanted a proper wedding in a church and it had taken my fiancé and I eighteen months to save the money needed for the grand scale wedding I had planned. It was an amazing day only slightly marred by the behaviour of my new family in-law. My new husband came from a family that was well known throughout the island. Private squabbles amongst themselves frequently spilled over into public life and a police presence was often needed to smooth ruffled feathers and restore the peace. I found myself feeling thankful that he was different as he desperately wanted to better himself and I was part of that dream. As the reception wore on his relatives, spurred on by free drinks, became an embarrassment to themselves and I couldn't wait for the evening to end so I could be alone with my new husband, naively thinking that we would live our lives separate to the rest of the clan.

We honeymooned in Scotland, where I was shocked to find that my new husband, aged 28, missed his parents and felt duty bound to call home and check on them daily, and this was my first inkling of the little boy I had married. That said, we had an amazing time. We visited Loch Ness, but alas we did not spot the monster, although we looked. Coming from a very superstitious background, he refused point blank to go out onto the lake in one of the "Jacobite" cruisers just in case 'Nessie' did appear, even though I teased him mercilessly about it – until I realised how strong his fear was. We rode on a double-decker bus (Guernsey does not have any – nor trains) and ate at MacDonald's: Guernsey does not have one of those either! The weather was glorious and we were well rested when we returned to Guernsey, via Mum's house in the South of England.

We bought a little Guernsey granite cottage on the outskirts of the St Peter Port and settled into married life. We both gave up smoking (finally!) and life looked good. He was a good provider and a keen fisherman, often heading for the rocky headland with his fishing rod after finishing a gruelling day working in hot greenhouses and returning a couple of hours later with fresh mackerel for tea. However, he was very much the 'little boy' that I had glimpsed on honeymoon and I found myself constantly having to mother him. The 'little boy' in him, incidentally, was also very comical and slapstick, and we would spend many moments during our marriage crying with laughter over some ludicrous thing that he had said or done. He loved crosswords, but any serious attempt at writing the answers always dissolved into hysterical laughter as he was dyslexic and would not only spell the answers wrong, but sometimes also jumble up the clue, making the answer impossible to work out.

"Ok, what's 'ten down', again?"

We were sitting in bed with the crossword book and he had decided he would read out the clues and we could then both work out the answers. We were on the last clue, and had been for days, but the answer was evading us.

"Male Volent" he answered.

"Male what?"

"Volent"

I had racked my brains for a week. I had no idea what a 'volent' was, never mind what a male one would be called. Finally, in desperation, I grabbed the book off him and scanned down to the clue in question. I sighed deeply.

"That says malevolent ..."

That incident became our favourite one to tell at family gatherings over the years, as it never ceased to make us laugh.

After a year or so of marriage we decided we would like to add a dog to our household. A few years before whilst still living with Mum I had acquired an all ginger female cat, which was quite rare as ginger cats are always Toms. I had been visiting a friend's aunt, who had begun telling me about the litter her cat had just had while she hunted for the kittens, one by one, to show me.

"There is another one, somewhere," she smiled at me, as I played with the four little balls of fluff, "but she's always hiding and jumping out on me. She's such a little madam!"

She sighed, exasperated, as she went off to hunt a little more for the 'elusive' kitten.

"Ouch!" I jumped up as a sharp pain shot through the back of my ankle. My foot shot forward and I looked down to see a ball of ginger fur hanging doggedly onto my foot. (no pun intended!)

"Oh, there she is!" 'Auntie' cried happily, disengaging the hissing, spitting fur ball from my foot, while I rubbed my now bleeding ankle, "She was under the settee!"

I fell in love with her and a week later took her home. She was a wildcat but utterly devoted to me and I named her Shani.

Later, when mum had moved away and I was living at the boarding house, my landlady's cat had a litter and I ended up the proud owner of a ginger and white bundle of licks and purrs, with a pointy tail that stuck up straight like an aerial making her look like a fairground 'bumper car' as she ran around. I called her Pickles and she lived up to her name, as she emptied my landlady's fishpond on a regular basis.

"I don't know where all my fish have gone," my landlady confided in me one afternoon, looking perplexed, " I have re-filled that pond twice in the past month."

I didn't have the heart to tell her that I had seen my little tea-leaf hiding up the tree that overhung the pond that morning, seen her rush down the tree trunk straight into the pond and scoop up what was obviously the last goldfish, and then seen her strut, purring, behind my landlady and back into the house soaking wet and licking her lips. She was definitely a 'pickle' but she loved her cuddles and always looked so innocent that everybody loved her instantly. Well, almost everybody. Shani detested her on sight as jealousy reared its ugly head, and constantly found new ways to clout her, pounce on her or steal her food. Years later, Pickles got her own back by waiting outside the cat flap for Shani to poke her head out – just so she could clout her back!

Growing up I had always had pets: Rusty was the family dog when I was small. He was a mongrel who was extremely suspicious of me, as he was part of the family before I was born and saw himself as above me in the pecking order – and I felt I could never trust him. He was very much my dad's dog, although he had actually been given to my mum as a present. He was only a puppy when they acquired him so Dad decided to take him to work everyday in order that he could do some training during his lunch hour. As his only form of transport at the time was a large big-engined motorbike, Dad had no option but to take him on that. So from puppy-hood Rusty learned to balance on the petrol tank, and every morning he could be seen leaning into the sharp corners with his ears streaming out behind him like Mutley! He never lost that sense of balance, and even when my parents later graduated to a car he would sit on the floor between the legs of the front passenger and begin to position himself as the corner approached, ready to lean into it. He must have learned to pick up the change in the movement of the vehicle from his motorbike days because he always leaned the correct way, usually squashing the person's leg in the process, even when he could not see the road.

When we lived at the 'Dump' my sister and I also had a blue budgie called Joey: a regular cheeky little chappie. He could say his name and when let out of his cage he would play his one of his favourite games, of which there were a few. Dive-bombing the dog while he slept was one that he loved. Landing on our heads and running up and down our shoulders was another, although I didn't like that game so much as he was prone to leaving little 'presents' on our heads, which usually sent me into squeals of "Mum! He's pooed on me again!" as I ran around the room trying to dislodge him before he could add to the insult.

Mum was the administrator/secretary for the taxi-business so there was usually wages to sort out on a weekly basis: and this was the time Joey waited for, for then he could play his favourite of all the games. He would sit quietly on the curtain rail, or the lampshade and watch as she began counting out the paper money into piles and stacking the coins in neat little towers ready to begin sorting out the wages. Gradually he would sneak closer and closer until he could steal her pen and run up and down the table with it, rolling it over and over in his beak. When he became bored with that, he would turn his attention to the towers of coins, which he would systematically knock over so he could roll the coins across the table and off the edge, including heavy 50p pieces, dropping more on her head with absolute precision when she bent to retrieve them. Sitting back up at the table with a handful of change Mum's eyes would narrow as she spotted the telltale chewed corners of the £10, £5 and £1 notes and a very agile budgie who resisted all attempts to catch him and return him behind bars!

He loved chewing paper and usually spat it out, which caused a little fuss when it was the paper-type lampshade above the dining table that he was chewing ... and the spat out bits floated into my sister's dinner! One day, Mum was reading the newspaper and a hole appeared in the middle, causing her to sigh...she never knew where he would turn up next! When he passed onto paper-chewing budgie-heaven (don't knock my theology!) we acquired two more budgies, a blue one and a green one, which we called Joey and Peter, but they never talked to us (probably because they preferred to talk 'budgie' to each other) and didn't do any of the antics that made the original budgie so endearing.

After Rusty died, I was allowed a golden hamster, which I called Chas. However, I had to rename her Chassie, after we discovered her true sex! She had a large plastic ball that she would run around the lounge in, but she had to be watched closely, as her favourite game was to bang the ball against any hard object (wall, chair leg, door post) until it split open. The sudden silence that advertised her Houdini-like tendencies was quickly followed by cries of "Chassie's out!" heralding yet another evening of playing the game of 'hunt the hamster'! She was a grumpy little thing – until she escaped and went AWOL for three days. She made it up a flight of stairs and found her way into the spare room, which was full of cuddly toys. We probably would never have found her but for the fact that, being extremely inquisitive, she investigated an antique jug and bowl set before looking for a nice cosy teddy bear to sleep in and managed to fall into the jug.

When I finally found her she was wet, cold, hungry and very weak after being totally trapped without food for so long. I reached into the jug and closed my hand around her, intending to lift her out, but the neck was too tight for both my hand and the hamster to come out together, so the only way to get her through the neck of the jug was to ...tip it up. After giving her a warm bath in the sink to thaw her out, I dried her and then wrapped her in an old tea towel and cuddled her until she fell asleep from exhaustion. She was so deeply asleep that she never stirred, not even when I unwrapped her and placed her warm little body in her bed and covered her up. It was nearly a week before her little face emerged from her 'igloo' bed looking for food, and when she did finally surface, she was the sweetest, best-tempered hamster that ever lived and would run to me for a cuddle whenever I opened her cage.

And now I was going to enter into the realms of joint dog-ownership, and wondered if I was ready. We had decided to offer a home to an unwanted dog, preferably a young Labrador Cross as we wanted something safe if we had children, so my husband set off to the local RSPCA shelter to make enquiries while I went to work. When he collected me at the end of my shift he seemed excited.

"What?" I asked, as he practically bounced his way to the car. He grinned at me like a little schoolboy and then announced, "He's in the car!"

"Who?"

"The dog."

I stopped dead in my tracks. "The...dog...is...in...the...car..." I repeated slowly, trying to take it in. We had no dog bed, no dog food and no blankets. Nothing. He was supposed to be going to look. Just look. Nothing else. I immediately went into mental overdrive, working out how we could acquire all the essentials on the way home.

"Ok," I sighed, "Well, we have him now. Is he a Lab Cross?" He nodded, affirmative.

"And how old is he?"

More smiles, though a little uncertain now, "About nine months," he answered, "but he looks big for his age, cause of what he's crossed with"

"What's that?" I laughed, "a Doberman?"

Silence....

We reached the car, and I opened the door to be confronted with a big black goofy looking dog taking up the entire front seat, with a truly dopey expression on his face. He was all nose, ears, legs and tongue. His name was Kal and he had a history of ill-treatment which, as we were about to find out, would make him a little of a challenge as he was very soft-hearted and craved attention (not unlike myself!) On arriving home, Kal and Pickles surprisingly became firm friends - while Kal and Shani unsurprisingly became sworn enemies. We found out that not only was he a Labrador and Doberman cross, but that there was also Greyhound in there somewhere. He had the Labrador shaped face and temperament, the floppy ears and speed of the Greyhound, and the nose, warts and fierce protectiveness of the guard-dog Doberman. What a combination!

But he was also a damaged soul, fearful of vacuum cleaners, Christmas crackers and squeaky toys. Raised voices would send him into his bed, where he would sit and shiver with his head down and his tail feebly thumping on the floor. It broke my heart to see. Unfortunately, he was also very naughty and it was a struggle to find ways of communicating displeasure to him without shouting, as he could drive me to distraction. He loved my swing-bin and treated it like a 'lucky dip', resulting in me having to lock it away in a cupboard to stop its contents ending up all over my kitchen.

He hated brass bands and would howl for the duration of their playing until they were well out of earshot, which made the Poppy Day parade that came past our house every year in November a deafening experience indoors. But he was also comical. I had two windows in my lounge that fronted onto the road with very deep windowsills, which the cats would sit in, one in each window. People would often comment in passing, as they looked very sweet, but one day I arrived home to find a small group outside my house giggling and pointing. As I moved closer to the house, I couldn't help but smile: in one window sat both cats and in the other, looking like a bunched up tarantula… was Kal.

Shani was disgusted that there was a dog in the house and never missed an opportunity to let him know that she considered herself the boss, often hiding on top of the kitchen worktops so she could take a swipe at him as he walked past. He never spotted her and so he was always totally unprepared for the hissing, spitting, growling angry face that suddenly loomed in front of him, making him back-step with a start and a bewildered look. He had a burnished orange blanket in his bed, not unlike in colour to Shani, and she thought it funny to hide amongst its folds, jumping out on him when he least expected it: until the day fortune smiled on him. Shani was asleep on the arm of the settee blissfully dreaming of mice and roast chicken when Kal wandered into the room. As he passed the settee he looked at her, as she was eye-level with him. He stopped; looked at me, looked at her, looked at me again, looked back at her - and with a triumphant air, gave a loud "WOOF!' directly behind her. There was a flurry of ginger fur, claws, and a loud 'YEOWL!" as she shot off her perch and streaked across the room and out of the door. Kal looked at me as if to say, "Sorted." and continued on his way to bed while I cried with laughter. Shani never played her trick again and I will never forget the look of delight on that dog's face when he had finally managed some payback.

Chapter 11
UNEXPECTED TURNS

Meanwhile life was setting up a nasty surprise. I was still working at the dry cleaners and one morning as I arrived at work, I was summoned to the office. Two years previously some money had gone missing from the in-store safe overnight. At the time, the police had been called and the three key-holders had been questioned: the Manager, myself and another girl who covered for me on my days off. As their findings were inconclusive, my employers were advised to sack all of us and start again, which they refused to do. Now two years later it had happened again, only now I was the only original staff member still working there. The manager had retired and the other girl had left to start a family. One and one was added up and the answer was.... I must have done it. No proof required, no asking, no searching, no investigation, just sacked on the spot. I was devastated, although I now see that I was simply reaping the dishonesty that I had sown in my earlier years.

I had begun to attend church again during the early years of my marriage, determined to connect with this God who I knew was real but I seemed unable to hold onto. And it was to Him that I finally turned. To my amazement, one of the members of Shiloh Church where I was attending, came forward and offered me a job in one of the branches of Le Riches Stores (Guernsey's answer to a supermarket/convenience store), of which he was the Regional Manager. I was amazed: firstly that he believed that I was innocent and secondly, that he would ask one of his managers to employ me. As it happened, this was probably the best move I could have made, as I loved working with the staff and management there and still count some of them among my close friends even now many years later.

Nigel, who was in charge of the fruit and vegetable section, had a very dry sense of humour and often wound up the regular customers until we cried with laughter. One lady who came in daily, was one of those people who ask questions about everything so that she could find something to complain about, usually the place of origin of the food.

"Where are these apples from?" she demanded to know one Monday morning. It had been raining all weekend and the downpours had continued into the new week so we were all a little fed up, but when we saw the twinkle in Nigel's eye we drew closer and waited for his answer.

"Pardon?" he said loudly, cupping his ear, and winking at us. She repeated the question.

"What?" Nigel said, louder. It was starting to look like my favourite episode of 'Fawlty Towers'.

A third time the question was asked and then finally with a straight face Nigel said with utter seriousness

"Off a tree, my love" and then proceeded in true Basil Fawlty style to wander off muttering to himself. The look on the lady's face was priceless and I could see that she really couldn't believe what she had heard!

A couple of years passed, and the problems with the dry cleaners faded into the distance as I moved on with my life. Then one day, by chance, I found out on the grapevine that the thief had finally been identified. I was shocked to find out that it had been one of my co-workers, but I couldn't figure out how she could have accomplished both robberies, as she had only been working for the company for six months at the time of the second theft, and I had never even met her at the time of the first. After some investigation however, it transpired that she was the daughter-in-law of the Manager of the dry cleaning section and had somehow managed to copy his key and orchestrate the original theft. When the second theft occurred, the Manager had retired, but now she was working for me in the shop. I was stunned when I was told this, as I couldn't get my head around the fact that she had let me be sacked when I thought we were friends.

I was a more than a little disappointed that although I now knew the truth, God had not yet vindicated me, so I continued to pray. But God's timing isn't the same as ours and I knew that I had to let go and let God orchestrate the vindication.

Sure enough a few weeks later the Area Manager himself, the one who had actually sacked me without allowing me to defend myself, came into the shop. It was Christmas and the shop was packed with people buying trolley loads ready for the holiday. He joined the queue for my till and as I saw him I was reminded that he had never contacted me regarding the fact that I had now been proven innocent and that I had received no apology: and now he had the audacity to come to my present place of employment and stand there as if nothing had happened – and I saw red. As he shuffled closer toward me with his trolley I grew angrier and angrier until, by the time he reached me I was shaking. I took a deep breath. I knew that I did not need to defend myself; that both he and I knew that I was innocent of the crime I was accused of, but that if I handled this badly I could end up sounding vindictive. So controlling the desire to scream and call him a few choice names, I decided to remain calm, not raise my voice, and behave like a mature adult. It took all I had!

Finally it was his turn to be served.

"Hi" I smiled, disarmingly. He smiled back and started some small talk. I let him rabbit on for a few moments and then, as he began waffling on about another topic I struck, cutting him off mid-flow.

"So, where's my apology, then?"

"Er...I beg your pardon?"

"I said, 'Where's my apology?'" I repeated, casually continuing to scan his items.

"I don't understand."

However, I could see he was beginning to feel a little uneasy at this point so, emboldened by the knowledge that he knew exactly what I was talking about, I leaned towards him and added, conspiratorially,

"I know who did it."

He looked a little confused so, as I tallied up his shopping, I enlightened him with my newfound facts and watched with great delight as he finally had the decency to look embarrassed. As I finished, a deathly hush settled over my queue, and I had the immense satisfaction of watching him frantically trying to find something to say, and failing.

"Ah… well… um…well, you see…"he stuttered, looking around him.

"I'll expect my written apology in the post then, shall I?" I prompted. Nodding, he hastily gathered up his shopping and practically ran out of the shop, without so much as a backward glance. I took a deep breath, composed myself and prepared to serve the next customer. I have been vindicated, I thought to myself, and only God could have planned it so precisely.

"Thank you, Lord," I whispered gratefully.

The next customer in the line looked down at me as she loaded her shopping onto the moving belt.

"Well done" she smiled. I returned the smile and looked over my shoulder to see my manager giving me the 'thumbs up' sign as he leaned out of the office door, where he had been lurking and listening throughout the entire proceedings. I never did receive the written apology but it didn't really matter. I knew that he was aware I knew the truth, and that was enough.

Finally, after five years of marriage we received the news we had been waiting for: we were going to have a baby, and we were overjoyed. Unfortunately our joy was short-lived as I miscarried early on in the pregnancy leaving us heartbroken. Although we continued to try for another baby, my husband was not mature enough to handle the disappointment and became an absent husband, preferring to spend his spare time fishing with his mates, or down at a friend's house, a choice that would later lead him into situations he was ill equipped to handle. I, on the other hand, was not only left to handle the miscarriage alone but also the desertion and the resulting loneliness. Unable to cope, I found that I was once again withdrawing into myself. I had never been slim, but since the assault in my mid teens my weight had gradually crept up and by this time, at 28 years old, I was wearing size 28 clothes and weighed in at seventeen and a half stone. I was also asthmatic and now, on top of everything else, I was childless and depressed and constantly blamed myself for the state of my marriage, convinced that my weight was the cause.

Finally one morning I looked in the mirror at the bloated, sad, hopeless, obese thing that I had become and was filled from my head to my toes with loathing.

"I hate you" I spat at my reflection with all that was within me.

"God, if you don't do something, I won't be around much longer," I sobbed. I knew I couldn't lose weight alone. I had tried every diet under the sun. I had eaten little, I had eaten lots, I had tried slimming clubs, I had tried fasting, I had tried.... well, you get the picture. God was my last hope – and thankfully He came through.

The next morning I awoke with an inexplicable unquenchable desire to walk the three miles to work, which, as you will remember from my early years, was not at all normal for me and all I wanted for breakfast was ...yoghurt. It wasn't a conscious decision; I was just not hungry. The walk to work wasn't easy but it was all downhill, which helped and it never entered my head to give up. At the end of my shift, I found myself once again donning my trainers and without a second thought, I set off to walk the three miles back home again. Uphill. It took me decidedly longer to get home than the 45minute trek in the morning! After a break and a cuppa, I took Kal out for a walk. This was a great move because, being a big dog, he could pull me up the hills when my legs would no longer move or I couldn't breathe.

Gradually, over the next three months the asthma stopped, I began to walk everywhere and I started to lose weight. The amazing thing was that I survived all this time on yoghurt for breakfast and an apple for lunch. I ate nothing else, but I was far from hungry. I walked three miles to and from work each day, another six miles with the dog and then, if I was bored, I'd walk for sheer enjoyment with my personal stereo for company (listening to tapes of my favourite preacher). God had intervened and answered my prayer of desperation and I was so aware of it.

It was a supernatural time, and even when I began to eat meals again the weight continued to drop off. My co-workers couldn't believe it when I had a bag of fish and chips one evening and the next morning I arrived at work so excited because I had lost another three pounds overnight! At this point I would like to stress that in normal circumstances this method of losing weight is NOT recommended. In my circumstances however, God chose to do it this way and so to anyone wanting to lose weight I will say don't copy me or anyone else. Ask God direct and He will show you the best way for you... He loves doing the same things - just differently. Just look at how He healed in the Bible... never the same way twice!

And so, in the space of nine months I went from seventeen and a half stone and a size 28 to twelve and a half stone and a size 18 - and I could breathe. I had my hair cut into a modern bob and changed the way I dressed. Out went the 'tents' and in came skirts and tops – and jeans. Aaaah jeans: I hadn't worn jeans for years, and I had promised myself a pair when I had lost weight. What a feeling that was! I entered a sponsored World Aid Walk of twenty miles, around Guernsey's perimeter, and completed it in five and quarter hours. I have never felt so elated. I had finally achieved something, and it had been hard, but I had persevered for the first time in my life – and it felt good. The next morning

I walked into work as usual and nobody believed that I had completed the walk because I wasn't sore and had no blisters; it took some persuading on my part to get them to part with their sponsorship money, and even then some of them weren't totally convinced until I presented my certificate for inspection!

My work uniform; a typical nylon shapeless overall made in bright colours to resemble a dress, worn with a tabard over, gradually became looser until it was so uncomfortable I asked my manager for a smaller one.

"Help yourself', he smiled, pointing to the box on top of the cupboard. Excited, I rushed into the 'ladies' with my 'box of delights' during tea break and tried on the next size down from my XXXL. It was huge, so I tried the next, and the next and the next. Finally I tried the medium size and it fitted like a glove. I teamed it up with a new tabard that showed off the fact that I did actually have a waist and proudly walked into the staff room to show off my new uniform.

"Ta da!" I sang, doing a twirl.

There was a stunned silence as the girls stared, open-mouthed at their 'new' colleague, a silence broken only by the sound of one girl spitting her tea out across the table!

A few days later I was working on the Wines and Spirits section when a regular customer who I hadn't seen for a while came up to me with a query. I directed her to the right department and turned back to my task.

"Thank you, my dear," she said. She turned to walk away, then backtracked.

"You're new here, aren't you?" she queried. I shook my head.

"Yes you are," she argued. Again I shook my head, telling her she was mistaken.

"No, I've worked here for five years" I explained. Looking at me as if I had lost my marbles, she smiled condescendingly and shook her head slowly.

" No, I'd remember you," she insisted. "I come in here every week, although I have been rather ill recently and haven't been able to come in as often as I would have liked"

"I know…" I began to say, but I could see this conversation was going nowhere. Then I had a brainwave.

"Do you remember the girl who used to work on this section?" I asked her, "She was really big," and I held my hands out at my sides to illustrate. She nodded, and her face took on a concern that was touching.

"Yes," she affirmed, "Such a shame for a young girl to be like that."

"Well, that was me," I smiled at the look crossing her face, "I've just lost a lot of weight." Her astonished look was priceless and, had I been able to bottle it, I would have made millions. It was worth millions to me either way, and I spent the rest of the day so encouraged it was intoxicating.

I telephoned mum to share my excitement, and she decided to come over and stay with us for a week so she could see for herself this new 'me'. The day of her arrival dawned and I found myself standing at the airport waiting for her to come through customs. Although Guernsey now has a state-of-the-art airport, back then it was not much better than a glorified packing shed. Passengers would walk across the tarmac from the plane to the terminal building and through a door directly into the baggage reclaim area, where they waited for the ground staff to 'post' the luggage through a large cat flap onto the conveyor. This was not a moving belt but a series of metal poles laid about two inches apart on a downward slope that rotated individually to bring your luggage – eventually - to a grinding halt at your feet. That done, you would hoist your bags onto a baggage trolley with supermarket trolley-wheels, and wander through the 'red' or 'green' customs channels, situated next to each other with no barriers and manned by one bored customs officer. Twenty feet later, through another door, and you were in the airport foyer, segregated from the general public by a couple of poles and a rope barrier. On average, the whole process took no longer than ten minutes.

I spotted Mum amongst the gaggle of passengers that had just alighted, smiled, and waited for her reaction. She scanned the waiting crowd, searching for me and looked straight at me... then carried right on scanning the rest of the crowd. I couldn't believe it; maybe she just hadn't seen me. Ah, now she was scanning back the other way – but no, her gaze swept past me again. The truth began to take shape – she did not recognise her own daughter. Another sweeping glance came in my direction ... and went.

"Mum!" I called, "I'm over here!" I waved.

Her eyes followed my voice and as she spotted my hand mid-wave her jaw dropped.

Overcome with emotion, her hand flew to her mouth and she burst into tears. So did I.

We hadn't seen each other for nearly a year and now here we were, sobbing on each other's shoulders in public! Wounds were healed that week and a new beginning was birthed for us in our mother/daughter relationship, as she confided that she had found it extremely hard to watch me constantly put on weight and be unable to say anything to me about it, thinking it would make me feel unaccepted: and I confided that she was right, but I had also thought she didn't care, because she had never mentioned it.

Unfortunately all these changes had the opposite effect on my marriage to what I had envisioned, as my husband's immaturity came to the surface. Unnerved by his wife's new look he began to spend even more time at his friends' house and, too late, I discovered that he was having his head turned by their teenage daughter. He was thirty-four. I thought it was ludicrous at first, but as the weeks passed I noticed with some alarm that they were obsessed with each other. Despite warnings from me and both our families and friends, they continued to move headlong into the embryonic stages of a relationship that was to have a devastating effect on our marriage.

Chapter 12
OLD LADIES AND CHEEKY SQUIRRELS

It was during this time that I finally learned, what Christianity was all about. I began to spend more and more time reading my Bible and talking to God, and I found that He listened – and answered. In the lonely hours of the night, I realised that I could share my deepest fears and feelings with Him; I could weep; I could shout; I could get angry; I could speak of my pain and I could speak of my heart's desires, and He would gently lead me to the Bible and speak directly into my life. Finally the truth dawned and I suddenly understood why I had struggled so much over the years with my 'faith': it had never been personal.

You see, God is an amazing Being and He wants to be in relationship with us, His creation. Once I grasped that, I found that He was the best friend I could ever have wished for. He knew me inside out and back to front; He knew how I felt, and He knew my heart. I could never be in a close relationship with Him while I was copying other people's faith, or just paying lip service to 'rules and regulations'. God knows that what we value most we place above all else and pay homage to it: just think about the sacrifices we make for our 'passions' in life. It is what I set my heart on that becomes my 'god', my 'treasure': and it is my heart that He wants. Nothing else will ever do, for if He doesn't have my heart, something else does, and that 'something', no matter how nice or good it is in its own right, will never earn the right to be worshipped. God alone is worthy of that honour.

But although I was moving forward in my relationship with God, I found that my relationship with my husband was going in the opposite direction. He was becoming more and more distant and did not want to be with me – and he wanted nothing to do with God. I was torn as I knew that, even at this late stage, had he allowed God to help, He would have restored our marriage, but his behaviour continued to change and I found myself living with a stranger, who did not resemble the man I married in any way, and I knew I would soon have to do something to keep my sanity, but it wasn't until he started to physically threaten me that I realised that I couldn't stay.

Mum arranged for me to stay with her in England and one Friday in November I packed my bags, wrestled Shani into her cat basket and headed for the airport. The hardest thing for me was to leave Pickles and Kal behind, as I loved them both. The airline had made it clear, however, that only one animal at a time was allowed on board the plane, and so it had to be my cantankerous Shani that came with me. Pickles and Kal had each other, but Shani only had me. Later, both Pickles and Kal were eventually rehomed together and lived out their lives happily in peace and quiet, with a lovely mature couple that my Dad knew.

Once I was in England, away from the whole situation, it became clear that the stress had driven me close to the brink of a nervous breakdown and I spent a few months in a state of severe depression, alternatively sleeping and weeping, unable to cope with anything. It was a dark time in my life, but once again God did not let me go, gradually bringing me back into the land of the living, where hope, love and all good things dwell. Meanwhile back in Guernsey things had progressed to the point that I knew it was time to begin divorce proceedings and carry on with my life. The healing would take time, but I was no longer on my own, and I knew it.

By now it was early 1995 and I had been living with mum for a few months while the strains and stresses of the disintegration of my life in Guernsey finally drew to a close. Gradually I began to feel ready to face the world again and started looking for work. A friend of my mum was working in one of two 'Abbeyfield' homes for retired gentlefolk in the neighbouring village and was asked if she knew of anyone who might be interested in becoming a part time dishwasher in the other Home, so she recommended me and called me to let me know that I could drop in the next morning for an interview if I was interested.

"Do I look alright? I asked mum nervously, as we walked across the small car park the next day. I glanced at the "Abbeyfield House" sign that bordered the grass verge and wondered again whether I was doing the right thing. After all, this was a home for elderly ladies and, like many young people, I had preconceived ideas of the sort of establishment I was entering. My appointment was with the housekeeper, Mrs Rogers: a lady with a formidable reputation, hence the nervousness. We were met at the door by a rather short, stout, grey haired elderly lady with an air of authority about her. My new boss, I wondered?

"Hello, do come in," she opened the door and motioned us inside.

"I'm Mrs Rogers," she announced, confirming my suspicions. We were ushered into the dining room and bade to sit down. I found it all rather formal and "upper class" and caught myself smiling at the sudden urge to mind my P's and Q's. Mrs Rogers, however, was a delightful lady with impeccable manners and an ability to put me at my ease immediately. After a lovely chat (it never felt like an interview!) I was hired and was requested to report for duty the next lunchtime.

12 till 2pm the next day found me scrubbing pots and pans, cleaning work-surfaces, stacking the dishwasher and washing the floor. Mrs Rogers was a very proficient cook and we worked well as a team: I washed-up as she worked, keeping her workspace neat and tidy. I noticed her watching me a few times, but she never commented, so I was unprepared and surprised when, as I finished my first shift, I was summoned to the dining room.

"How would you like to train as relief cook, Alison?" Mrs Rogers asked when we were seated at the table. I was speechless. I had only washed dishes for two hours and I was being offered promotion already!

"You see," she continued, "Moira is the main cook, but I cover her days off and, to be honest, it is getting a bit much for me. I am seventy four, after all." She smiled at me.

"And, "she added, "I like the way you work. I think we shall get along famously, you and I." I was delighted and looked forward to beginning my new job.

The next day I was introduced to Moira, the cook, who made it obvious she didn't approve of Mrs Roger's idea, and that when I worked with her, it was in a dishwashing capacity only - and I had better know my place. I didn't mind, for God often teaches us humility in the unlikeliest of places, but I soon found out the reason why I had been needed in the first place. She was the untidiest, messiest cook I had ever met and the kitchen resembled the aftermath of a food fight – every day. The cupboards had flour handprints inside and out, as did the clean stored dishes; the ovens had spilled food inside and out; the bin looked like a health hazard waiting to explode, and even the windows were known to have custard splashed up them.

"I can't believe how clean the kitchen is," Mrs Rogers nodded in approval as she surveyed the gleaming worktops a week later, "It never looked like this when Moira was on duty before. Actually, sometimes I despair of her," She paused for effect, "Do you know what she did a couple of weeks ago when we were having jacket potatoes for lunch?"

I shook my head, wondering what was coming next.

"Well, she decided that she wanted the potatoes all the same size."

I nodded, waiting for the punch line.

"I walked in and found the silly goose had emptied the (half a hundred weight) sack of potatoes in the middle of the kitchen floor, and was rooting through them to find the size she wanted. What a mess! A pile of potatoes and ground in the middle of the floor! Honestly, Alison, I don't know what she will do next"

I must say that, at the time, I thought she had exaggerated, but a few weeks later jacket potatoes were once again on the menu when Moira was the duty cook and I walked into the kitchen to find a potato mountain and half a field by the sink. It took me ages to clear it up and I began to realise that this was just how Moira worked. She was always in a hurry, a law unto herself and totally unteachable. Mrs Rogers despaired of her white sauce, which tasted like wallpaper paste because she would not cook the 'roux' first (flour and butter), claiming it took too long. The residents would grimace as it was placed on the table and it would always be returned to the kitchen, untouched, at the end of the meal. It was very frustrating to work with this lady, as she would not accept advice or suggestions: not even from Mrs Rogers, and even the puff pastry lids of her pies would shrink away from the sides of the dish, leaving an unsightly mess because she would not do the basic preparation needed to ensure a good presentation.

Unfortunately for her, when Mrs Rogers began to teach me how to cook for the 15 residents and staff I was keen to learn, as I wanted to be able to make the mouth-watering dishes that I had seen her serve up. But I listened and as I put into practice what I learned many of the ladies began to compare Moira's cooking unfavourably with mine. Although she resented the comparison, she still would not change the way she prepared and cooked the food and the grumbles continued. Meanwhile, I was learning how to make huge sponge cakes and fruit cakes ready for the annual fund raising cream tea, a day in the social calendar of the house which was legendary within the village. That year, when the cakes were auctioned off at the end of the day, Mrs Rogers was complimented on her cake making skills, being told, 'Once again, you have surpassed yourself!'

"I had to swallow my pride and tell them that, actually, you had made the cakes this year, not me." She later told me, although I must confess I could see how difficult it was for her to admit it, and I admired her for it.

I began to get to know the ladies who were resident in the home and found myself growing quite attached to a number of them. The house was split into two halves: one half was for ladies who were able bodied and still quite independent; indeed some were simply retired and just had no desire to live alone; it amused me that Mrs Rogers was older than most of her 'residents'. As well as housekeeper for the entire house, Mrs Rogers was also the manager of this side and ruled her 'ladies' like a hospital matron, keeping everything running smoothly. They viewed her rather like a strict headmistress and lived in fear of her disapproval although at times, when they behaved like naughty schoolgirls, her stern look was all that was needed to instil silence. Lunch times could be rather an ordeal as Mrs Rogers had been brought up in a very grand house with servants, and expected the correct etiquette at the meal table, which could produce a little tension: woe betide anyone who spoke out of turn or put their elbows on the table! But even so, she was a very fair and honest lady who, although she expected respect, earned every ounce of it.

The other side of the house was more like a care home with a manager and care staff, for ladies who were infirm and unsteady, needing help in their daily tasks. Later on I worked extra shifts in this side of the home and discovered one lady had been to Guernsey in the 1920's; we spent many hours chatting and poring over an old photograph of her sitting on a rock on a Guernsey beach with Castle Cornet in the background, sipping Coca Cola through a straw.

Whilst working on the 'care' side I became friendly with a few of the staff there, including a lady who was a spiritualist. Interestingly enough, we got on rather well, although our spiritual lives were extremely different, and we would often sit in our break times and discuss the Bible. She had some very strange ideas about Christianity and God, and could not grasp the idea that God wanted a relationship with His creation, including her. One morning she began telling me about the 'healing meeting' she had attended the previous week and was talking about the energies and forces; it sounded so cold and distant. God just was not personal and it saddened me that she was missing out on so much, especially as I had struggled so hard to finally grasp the truth that God is real and wants to be involved in out lives.

"We said some prayers for absent healing," she beamed.

"Uh... absent healing?" I queried. " Is that when the healing is absent from the meeting?"

"Oh no, that's when we pray for someone who isn't present to be healed"

"Oh right," then a thought struck me - "and were they healed?"

"No, actually, " she said, looking a little embarrassed, "she wasn't"

"Well, there you go then, I was right!" I smiled smugly and left the room. As I walked away, I felt the Lord speak a rebuke to my heart and knew that I had not only just missed a huge opportunity to share the love of my Saviour with this lady, but I had also belittled her by ridiculing what she believed in. My hollow victory over her beliefs was very short-lived, and indeed, from that point in time she became more and more distant from me. I was ashamed of myself and knew that I had damaged whatever witness I had been to her and so I too, kept away from her, not knowing how to make amends for the offence. I often wonder how things would have been different had I had the grace to apologise to her and seek forgiveness, but that is, sadly, something I will never know this side of Heaven.

"Well I never!" exclaimed Mrs Rogers one morning. I followed her astonished gaze and, as the situation dawned on me, I laughed out loud.

"Alison," she admonished me, "It isn't funny, that cost rather a lot of money. What a cheeky little devil!"

"Sorry," said I, looking anything but, " but you have to admire its ingenuity!"

"Hmm," she grudgingly agreed, making her way out of the back door to survey the lone pole standing tall and proud in the centre of the garden, a testament to a resourceful thief.

Mrs Rogers had a squirrel problem. The care home was the proud owner of a fine bird table in the rear garden and the ladies loved to sit and watch the small garden birds chatter and squabble as they feasted on the ample piles of seeds and scraps that were offered on a daily basis. They also loved to watch the antics of a particularly clever squirrel on its constant quest to eat the food on the table before the birds. Mrs Rogers, quite perturbed by this cheeky intruder, had tried everything, in vain, to halt the squirrel in its tracks. Finally, in desperation, she had invested in an expensive 'all-singing all-dancing' squirrel proof bird feeder, consisting of a food dispenser encased in a squirrel proof cage which hung on a pole...and Mrs Rogers had just witnessed the squirrel knocking the cage off the pole and bounding away with the entire weeks supply of bird food, cage and all.

It wasn't long before I was officially the relief cook, at which point I acquired an added task of taking Mrs Rogers to the supermarket on a monthly basis to bulk buy, not only for the Abbeyfield House we were in, but also for the other one on the other side of the village. She was unable to drive due to cataracts in both eyes and was extremely pleased when she found out that I had a licence, immediately press-ganging me into service. The unexpected perk of this was that I was given the car to run around in for the rest of the month as well, for which I was extremely grateful, on the condition that I became a chauffer whenever she visited her family. It was a fascinating time. I met all three of her daughters and all of her grandchildren, and I felt that I almost became in some way, an addition to her family. I would drive sometimes for sixty miles or more to enable Mrs Rogers to visit a daughter for Sunday lunch, only to find that I was included in the lunch invite which more often than not happened to be a banquet. I met the family pets and their puppies, I gazed in awe at the luxurious homes they lived in, the antiques they collected and the vast gardens they relaxed in; but most of all I was amazed at the way they all embraced me like a long lost friend. After what had happened in the last few months in Guernsey, I was really touched to be treated in this way and I will always remember them all with the fondest memories.

Shopping trips were never dull, as I drove and parked Guernsey-style. If I took a wrong turning I would simply stop, reverse into the nearest driveway and then resume the correct route, much to Mrs Rogers' concern.

"Alison," she complained one afternoon as I was once again emerging from some stranger's driveway, after taking the wrong turning on a roundabout, "I do wish you wouldn't do that. It makes me quite queasy when I suddenly see a brick gateway looming up in front of us when I am expecting a roadway. You know my cataracts distort everything and make it all fuzzy. It is all very disconcerting. Have a little compassion!" I assured her that I would try and be more thoughtful and the drive continued quite peaceably. That is, until we got to the supermarket... I drove into the car park slowly, looking for a parking space near the entrance, as I knew the trolley would be heavy and it would be me who would be pushing it. Aha! I spied an empty space just ten feet away from the door and, after checking that no cars were moving in the vicinity, I aimed the car and put my foot down. Mrs Rogers was totally unprepared and, as we took off she was pressed suddenly against the back of her chair and, as she was less than five foot tall, her feet came off the floor.

"Merciful Heavens!" she cried, "What are you doing now?"

"Parking" I said meekly, realising that I had, once more, been more than a little thoughtless.

She was very forgiving, and after we had sat in the car park for a few minutes to allow her nerves to relax, we made our way into the supermarket. Her method of shopping was simple: make a list of what you need; take said list to shop; add a few extras that she fancied at the time; and then... double it! So two hours later we emerged with a trolley (or two) overflowing with food that we probably didn't need and that I was going to have to find a space for when we returned to the Home. Personally I think she rather enjoyed the excitement of my driving, although she would never admit it. However, when she had her cataracts operated on and could see clearly for the first time in years, she asked me to take her to visit her daughter who lived fifty miles away and although she never said a word, she did look rather alarmed most of the way!

My time at Abbeyfield was not without mishaps, however, as my first 'lone' Monday proved. The Monday lunchtime menu was always salad, with a jacket potato and whatever meat had been left over from Sunday's roast. I loved Mondays as it was an absolute doddle and I had plenty of time to bake cakes ready for freezing for the rest of the week. Humming around the kitchen, checking the potatoes were cooking evenly, the sponge cake wasn't rising lop-sided and the fresh egg custard for pudding wasn't burning, I was in my element. I loaded up the trolley with half the coleslaw, lettuce, beetroot, spring onions and cucumber, ready to wheel into the dining room when the potatoes were done, then arranged the rest on the table for the 'care-home' side.

"Beep! Beep!" the alarm on the large eight-ring gas cooker sprang into life, and the manager of the 'care home' emerged from the kitchen doorway, where she had been waiting patiently to begin stacking her trolley to take to her ladies. I carefully transferred the potatoes to the waiting serving plates, placing one on my trolley and leaving the other two for her. After performing a mental inventory: table empty; trolleys loaded, ovens empty (i.e. nothing left in that should be out!) I turned to make my way to the dining room, pleased with myself for managing all by myself. The corridor that led from the kitchen to the dining room was on a slope. Downwards. As it reached the bottom of the slope the nice shiny tiles came to an end and became lovely carpet…with a metal divider separating the two.

My trolley was a rather old rickety wooden one that one of the Trustees' wives had donated, and it had small metal wheels, making the necessity of lifting the front wheels over the lip paramount. As I was pushing my trolley down the slope, the manager who I had left in the kitchen asked me for some salad cream, so I turned my head to advise her where it was. Consequently I wasn't looking where I was going and as the wheels hit the metal strip head on I closed my eyes as everything… and yes, I do mean everything sailed through the air like a spectacular firework show, landing with a splat, a few thuds and lots of clashing crockery… right in the doorway of the dining room. I was mortified! There was a stunned silence from the dining room as each resident stared in horror at their lunch, then Mrs Rogers rose to the occasion and took charge. Together we picked everything up, binned the salad and made fresh, salvaged the potatoes and, within ten minutes she was back in the dining room, cool as a cucumber, dishing up as if nothing had happened.

I really connected with one of the ladies, whose name was Miss Shoesmith. She would often come by the kitchen for a natter in the doorway if I wasn't too busy, and would share lots of stories of her life. One day homemade curry was on the lunch menu. I had made it once before dutifully following Mrs Rogers's instructions, but this day she was out with friends for lunch. I hummed and sang around the kitchen as I added a little bit of this and a little bit of that, but I never tasted it to check how it was spicing up. Subsequently, when I dished it up, there were a few raised eyebrows at the spicy smell that emanated from the serving dish. I escaped to the kitchen, leaving the ladies to enjoy their lunch and sat down to eat the little bit I had put aside for me.

Whoosh! The flavours hit my taste buds like a jack hammer, but after the first mouthful I could no longer taste anything, so I finished it all, wiped the dampness form my forehead and around my eyes and sat down with a large glass of ice cold milk. And waited. Sure enough, once lunch was finished the ladies started to filter their way back to their rooms, and each one stopped at the kitchen door:

"Thank you"

"That was lovely"

"It was ok but not as hot as usual" (I realised this day that some people lose their sense of taste as they get older!) and then Miss Shoesmith poked her head around the door.

"That was lovely, my dear," she smiled,

"But," she added with a twinkle in her eye, "It couldn't have been much hotter, could it?"

Chapter 13
BIKER CHICK

Life away from the care home, in the meantime, was ticking along nicely. I was now attending the local Elim Pentecostal Church that met just around the corner from mum's house, and making new friends - and I had finally realised an old dream. I had wanted wheels for as long as I could remember: not four wheels, mind you, but two. In Guernsey the legal age to ride a 50cc motorbike is fourteen, but my request for one for my fourteenth birthday had been met with a resounding "NO!' Well, what did I expect after trying to kill myself on a pushbike for years? Well, now I was twenty-nine and maybe, just maybe, I was becoming sensible enough to own a motorbike; not a sleek fast one like my dad's dream bike, but a low-rider Harley Davidson type. After praying for a while, I felt that I was getting the go-ahead from God, and so I decided to look around some bike shops to see what was around. I fell in love with a burgundy 250cc Yamaha Virago but couldn't afford it on monthly payments, so Dad offered to buy one in Guernsey for me and arranged for me to pay him back at a rate that was within my budget. Excited, I bought my leather jacket, burgundy helmet (to match the bike) and booked my Compulsory Basic Training (CBT) lesson. However, things did not go as smoothly as planned...

"What on earth happened to you?" bellowed John, my instructor, as we pulled into a lay-by, "You look like you've taken one look at the road and freaked out!"

I nodded, indicating that his assumption had been correct.

We were nearing the end of the CBT lesson, which had spanned an entire day. The first part had taken place within the safety of a school playground, where I and three other novices had learned to change gears, change speed, approach roundabouts safely, look behind us over both shoulders (but not at the same time!) and stand our bikes up so they didn't fall over. We had passed the first part of the test set out for us and now, in order to complete the test and obtain our certificates, we were putting what we had learned into practice on the road. And this is where, for me, it had all fallen apart.

I had been the star pupil all day. Having no biking experience whatsoever I just did what I was told, unlike the other guys who were having to unlearn a lot of bad habits picked up from larking about with mates' bikes. Unknown to me, the three instructors were fighting over who was going to take me out on the road for the final stage, as I was going to be a 'dead cert' for a 'pass'. John, being the owner of the riding school, had pulled rank and obtained the privilege of escorting me on my debut ride. However, he had not accounted for the fact that I had only driven a car for a few months on England's roads (with Mrs Rogers) which were very different to the small Guernsey ones I was used to, and I had never dreamed I would be so scared to do seventy miles an hour on a 125cc motorbike, which felt like a glorified pushbike. I was absolutely petrified! However eventually, after a few deep breaths and a lot of persuasion, I gained a little confidence and with much trepidation, I managed to complete my CBT with a 'pass'. Just. I was now deemed safe enough to learn to ride a bike on the roads, but in actual fact the fun was only just beginning.

"That's got to be it," Mum pointed to the house with half a dozen motorbikes in the front garden. Some were complete; some were in different stages of repair and some were, well… bits. John and his wife, my instructors, ate, slept and dreamed bikes. John was a twenty-plus stone hulk that dwarfed whichever bike he sat on – a fascinating sight on a 125cc – while his wife weighed six stone, at a push. I had arrived for my first lesson. I was fitted out with an earpiece which was worn inside my helmet; a one-way device that allowed John to communicate with me and direct me while on the road, but did not allow me to talk back, and we set off on our first session. I was so nervous that I couldn't relax, and found out pretty quickly that a tense rider will find it extremely difficult to control the bike. After twenty minutes we returned to the house for a coffee break, allowing me to loosen up and for John to take deep breaths. The second half of the lesson was much better, although we spent half of it standing at a roundabout watching cars entering and exiting.

"You really don't have a clue about roundabouts, do you?" John commented, after I had sat for ten minutes trying to work out when to move, and then shooting out in front of an old lady in a Honda Civic, "It could be a watermelon in the road, for all you know, couldn't it?"

Well, what did he expect? Guernsey only had one roundabout, and that was newly built just before I had left. Nobody there knew how to use it, and would drive around it twice – once to decide which turn off to take and the second time to actually perform the manoeuvre. In fact, when the original traffic lights were first replaced by the offending giant spaceship most people would simply turn right, as they had always done, totally disregarding the concept of skirting the roundabout, resulting in the screech of brakes and shouts from the people they had almost run off the road, or head-on into.

Still, he must have seen some potential, or maybe he just enjoyed a challenge, (or maybe he was just desperate for the money?) but either way, another lesson was arranged for the following week. However, after a few weeks it was obvious that I was not a natural 'biker' and after I had burst into tears over taking a wrong turn, John questioned whether I really should be attempting to learn to ride.

"Yes," I sniffled, "It's something I have wanted to do since I was fourteen." It sounds silly, but I had realised that I had nearly always given up on things when they became difficult and I was determined to finish something no matter how hard it became. This was to be another turning point in my life, one of many milestones to maturity. He looked doubtful, but agreed to continue to teach me. During coffee, it dawned on us that I was trying too hard and making everything a big deal, which was why I was so tense: so a new tactic was devised.

The next week, whilst I was nervously attempting a U-turn, John began to sing through my earpiece– loudly. I wouldn't have minded, but this man who looked like a 'Hells Angel' sang 'The Wheels on the Bus", "Twinkle, Twinkle Little Star" and other nursery rhymes! It worked, as I could do nothing but listen and I laughed so hard that I relaxed; and the rest of the lesson was fun. This became a regular part of the lesson and I still have the sight etched in my mind of him weaving along behind me one day while he sang, "I feel good...dananananana... I knew that that I would now... I feeeeel good... I knew that I would now... so good, so good, I got-a-you...da da da DA!"

Unfortunately, I still had days when I was nervous, and these caused some hairy moments. I hated riding over speed humps, as the bike would shake and I felt that I was going to lose my grip on the handlebars. Riding one afternoon through the estate where John lived, which had lots of speed humps, I found myself growing tenser and tenser as we approached the sharp bend just before the dual carriageway turnoff. I tried, in vain, to relax, and to my horror realised too late that my elbows had locked and I couldn't bend my arms, resulting in the road veering away to my left as I rode straight across the road, at an angle and up the pavement, coming to a shaky halt with my front wheel resting against somebody's garden wall.

"That was scary," John commented, stopping beside me as I removed my helmet.

"You should have been sat where I was," I answered sulkily, seeking sympathy.

"It wouldn't have happened if I had been sat where you were!" he countered dryly, with sympathy obviously not on the agenda.

My riding skills (?) had no choice but to improve and as they did so John began to think about booking my test. To get me used to the test route that was most often used, he decided to take me along Titnore Lane, a narrow winding 'A' road on a steep hill with a speed limit of 60mph, and a reputation for accidents. Going up wasn't too bad. I enjoyed leaning into the corners, although I felt that 60mph was much too fast for the camber of the road, and was much happier at 40-45mph. Then we reached the top and I was instructed to go around the roundabout and come back down the hill. I was also advised that the examiner would be looking for confidence in a rider at 60mph, so I opened the throttle and took off. The camber of the road on the way down was much worse than going up however, and I found that I was struggling to stay on my side of the road. Given that the road is one blind corner after the other, I began to feel myself tense up, and as I approached the final bend I overshot the continuous white line separating me from the Mercedes racing straight toward me. I shut my eyes (as you do!) and prayed. Hard. I have no idea how I missed the Mercedes, but I am pretty sure God had a big hand in it. Reaching the bottom of the hill, I pulled into a car park at John's request, and sat quietly as he removed his helmet and stared at me, his face the colour of ash.

"I thought you were going to be that guy's hood ornament," he said, shaking his head. I had really scared him and it showed. The next lesson was spent entirely on Titnore Lane, going up and down, up and down, till I was utterly sick of the sight of the place, but able to ride smoothly in and out of the corners with confidence.

"Alison, that was excellent, I am impressed" John's voice echoed in my earpiece as, a few weeks later,I confidently performed a perfect U-turn.

"In fact," he added, "my 'press' has never been so 'immed'!"

I smiled with delight, as praise from my instructor was rare. I was on an hour lesson before my test and I was vigorously being put through my paces. He came with me to the test centre and booked me in, giving me a thumbs-up as he left. An hour later, after a tranquil test ride to the seafront and around familiar quiet roads the opposite end of town to Titnore Lane, I sat in the office in shock as my examiner handed me my 'pass', which would enable me to send off for my new licence. I was ecstatic. I jumped onto the bike and rode straight round to John's house, abandoning it in the front garden as I rushed to the front door and excitedly rang the doorbell. John's wife finally answered the door to find me hopping up and down impatiently.

"I passed!" I shrieked, and then stopped in my tracks, taking in the two shocked faces, as John had, by now, also appeared.

"What?" I demanded.

"I never thought you'd pass, "John stated, shaking his head in amazement.

"Well, thanks for the vote of confidence, but I couldn't have done it without you." I answered as we began to laugh.

"And," I added, "After all that, I didn't go anywhere near Titnore Lane!"

Two days later I returned to their doorstep to deliver a bottle of wine and a 'thank you' card: signed by "The Guernsey Hood Ornament, the Expert in Straight Cornering". We had shared some hairy moments, but they had stuck with me all the way, encouraging me and pushing me forward when lesser beings would have called it a day and run for the hills, and I was grateful.

Within three weeks I had a call from my dad.

"I've got a nice shiny new motorbike sat in my garage," he said quietly, while I shrieked and jumped up and down whilst trying to disentangle myself from the wires. (I was so glad when Mum got a cordless phone!)

"It needs an adjusting service after the first five hundred miles" he added," So, as it needs to be done at the garage which supplied it, I'll ride it around Guernsey and run it in, get the service done and then bring it over."

"Ok," I said, a little disappointed. It'll take him ages to do five hundred miles on that pokey little island, I thought.

A month later he called again.

"The bikes going in for its service tomorrow,"he announced, "So I'll be over at the weekend." I was flabbergasted!

"How did you do five hundred miles in just one month?" I asked, incredulous. He chuckled.

"I just took it out in between driving the taxi, and rode it at every available moment. Actually," he admitted, "I really enjoyed riding it. I didn't think I would, as I've never been one for the 'sit up and beg' type of bikes, but I was pleasantly surprised. It is very comfortable, although I almost came a cropper one night." He chuckled again, but didn't elaborate, so I had to ask.

"What happened?"

"Well, I'm used to the motorbike and sidecar, and the other day I was out riding and as I slowed down at the junction I only just remembered in time that I was on your bike, which doesn't have a sidecar attached and that I needed to put my foot down!" Now I could hear him roar with laughter as he could picture himself lying in the middle of the road, trying to explain himself to a curious policeman!'

That weekend, after getting more and more excited by the day, the moment finally arrived. I waited in all day but it was past ten o'clock in the evening when I finally got the phone call.

"I'm lost" Dad admitted, laughing, "I think I took a wrong turning at a group of really confusing roundabouts and I've ended up in a little country road by a red phone box…"

I knew exactly where he was. At the turnoff from the A27 into the neighbouring village, there were two roundabouts, set on a funny angle from each other and they were indeed, very confusing. And this village (in the wrong direction) had the only red telephone box around for miles.

"Stay where you are," I smiled, "We'll come and get you."

Mum and I both jumped into her car in our pyjamas and

drove to the village. We hoped we wouldn't suffer a breakdown or get stopped by the police, as we didn't fancy explaining what we were doing out on the A27 in our pyjamas at ten o'clock at night in October! Sure enough, there he was, sat outside the phone box, looking frozen.

"Did you bring your helmet?" he called out, as we drew up alongside him. I looked down at my pyjamas and shook my head.

"That's a shame," he added, "You could have ridden your bike home while I sat in the warm car!" I remained silent, secretly relieved that I hadn't been dressed, for I was still very unsure of myself and the thought of riding my new bike for the first time at night with an audience horrified me. He followed us home to a hot coffee and lots of hugs, and I beamed with delight as he handed me my bike keys. The next morning was sunny and the first thing Dad did was to offer to take me for a pillion ride on my new bike, to get used to the movement again, as I hadn't ridden for a few months. Never comfortable with riding pillion, I declined, so he looked at Mum.

"Game?" he queried. She nodded, and asked if she could borrow my helmet... then sat astride my new bike behind my dad as if it was the most natural thing in the world, and off they went!

I was glad that they had managed to remain friends after their divorce but it was still a strange sensation to see them go riding off into the wild blue yonder... on my new bike! Actually I did feel a little gutted for a while and wished I had been brave enough to go on the back myself, but it didn't last long, for when they returned a short while later, Mum was smiling with pleasure and nostalgia.

"I had forgotten how it felt," she explained." It was just like it had been all those years ago when we were teenagers..."

Later on that day I plucked up the courage to grab my helmet and my keys and, dressed in jeans, boots, gloves, scarf and leather jacket, I wheeled my new shining burgundy 250cc beastie (with lots of chrome for me to polish) out of the garage and sat astride the sumptuous padded seat. I started the ignition with a little button (no kick-starting for me!) and, with only a brief backward glance at my spectators, cruised out of the driveway and turned left onto the main road. I made my way to the A280, a long winding road that snaked between the South Downs; with open fields and farms on one side and hills and woods on the other; and opened up the throttle. I banked into the first corner and I could hear the engine purring, changing to a powerful thrust as I accelerated out of the bend and onto the straight. I could feel the power of the motor as I opened the throttle a little more and changed up another gear. My heart and soul rose within me and I found myself singing praise and worship songs to my Creator, who had made all of this possible, and my eyes began to stream, but whether it was from the wind or extreme joy I am not prepared to elucidate! But I had persevered and gained my license against more than a few odds: and now I was flying free as a bird... and it was exhilarating. I was in seventh heaven.

Chapter 14
WHERE PAST AND PRESENT MEET

It was a beautiful day in May; the skies were blue, the sun was shining, the birds were singing, and my heart was soaring like an eagle – and my burgundy 'beastie' was purring. I was hurtling at 70mph along the M27 on my way to Weymouth and life was good. As usual, I couldn't help but sing loudly all the way along the motorway, but thankfully I wore a scarf about my mouth or else I would have eaten more than I had bargained for that day, as the bugs were plentiful. I had been in possession of my bike now for a few months and it was due its first proper service: Dad had pre-arranged with the garage that he had bought it from that this first main service would be free of charge for me, provided I took it back to them to do the work. I still could not grasp that he had managed to ride 500 miles in just a month on an island that can fit inside Loch Ness but he had, and now I was on my way back home to Guernsey, a new me with a new bike. Or so I thought...

Dad was away from the island that week so I stayed with my Nan and Pop next door. I had a fantastic time the first few days, driving around the island and revisiting old familiar haunts. On the scheduled day I dropped my bike round to the garage on the West Coast and caught the bus back to Town. I wandered through the cobbled High Street, no longer boasting a 'Lipton's' but now with many banks and fashion shops. Having spent a pleasant hour or so browsing and window-shopping, I began to make my way through the pedestrianised Arcade, with its familiar jewellery shops and cafés. I noticed that the drainage grids still ran along the centre of the paved path and remembered with wry nostalgia the many shoes that had met their demise there, as stiletto heels were all the rage in my teenage years and most of them had ended up stuck in one or the other of the grids. Recalling the embarrassment of walking barefoot with my 'heelless' shoes in my hands, I was glad that I was wearing my biker boots and did not have to watch where I was walking.

Turning the corner, I found myself going past the baker's shop where I had begun my working life and stopped to peer in through the window. The shop had had a major makeover and I hardly recognised the place. It looked ultra clean and smart and very modern, but sadly I thought that it had lost some of its charm in the overhaul of its image. Deep in thought, I turned away from the window and began to make my way towards the Market. As I approached the Market Steps I heard my name being called. Automatically I turned ... and found myself face to face with my old flame Robert.

"Alison?" He was staring at me, and I was a little perplexed until I realised that the last time he had seen me had been before the weight loss. And now I was five stones lighter, wearing jeans and leather jacket, and carrying a crash helmet. No wonder he stared! I smiled and my heart gave a little lurch, a sure sign that I was heading for trouble. I wisely began to walk away, but it was made difficult when I realised that he still held that special place in my heart, even after all this time and all that had been in our past. But I was aware that he was a non-believer, and without that basic strong foundation a relationship would be doomed from the start. I carried on walking.

"Alison!" he called. I kept walking.

"Alison, you look great. Come for a drink for old times sake, please?" he persisted, following me. I kept walking, a little slower this time.

"I don't drink!" I called over my shoulder, stepping up the pace again. But I was weakening, as I suspected I would. Oh why did I not stop and ask God for strength?

"Then come for a coffee." He laughed. I stopped, hesitated, then turned, and walked resolutely straight into my next season of trials and tribulations. We spent the rest of the entire week together. He took me out for meals, to the cinema and for romantic walks to watch sunsets; and Guernsey has sunsets like nowhere else on earth. He was the perfect gentleman, treating me like a lady, and I relished his attentions. When, at the end of the week, he mentioned marriage, I thought I had died and gone to Heaven; my deepest desires were coming true and I was floating on air. I was still as obsessed with him as ever and although something (or Someone) was niggling at the back of my mind, telling me to slow down, take it easy and test the waters, I set my will resolutely to follow my heart - which was another way of saying that I stubbornly opened my vulnerable heart to the person who could damage it most ...again. It was a tearful goodbye that was said as I boarded the ferry back to Weymouth, amid promises of his following me at a later date so we could get married.

It took a few months and a few major legal hiccups, but eventually the day dawned when he was due to arrive in the UK and I waited, heart in mouth, at Gatwick airport, terrified he wouldn't come. It was a huge sigh of relief that I breathed as he emerged through customs with open arms and a smile the size of England. He moved into Mum's spare room, and began looking for work as we planned our wedding. We decided on a date in February and I began to organise and post invites. Mrs Rogers was at the top of my guest list, and the 'ladies' were excited to hear all about my plans. The housekeeper of the second Abbeyfield House on the other side of the village had recently retired and Mrs Rogers had taken over her position. She had taken me with her - a move that pleased Moira ... and promoted me to main cook/housekeeping assistant, which didn't please Moira one little bit. But it meant that I had longer hours and more money, which was a godsend.

However, at the beginning of December, all peace was shattered. Robert was watching television and as I walked past him toward the patio doors, he eyes followed me.

'You're pregnant," he announced. I was stunned, and shock

quickly turned to anger. After all that I had gone through with the miscarriage just a few short years ago, and knowing how much I still yearned for a baby, I thought he was teasing me, and it was a cruel thing to do.

"That is not funny," I hissed, glaring at him. He shrugged and repeated his statement.

I did not believe him, although there was no reason why I shouldn't have been. I couldn't wait for the wedding day after waiting so long to be with him, and so, against all my Christian convictions, we had been sleeping together regularly without any precautions. After all, I naively thought that trying for six years with Jason without results meant that I would probably take six years again. Wrong.

A few weeks later, still denying any possibility of being pregnant, I developed a cough and made an appointment to see my doctor, as asthma still reared its ugly head if a cold went to my chest. Robert came with me, and after my examination, sat with me while the doctor prescribed some antibiotics.

"Now, before I prescribe these," the doctor said, smiling, "I need to know if you are pregnant."

Red rag. Bull.

"What is it with everyone?" I raised my voice ever so slightly, causing the doctor to do the same with his eyebrows. I turned to see Robert nodding at him over my shoulder, and mouthing 'yes she is' to him. Spitting feathers, I turned and stalked out of the surgery, stomped home in a foul mood, and stewed for the rest of the morning. After lunch I looked at Mum, who was chatting on the phone.

"I am going to the chemist to buy a pregnancy testing kit to prove I am not expecting, and then everyone can shut up," I declared. She nodded and I swept dramatically out of the house, slamming the door as I went. I returned fifteen minutes later went straight into the bathroom and opened the kit.

The instructions stated to wait three minutes before checking the result, but as I placed the stick on the side of the sink I watched the blue line make its way across the little window and my eyes became like saucers. In shocked silence, I walked into the kitchen, where mum was still chatting on the same call and waved the stick in front of her. Her mouth dropped open and, after muttering a 'goodbye' to her friend, she hung up. Inside I was so excited that I was pregnant, as this baby was so wanted, but at the same time I was terrified as I was not yet married and I knew that if things went wrong with Robert and myself, I would be an unwed mother. Although it was now the late nineties and single parenting wasn't considered a big deal, I knew within my heart that it was not God's best for me, or for my child.

Robert, meanwhile, had registered with some employment agencies and finally work became available with the local refuse collectors. Although it was good pay and hours: he finished early in the afternoons, he hated the smell that was so much part of the job and would dive straight in the shower as soon as he returned home. The stench, however, became so bad that he decided not to even bring it into the house, preferring to strip down to his underpants on the front doorstep, much to the delight of the neighbours!

February dawned wet and cold, as it usually does, and the day of the wedding finally arrived. Robert was nervous, anxious that his parents should like his choice of wife, especially as they had travelled over from Guernsey for the day. Dad had also made the trip over to give me away at the registry office, but although he seemed pleased for me, I could tell that he was a little disappointed that I was marrying someone with such a chequered past: some of it rather too recent for comfort. My sister and her husband did not come as they disapproved strongly of my choice of partner and would not be hypocritical by attending the wedding and pretending to be in agreement with it. However, it was still an enjoyable day and I was every inch a bride in her element, even with the extra inches that I had acquired over the last four months.

"Let's listen to the heartbeat," smiled my doctor, a few weeks later, getting the little heart monitor out of her desk drawer, "It was low down last time, so it should be higher up this time, with the baby turning."

She looked a little perplexed as she scanned my tummy in the expected area and found no sound.

"Hmm, let's try down here. Oh, there it is." She made a note and continued with my check-up. Another appointment was made, and again the heartbeat was in the same place. As the weeks went by, and the heartbeat was not changing position, it was becoming obvious that my baby was not turning and she began to talk about the possibility of a caesarean birth. An extra scan was scheduled and I wondered what I would see this time. Robert had missed my first scan due to work commitments so Mum had experienced the privilege of seeing her grandchild earlier than most grandparents. As the picture on the screen had become clearer, it had revealed a curled up little person, who waved at Mum and I, then promptly turned over until all we could see was a beautifully formed back. No amount of manoeuvring with the scanning tool could show us whether we were looking at a boy or a girl. I was convinced I was having a boy, but I guessed I'd have to wait and see. The second scan was also rather ambiguous, leading the radiologist to believe she was looking at a baby girl. I thought of all the blue baby clothes at home and disagreed with her. So did Robert, who had managed to be present this time.

Now I was going to have a scan when nearly full term. Surely I would find out today? But, no, this baby was determined to be a secret until the very last minute. In actual fact, I really didn't mind, as I preferred not to know the sex of my baby until it was born. What the scan did do was confirm that my little person was not moving an inch, let alone turn over! Sitting down comfortably, head behind my ribs (ah, so that was why I couldn't bend down to do up my shoelaces!) and feet struck out straight, which explained the constant kicks in the bladder, meant that a breach birth was inevitable and so an elective caesarean was unavoidable: a date was arranged and I was sent home to wait.

July 17th dawned bright and sunny – I could see it through the hospital window as I was wheeled out of the ward towards the operating theatre. It was plain sailing from there, apart from the extremely unpleasant epidural, which does not bear thinking about, let alone putting into print. The surgeon did all the hard work, although I had a couple of scary moments when I reacted to the anaesthetic, resulting in my blood pressure suddenly plummeting and making me sick – not much fun when the only part of my body I could move was my head... A short while later I was presented with a beautiful pink noisy boy. A boy... I sighed in contentment and drifted off to sleep, while Robert, who had been at my side throughout (with a little bowl in his hand) was escorted back out of the room to change out of his theatre greens.

I awoke to find myself back in the ward, with Robert asleep in the chair next to the bed, our son in his arms. Aaron. That was the name chosen when he was still a little mystery. Blue-eyed and smiley, he captured the hearts of all the nurses and, over the next few days there would be many a time I would have to hunt for him, only to find him being passed around and cuddled at the nurses' station. They nicknamed him 'Snuggle Bug' due to his fondness for snuggling into a nice warm neck, and I was so proud of him. So was Robert, who wandered around in shock for the first week or so, telling everyone about his 'beautiful' son. Like all first time mums, I spent hours studying his tiny fingers and toes, and examining his long eyelashes. Everything was so perfect, and I was constantly gazing in disbelief at this tiny person who I had made (well, with a little help).

"Drrrrrrrrrrrr!"

I awoke to the sound of drilling. Loud. Somewhere in the wall directly behind where all the newborns were sleeping in their little see-through cots. They remained asleep.

I couldn't speak to the lady in the next bed without sounding like a fishwife, but our little darlings slept soundly.

"What's going on?" I bellowed to the nurse, when she came to check me over. She grimaced.

"They're putting in the air bricks!" she hollered back. I shrugged my shoulders, not understanding the significance of this. She went on to explain. Loudly.

"This is a brand new wing of the hospital, but they have just realised that they didn't insert the air bricks when they built the back wall, and the building can't breathe. So they are doing it now."

So for two days I sat in my bed while my head reverberated with the sound of drills and my little cherub slept peacefully next to a vibrating wall.

Finally I was given the all clear to go home. Dad had travelled over from Guernsey within a day of the birth of his grandson, visiting with Mum every day and taking loads of photos, and it was he and Mum who came to collect us, as Robert was now working in a different town for a security firm and his shifts determined when he could visit.

Settling into life as a mum was fun. I spent most of my days gazing at my son, singing to him, cuddling him and feeding him. However, I was beginning to notice that things were changing between Robert and myself. He started working away for longer, sometimes for days at a time, drinking a lot and becoming very elusive, and I began to suspect that there was someone else in the picture. Haunted by feelings of inadequacy, I realised that Robert was still the same Robert from my past, with the same roving eye, the same attitudes and the same excuses and, as usual, I concluded that I was to blame for not noticing it sooner.

We all have skeletons in our cupboards, and belief systems that we surround ourselves with and adhere to. Mine was the belief that I was unacceptable, although I knew that God accepted me; it is possible to know something in your head, but it doesn't become part of who you are until it gets into your heart. Robert's belief system dictated that he was always going to make a mess of everything. So when life was looking good and he was happy, he was scared that he was going to do something to spoil it. So he ran before it happened, not realising that the very act of running away just created the scenario that he was running away from to avoid. Outwardly, he still lived in the same house as me, but inside he ran from responsibility and he ran from maturity... and he ran from himself.

And once again I ran back to God, whose grace far exceeded my self-judgement.

However, although God may have forgiven me for my stubbornness and wilful disobedience, there is a law of nature, both physical and spiritual, which states that 'whatever you sow... the same shall you reap', and I began to come to the realisation that what I had been sowing had not been good – and therefore one day I would reap the harvest of my actions. It was a sobering thought. One afternoon, a few weeks later, I looked at my beautiful little baby boy, in the middle of a feed, and wondered what all this was going to mean to him. What sort of life was he going to have, growing up? What role model was he going to have? I realised that I hadn't taken my precious little child into consideration at all, and I was suddenly overwhelmed with the seriousness of the situation. Here was an innocent little baby, who did not have any choice who his parents were, and I had given him a dad who was going to constantly let him down, whose word could not be trusted and whose behaviour damaged all those he held dear. And the scariest thing about it was that the negative influence that Robert would unknowingly exert would encourage him, by example, to be the same.

And I was devastated.

Chapter 15
PARENTHOOD

"Alison", Mum screwed her nose up as she nodded towards Aaron, curled up in my arms.

"He needs changing." She explained, seeing my questioning gaze.

"Oh, does he?" I drew in a deep breath and smelt nothing. Exasperated, she fetched the nappy bag, returning to find me chuckling gently; having no sense of smell was great for times like these! Aaron was a delightful baby. He smiled, gurgled, snuggled and slept. I was determined to enjoy every stage of his development and growth, as I realised that his 'firsts' would only happen once. He had a fascination for walls and, as he learned to sit up, would brush his hand against any brickwork he found as I pushed his pram along the pavement. This, of course, made every journey extremely long, as I had to walk at a snail's pace to ensure he kept the skin on his fingertips! He learned to talk very early on (and indeed, has never stopped!) and both Mum and I spent hours teaching him the correct pronunciation of words, resulting in strangers stopping and commenting on his clear speech.

By now I was working for a bed company, having left my 'Ladies' behind during my pregnancy, as I had found the long hours of standing in a south-facing kitchen during the hot summer of 1997 unbearable. Mum would look after Aaron for me and they would come to collect me at the end of my working day, where she taught him to recognise colours by waiting in the car and chanting the colours of the cars that drove past. He was very bright and picked things up quickly, again to the astonishment of people we met. I was now single again as Robert and I had finally separated after my suspicions were confirmed as fact, and divorce proceedings were underway. He would sometimes come around to see me and Aaron, but gradually the visits became less and less frequent until they stopped altogether. I was relieved when this happened, as I was finding it hard to adjust and move on with the constant reminders of what I had lost.

I loved being a mum when Aaron was a baby, and never tired of watching him sleep. As he grew older, that habit never changed. As he hit the terrible twos with full force, I relished those rare sleeping moments when I could study his pink cherubic face and long lashes, without getting an ear bashing "NO!" every time his mouth opened. From the time he had learned the word 'no', he had practiced it at every opportunity, backing it up with explanations of why he was going to disobey. He was convinced that he always had a valid reason and it drove me to distraction. More than anything else, motherhood taught me that each life is so very precious. I had always spoken out against abortion in the past because I couldn't agree with the idea that the adult could choose, while the child could not. But it wasn't until I had a little baby of my own to care for that I realised what a privilege I had been given; to be responsible for another little person, so dependant on my love, wisdom and protection. I began to see what a heinous crime it was to abort, not just a collection of cells, as we would be led to believe, but a unique, 'once in eternity' person, along with his or her potential to love, and the plans that God had for that individual life. I began to spend time in prayer, asking for mercy for those hurting souls who were living with terrible guilt after buying into the lie, and also just thanking God for bringing my boy safely into existence and trusting me to bring him up. I knew I wouldn't be able to do it without God's help, after all my own life had been one disaster after another, but I was aware that God had brought me this far and He wasn't going to let me down now.

Shortly before Aaron's 2nd birthday I was at work when one of my co-workers called out to me from down the stairs.

"Alison, there's a guy here, says he wants to see you."

I squeezed out from behind the desk; still laughing over the silly joke I had been sharing with my colleague.

"Coming!" I called, turning my head to giggle again with my friend. I turned the corner, hand on the banister and clattered down the stairs to find myself face to face with…Robert. The shock must have shown on my face, as the laughter died on my lips and old feelings I thought I had dealt with came rushing to the surface with a vengeance.

"What do you want" It was a demand, not a question.

"I'm sorry," he blurted out, "I made a mistake and it's not her I love, it's you."

Once again I was faced with a choice. Do I take him back; try again, or do I tell him to go away. After all, the divorce proceedings were well underway. And once again, I made the wrong choice. I still loved him and I couldn't let go. He was like an addiction that I would run to, knowing it was going to hurt sooner or later. But if there was a chance that he really did love me…

He was living in a flat in the town centre and I agreed to visit one afternoon with Aaron. The meeting went well and he was besotted with his son. After that I began to visit regularly with Aaron, but also alone in the evenings when we would talk about our future. I almost convinced myself that things were different now; surely he was different now: but still something niggled and I couldn't trust him enough to blindly give myself to him as wholeheartedly as before. Within a month he had moved back into mum's house with me, but within two months the old patterns emerged, as he began staying away for two, sometimes three days at a time and drinking heavily. As another affair reared its ugly head I finally came to my senses and we parted company permanently. It was hard, as I had loved him ever since the first time I had set eyes on him when I was fifteen; and now I had to admit that it was well and truly over – and I grieved. What became of him I may never know, but I had finally learned my lesson (even if it had taken a lifetime to do so). I made the decision that I was never going to put myself, or my child, through this ever again, even if it meant staying single forever. After all, I could treat myself better than this, and if my marriage partner was not prepared to treat me with respect, then I would be better off without one. I knew now that I had to concentrate on raising Aaron to the best of my ability with God's help, and I threw myself into being the best mum I could be.

I sold my motorbike; a painful decision, but one which had to be made as I could not afford to continue with the monthly payments as well as pay the mound of debts that Robert had run up and kindly left me to pay. Not long after, however, God provided transport for me in a way I had never dreamed of.

"I've got a new taxi," Dad told me over the phone one afternoon.

"That's nice," I commented, wondering what that had to do with me.

"And I have an old taxi, the Proton, sitting in my driveway, doing nothing," he continued. The penny began to drop and I gratefully answered 'yes please' when he offered it to me. Free. He brought it over on the ferry and drove it to the house. Free. We went halves on the petrol and, after spending the rest of the day with him, Mum and I drove him back to the ferry for his return home. I thought it quite ironic that the taxi Dad had brought over to collect my newborn son and me from the hospital some years before was now sitting in the driveway, and was mine.

Meanwhile, once again I was feeling unsettled in the church that I was attending and so I began searching for a new church where I could feel I belonged. I had loved Shiloh Church in Guernsey, but I found that I was constantly comparing all the English churches with it – and they were found wanting in some way or another. However, eventually I started attending a lively church not far from where we lived that was in the throes of employing a temporary Pastor. The people there were very friendly and I found myself being accepted willingly, although they found Aaron, my self-assertive chatterbox, rather a challenge; or rather, some of them did. Others just loved him.

"Hello, young man," smiled one of the elderly ladies, looking down at him. It was our first Sunday and we were just finding our way around. Aaron stared at his shoes, suddenly fascinated with the laces.

"What is your name?" she pressed. Silence. Shoelaces.

"Aaron" I replied for him.

"And how old are you Aaron?"

"Four" he finally answered, although to his laces, not to the lady.

"And when are you five?" She smiled reassuringly at me, pleased that she had finally made contact with him. He stopped scraping his toe across the carpet, looked up into her enquiring face, and with a look of incredulity at her obvious silliness, announced,

"On my birthday."

She looked a little bemused, and left us to find a seat for the beginning of the service.

There were a few children at the church and one of them, Tristan, became Aaron's friend, keeping him company in the crèche. I settled in very quickly, and came to view the church as my extended family. Eventually, I did what came naturally and became part of the worship team, singing alongside Tristan's mum. This was the second worship team I had been involved in as it was something I had also done at the church in Guernsey. It was while I was being involved in this aspect of Church life that I suddenly realised that God had given me a 'talent' and that, in doing what I loved most, I was pleasing Him. I had loved singing all my life. I had joined the school choir at the Grammar School just because I wanted to sing the Hallelujah Chorus at the School Carol Service. I sang when I was happy, I sang when I was sad, but now I had a reason to sing that went beyond normal daily life. I was singing to the King of Heaven (and my baptism verse was etched in my memory). I was still writing songs at home, but like before, I was too self-conscious to play them to anybody. Surely one day, though, I would do something with them?

The PA system at the church was a little ancient and temperamental, but one of the guys who ran it, Kevin, saw early on that Aaron was bright and interested in anything electrical (well, anything with wires, buttons and lights!) and asked if I minded if he took him under his wing and encouraged his interest. Readily I agreed and so Aaron was introduced to the PA system. I had taught Aaron to call adults by 'Auntie and Uncle' out of respect, and so Kevin became 'Uncle' Kevin. He was fantastic with him, not only showing him which buttons and knobs did what, but actually allowing him to push and twiddle them. He was very patient and gentle, and Aaron loved being with him, running to him whenever he saw him. However, the other guy who ran the PA on alternate weeks was the opposite of 'Uncle' Kevin. He did not like children, especially ones who asked lots of questions and wanted to touch all the buttons. Aaron was told to "sit there and don't move" on the first, and every subsequent, occasion that he climbed the steps to the raised platform where the PA was situated and it was a most disgruntled boy who finally came downstairs at the end of the service.

Aaron still insisted on going to sit on the PA however, no matter who the sound man was and we soon settled into a routine of 'this week it's Uncle Kevin" with a smile and 'this week its Uncle Clive" with a scowl. However, one week due to holidays and illness we were unsure and walked into church, coming face to face with Clive instead of Kevin, and I drew in a breath as Aaron approached his nemesis.

"Uncle Clive," he enquired, with his singsong voice. Clive looked down at him, openly showing his distaste at being called 'Uncle'.

"Yes" he growled.

"Are you doing the PA today?" I could hear the desperate hope in Aaron's voice that he was wrong in his assumptions.

"Yes, Aaron, I am." And my 'sweet' little boy stamped his foot, clenched his fists, and with tears of disappointment in his eyes, wailed:

"And I prayed SO hard that it would be Uncle Kevin!"

I prayed at that moment for the ground to open up and swallow me and I was reminded of the times that I had done similar things to my mum…

Like the time I had burped really loudly standing next to her in a crowd, waiting to cross the road at a Pelican Crossing. Being a teenager, I kept silent, not wanting to own up by requesting pardon, and she turned slowly to me with accusing eyes.

"Pardon Me." she announced loudly, attempting to shame me into using my manners. I leaned towards her and whispered, "Thanks Mum" with a smile, as the crowd turned as one man to stare at her. With an incredulous look on her face, she narrowed her eyes.

"I'll get you back for that." she promised. I had thought it hilarious at the time, but now that my son was doing it to me it wasn't quite so funny!

And it didn't stop there either. Aaron, as mentioned earlier, could be rather outspoken, and like most children it was usually at the wrong time. A short while after the incident at church, while holidaying in Guernsey, we visited my cousin whose son was six weeks older than Aaron, and whose favourite game was to empty the contents of his toy box all over the floor, watch his mother put everything back, and then re-empty it again. I hadn't seen her for a few years, although we had grown up more like sisters than cousins and I was really looking forward to spending some time with her. As we were staying in a self-catering chalet and had no transport, she collected us and drove us to her house, where she proceeded to lead us up the steps to the front door.

She unlocked the door and opened it, motioning to us to go through into the lounge, and stepped aside to allow us to enter first. Aaron looked at me, a little hesitant, then stepped slowly through the lounge doorway to come face to face with 'wall to wall' toys, as her son had outdone himself just before they had left to pick us up. As we followed him, he took one look at the pile of toys strewn from one side of the room to the other and stopped, turning around with an overwhelmed look on his face.

"Auntie," he asked politely,

"Yes," said she, bending down to him so he could speak to her properly.

"Could you tidy up please, so I can find something to play with?"

Again eternity seemed to stretch endlessly before me as my heart sank into my boots, but without hesitation she just laughed and straightened up.

"No," she replied, "you just go and play with something!"

And, without a backward glance at his bewildered face, she made her way into the kitchen to put the kettle on. She never commented on my embarrassment, for which I was extremely grateful. Not too many years later, she moved with her husband and, by then, three children over to the UK to within a ten minute car's journey of mum and I, and our friendship picked up where it had left off and grew until it became one that far outweighed the blood ties.

My mother had a saying: "You can always rely on your children to show you up."

I had always laughed, never thinking how true it was until I found myself saying it too!

Hmmmm… self- fulfilled prophecy, I think!

Chapter 16
LEARNING THROUGH LIFE

At this time I began seeking employment away from retail. The bed store I worked in had originally been a concession within another well-known furniture store, but that had gone bankrupt overnight, leaving us out in the cold – literally. On that day I received two phone calls. My area manager wanted me to move, with my manager, to the new store in Bognor Regis, fifteen miles west of my home town – and my previous area manager wanted me to move to his store in Crawley, about twenty miles north. The two area managers were known to be fierce rivals and I was not only a natural salesperson, but also very organised and prompt with my paperwork: a much appreciated talent when dealing with sales commissions! It was nice to be wanted and fought over, but after some thought, I decided to move to the Bognor shop; a decision helped by the fact that the drive west was very pleasant and I detested the arrogance of the Crawley area manger!

"My neighbours think I'm strange," announced my new colleague, Adam, one frosty morning, stamping his feet and blowing on his hands, as we waited for the manager to unlock the door to the store.

"Really? Why is that?" I asked, eagerly awaiting the unfolding of the story. Considering the usual catastrophes that surrounded Adam's life experiences, this could be interesting. After all, how many people do you know who, when unsure of the turn-off on a roundabout will drive around it extremely slowly two or three times, stopping at each exit to re-read the directional signs before continuing to the next exit to repeat the procedure... passing a waiting police car each time until, in disbelief they stop him, lights flashing, to breathalyse him?

"Well," he began, "This morning, I ran downstairs from my flat into the car-park, unlocked my car, jumped in and put my seatbelt on. It was only when I went to take hold of the steering wheel and put the key in the ignition that I realised I had got in the passenger side - and I had to get out, run around to the driver's side and do it all aver again."

"Well, anybody can have one of those days" I sympathised.

"Yeah, but I do it every morning," he whined, "and I've had the car three months!"

I have many great memories of working for this company: one of my favourites being the day pandemonium broke out over a spider. Adam, by this time, had left and been replaced by Heidi, a very self-asserted young lady, fresh out of college, with a degree in HR, no experience, and big ambitions. One afternoon she was sat on the edge of the desk, chatting with a customer over the phone while I served a young couple that were interested in a bed in our 'expensive' range. Lying side by side, testing the firmness of the bed, they listened as I took them through the customer journey of information, which would, hopefully, lead to a sale.

"...and this is the sprung base" I advised. I lifted the corner of the mattress while they sat up and leaned over the side to look – and stared straight at the biggest spider I have ever seen in my life – as it made a dash for the safety of the bed next to the desk. And Heidi. The scream that emitted from the desk area was ear splitting and within seconds Heidi was standing on top of the desk, jumping from one foot to the other, hysterical. The manager, thinking someone had been murdered, came thundering out of the staff room where he had been relaxing with a cuppa and a packet of biscuits, only to turn white at the sight of the spider and hastily make his way out of the front door to the car-park, to view the proceedings from a safe distance.

"Oh my goodness! It's got KNEES!" Heidi shrieked, as the spider lifted itself up on its extremely long legs and made a beeline for the underneath of a bed the other side of the showroom. I don't blame it, really, considering the noise level in the building.

It was at this time that I realised Heidi still had the phone in her hand and was trying to explain the proceedings to her poor confused customer, whilst hyperventilating. The situation was beginning to take on surreal qualities, with overtones of being slightly ludicrous and, as usual, I began to see the funny side. I was the only one – which made me worse. Finally, everyone calmed down, but when we went to hunt for the spider, it was nowhere to be seen. We never did find it. I did, however, close my sale and my customers even managed a smile when I not only asked if they wanted the two-drawer or the four-drawer base, but also gave them the choice of delivery with or without a spider!

I found that I had a natural God-given talent for sales, but only when I believed in the product I was selling. I would not sell the latest promotion when it was not what the customer needed and would always strive to match the right product to each individual customer, even when that meant lower commission for me. God honoured my integrity and I found that often in the monthly statistics I was the top seller in the store, even though I only worked four days: the full time staff worked six and the manager worked seven on most weeks. I really enjoyed the challenges of the job and loved the rapport I could build with my customers. But, as with all things, there was a fly in the ointment: my manager seemed to be devoid of any scruples. He would say anything to get a sale, usually making outrageous claims on behalf of the company, then discreetly disappearing when disgruntled customers returned for a show-down – emerging innocently from somewhere obscure after his staff (me) had calmed the situation and smoothed ruffled feathers. Then he began to steal orders. Being commission based, every salesperson worked hard to close their sales. However, sometimes the customer would want to bring a partner, friend or parent back in to get their feedback before making the final decision. On those occasions, it was standard practice to give written details to the customer, with the salesperson's name added, ensuring the sale was credited to that salesperson. Everyone honoured the unspoken rule – or so I thought.

I began to be suspicious after one of my colleagues' customers returned and the manager placed the order in his own name.

"Wasn't that _____'s customer?" I queried.

"They didn't show me his card," he answered.

"But you were here when he spent an hour with them last week," I reminded him. He shrugged his shoulders as he sauntered casually towards the staff room. Conversation over. I fumed all day. When, a few weeks later, I returned to work after my day off to find he had served one of my customers and deliberately placed the order in his name to the tune of £3500.00 I knew I couldn't work for him any longer. This time I had proof, as I had left a message in the diary that this (named) customer was bringing his wife in on Sunday and requesting that the order be placed in my name. It had been my largest order to date, and I was so excited I had been talking about it all week! When I confronted him he laughed.

"That's what you get for not working Sundays."

I was speechless. It wasn't just his greed that upset me; as manager, he earned commission on all sales, not just his, but I was shocked by his complete lack of a sense of honour. The atmosphere became very strained thereafter when he and I were working together, and although I spent many long hours before God, forgiving this man, (usually every day that I worked with him) I found that I could not enjoy the job as I once had, and that, along with the 45-minute drive each way and an astronomical petrol bill made my mind up for me. It was time to move on.

Changes at home also meant that I needed to work nearer, as Aaron's school days were taking a turn towards unchartered territory. He had been attending a semi-private school (which is where all my commission had gone!) and had loved it. The headmistress was a Christian and the school had been run on

Christian ethics. However, she had recently retired and with the changes of leadership had also come a change of staff and attitudes. Bullying between pupils came to the fore but was denied by the school board until one parent whose child had been bullied incessantly took the board to court – and won. Unhappy with the way the school was now being run, I began to look at other options and surprisingly, Home-Education was the route I felt God lead me down. The day I told Aaron that he was not going back to the school, he stopped having nightmares: something I had not even connected with the situation. He was in reception year.

I was, however, still in for a shock. Bullying affects people in so many ways and I was advised by the other home-schooling mums to 'de-school' him, allowing him time to make adjustments and then move forward at his own pace. I discovered I had a very angry little boy on my hands, a powder keg of frustration, fear and clenched fists. The treatment of his friends, and himself, at the hands of the cowardly bullies had upset him deeply and it was to be almost six months before he could function normally again. During that time, he spent the majority of his days going on field trips, learning through hands-on experiences, discovering the world around him using his senses and exploring God's creation. In short - he was learning without realising it.

We did no formal schooling of any description. No pen-work, no maths and no reading, although all three were tackled in his day-to-day experiences and naturally worked through. During his time at school I had looked through his reading books and was horrified at some of the subjects covered at such a young age, while he had struggled with a new reading curriculum which jumped from easy words to hard words at random and left him confused and frustrated. Money was very tight, so my first port of call became the local summer fairs where I could pick up books cheaply. I sought out all the old 'Ladybird' books with 'Janet and John' and started reading to Aaron in the evenings. He still resisted any attempts to persuade him to read, but would sit and listen for hours. Then one day, he surprised me by walking purposefully toward me with book in hand and announced,

"Today I am going to read to you."

He positioned himself next to me on the settee, sitting upright as if giving a performance, opened the book I had been reading to him and read it out loud, with perfect pronunciation and emphasis, while I stared at him open-mouthed.

'He's memorised it,' I thought to myself, thinking of how many times I had read it to him. Fetching the next book in the series, that I had only read twice, I passed it to him.

"Can you read that one, please," I asked, and without hesitation he opened his mouth and launched into another performance. He never looked back.

I discovered that he was fascinated with road signs, and would read them to me every time we went out. He studied the 'Highway Code' and used up reams of paper making copies of his favourites, and inventing his own and posting them all around the house. When the gas fire in the lounge had to be dismantled and taken out, he posted a warning sign in its place. If the current owners look behind the replacement fake fireplace, they will find a huge sign, covering the hole, which reads "Danger! Big Hole!"

"No Entry" signs were everywhere, along with "One Way" signs, creating fantastic icebreakers for any visitors. Then he began to notice advertising and the look of pure delight on his face when he read 'buy one get one free' on a poster next to his favourite pudding in the supermarket was priceless - and expensive. From that moment on, he would rush around the store hunting out all the 'deals' and insisting we buy them, until I had to start shopping alone!

"Okay Aaron, any ideas?"

We were sitting at the kitchen table, deciding on a name for our 'school'. We had a lot of single words, lots of scribbles, lots of doodles and ink spots on our piece of paper, but nothing we could use that would have any meaning.

"What about 'New Life'?" I suggested, "Especially as you have a new school life."

Aaron nodded enthusiastically, jigging up and down on his chair. Hmmm... so far so good. But we needed a school motto. And then it came to me.

New Life Homeschool
Learning Through Life.

And so our 'school' was born. I realised I needed to be up to date with technology and finally, with much fear and trembling, became the proud owner of a computer. The man from 'Currys' computer shop came to the house to set it up for me as part of the deal, and was very efficient. He pressed buttons and gadgets, spoke a form of Klingon which I presumed was 'computer speak', seemed pleased with what he had achieved, switched the computer off, shook my hand and left. The front door closed and I turned to mum, laughing.

"I don't have a clue how to switch it on!" I announced, shrugging my shoulders helplessly. I enrolled at the local sixth form college for a 10 week 'IT from scratch' course where I learned the basics, and began spending my evenings designing colourful worksheets for Aaron. I finally found a use for my ability to make up rhymes and soon our walls were dotted with all manner of poems, songs and sayings to help him learn his alphabet, multiplication tables and spellings. His favourite was a rhyme I made up to help him remember his vowels and consonants, to the tune of "one, two, three, four, five, once I caught a fish alive". I was amazed at how it all fitted easily into the tune and Aaron found it easy to remember. Years later, he can still remember it! (Sadly, as you can see, so can I!)

'A, E, I, O, U, I know my vowels, what about you?
I know my consonants too, they're in the alphabet: it's true.
B, C, D, F, G, H, J, K, L, M, N, P
Q, R, S, T, V, W, X, Y, Z (yeah!)'

Chapter 17
WATER COMPANY

In the midst of all this, I applied for a position in the call centre of the local water company that was based at the end of my road, and had to sit a written exam for Maths and English before I could be granted an interview. The English didn't bother me at all, as it had been my favourite subject at school and I found that logic would usually find me the right answer in a multi-choice question. But maths? Oh dear...

One look at the example of the test paper I was sent by post, and I knew I was in trouble. Fractions. I did not understand fractions at all. But God had it all in hand, as He always does. I had made friends within a circle of local Christian Homeschoolers and one of them, Jennie, became my lifesaver. We hit it off the first time we met and I still class her as one of my 'best' friends. And Jennie loved maths. Passionately. So the evening before my test found me sat at her kitchen table while she helped me get to grips with fractions, algebra and other maths 'nasties'. It paid off, and I advanced to the interview stage.

"So, Alison," Rose, the call centre manager, smiled, "Tell me what you do in your spare time?"

"I go to church and I home-educate my son, so I don't really get any spare time!" I laughed.

The next hour was spent explaining about my belief in God and my reasons for home schooling. And I got the job!

Eight weeks of intense training ensued and school became back to front for a while with Aaron drilling me on a list of task names and functions as I filled my head with computer systems and water bills and learned to handle calls in a call centre without pre-written scripts.

I became firm friends with Patricia, who sat in the row in front of me and laughed loudly all throughout the training: I have never, before or since, heard such an infectious laugh, the result of which was that many training sessions dissolved into happy chaos. She was a breath of fresh air, one of those few people who are fiercely loyal, with true grit and someone I am proud to call my friend. Later on, after another six weeks training, we progressed to the next level of competency together and I was delighted that we laughed as much, if not more, during the second round of training as we had in the first. Wisely, the water company did not allow us to sit together once back in the call centre, although I could hear her laugh echo around the office wherever they put her!

A short while later the water company decided to team up with a well-known emergency insurance company that dealt with burst water pipes, leaks and such like. Consequently, all the call centre advisers were instructed to sell insurance as part of each call, although we could only offer the deal to homeowners. This made each call a little longer, due to the quiz we had to subject our customers to each time they called...

"Hello, I'd like to pay my bill"

"Yes, that's fine, I can do that for you right away. Before I do, could I ask if you own your property?"

Confused silence.

"Er... yes"

Tick that box

"Would you be interested in taking out an insurance against water leaks, burst pipes...."

Stunned silence.

"...and if you do have an emergency," I would continue, " they will pay out for overnight accommodation for up to two weeks. And it will only cost..."

"No, I just want to pay my bill!"

As an incentive, we were paid an extra pound for every customer who signed up, which in my case amounted to rather a lot, as my salesperson past came into its own. I quickly became one of the top sellers in the centre, although I never pushed the sales: I would simply ask. More than once I finished a call where the customer had taken up the offer to find Sarah, who sat on my left, staring incredulously at me.

"I try and try to sell this stupid insurance," she cried indignantly, " and I tell them all the benefits and everything, and they always say 'no'. And you just say 'Do you want it?' and they fall over themselves to have it ... and you haven't even explained anything about it yet! Look!" she said, pointing to my tally sheet, which was rapidly filling up and then pointing to hers, which had four on it. I did feel sorry for her, but she wasn't the worst salesperson in the office...or the most feared. No. That honour had to go to my friend, Patricia. I shall explain.

As an extra incentive, the supervisors decided to keep a large tub of sweets by their bank of desks in the centre of the room and when we had sold a policy we were requested to print off the relevant customer reference number and policy details and present them in order to collect our sweet. When this became boring, they decided to spice things up a little and brought in a dartboard, and only if our dart hit the board we could help ourselves to a sweet. Patricia finally sold a policy and made her way over to the board. She collected her dart, positioned herself ready for the throw and launched her missile. It hit the board and bounced out, just missing her foot. Taking pity on her, the supervisor advised her that she was permitted to have another go. This time it bounced out and skewed sideways... onto the bank of desks nearest the dartboard, narrowly missing the person sitting there and knocking over his coffee. She exploded into one of her infectious laughs and within seconds the entire call centre was in hysterics. She didn't get her sweet, but later on when she managed to sell another policy, it was noted that as she made her way to the dartboard those sat nearest to it began to inch their way further and further away from it, ending in a mad dash for safety as she picked up the dart!

Call centre work, I discovered, was an eye-opener. As first

point of reference for any complaints, queries, apologies for late bills, excuses for not paying bills, house moves and stupid questions, for example:

"Why am I charged for wastewater? I don't waste any." I was in the firing line every time I answered a call…

"Good Morning. You're talking to Alison today, may I take your customer reference number please?"

"@#! @#*!@*!!!!!"

I pulled my headphones away from my ear as a barrage of expletives exploded out of the earpiece. I let the customer finish what he was shouting, and then took a deep breath.

"Ok sir," I answered, "Maybe you would like to explain the problem to me and I'll see what I can do"

More expletives.

"Sir, I cannot deal with the issue if you keep shouting. Please calm down."

Eventually the gentleman took a deep breath and began to explain what the problem was. As it turned out, he had called on numerous times, and had always been promised action. However, when I looked at the notes on the account, what had been written was not what had been done. The more I looked at the account, the more I could understand the man's frustration, even if I didn't condone his language. I explained to him what I was going to do, gave him my telephone extension number, and assured him that I would call him back once the much needed adjustments had been actioned on his account. The call ended with a happy customer, who was able to joke about the situation just before hanging up.

As I began to print off the computer screen to hand in to my supervisor; it was too big a problem for me to deal with personally, I looked up to see Joni, one of the supervisors, watching me intently, pen in hand and paperwork on her desk, and I realised I had just been monitored, and groaned. Of all the customers I had spoken to that morning, why did it have to be that one? I handed my request to the supervisor and stood by her as she clicked in and out of this gentleman's account, righting all the wrongs, adjusting all the meter readings and re-typing his bill, which now showed a hefty credit. Back at my desk, I set his refund in motion and called him back, explaining what changes had been made and advising him of the amount of credit that was due back to him. He was extremely grateful, and I had a tangible sense of a job well done as I hung up. I looked up to see Joni walking towards me with papers in her hand and I sat back in my chair, ready for the usual grilling. Instead Joni sat down, took a really long hard look at me and slowly shook her head.

"I can't believe you had him joking by the end of the call," she smiled. "That was absolutely textbook, Alison. You deserve a 100% on your form, but I can't give you that, because I'm not allowed – that would make you as good as the manager."

I shrugged my shoulders. I didn't work this way because I wanted recognition on my monitoring forms; God had done too much work in me for that, but I did feel a little cheated that credit was not given where it was due. It was at this moment that I realised that I wanted more out of my job. I wanted to be able to get my teeth into problems to solve, and situations to change, and to do what I had seen the supervisor do.

One morning as I slid back into my seat after a toilet break, Sarah looked up. She seemed a little anxious.

"Did you wash your hands?"

I stared at her, incredulous, but I nodded to be polite. But it happened the next time I went - and the next time - and the next time. It wasn't just me that she asked, though. Everyone on our bank of desks was interrogated about their cleanliness on a daily basis and I could see that my colleagues were beginning to resent the implications that were unsaid, but made nonetheless. Always one to make a point with a bit of humour, I decided to wait until it was my turn in the inquisition before I said something. I didn't have to wait long.

"Did you wash your hands?"

I didn't answer straight away but pretended to think hard.

"Hmmmmmmm, I think so," I said slowly and then I licked both of my palms, smiled sweetly and confirmed, "Yes!"

The look of horror that spread over her face was priceless. She stood up in absolute disgust and, with a slow shake of her head announced, almost choking on each word:

"I can't believe you just did that"

"Sarah," I laughed, "Do you honestly think that I would have done that if I hadn't washed my hands?"

However, she did not take too kindly to my humour and within an hour she had relocated to the far side of the call centre, where occasionally I would see her staring at me with utter disbelief written all over her face. We did manage to remain friends but she always viewed me with a kind of 'terrible' fascination from that point!

As I became more proficient at my job I began to take extra notice of what the supervisors did when I handed them accounts to amend or adjust. I was fascinated when I watched them work and I decided that I still wanted to be able to do more than just take calls, and began keeping my ears open for opportunities to move to a new department and learn new skills. Three months later I had my chance to do just that. A position in the metered billing department was advertised and, after passing the interview stage, I moved out of the call centre to a 'back office' and a whole new work experience opened up for me.

Chapter 18
A NEW DIRECTION

Meanwhile my 'church feet' were beginning to get itchy again. The numbers at my church had been dwindling steadily over the last few months as the stress of having no permanent Pastor began to take its toll on the believers there. All the youth and nearly all the families had moved to a new dynamic church which had started up just around the corner, leaving the Sunday school just a skeleton of what it had once been, consisting only of Aaron, Tristan and a family of three siblings. Feeling a little faded around the edges I began to look around for a new spiritual home and was invited by Jennie to go to her church, which had a thriving children's work. On my first visit there I knew that this was the place where God wanted me for now. I joined a women-only housegroup, which met on a Wednesday afternoon, and God began the healing process of a lifetime of sadness. Many tears were shed and much forgiveness was given and received, allowing my hurt, closed heart to finally begin to open up and trust. Unlike most church meetings I had ever attended, our Wednesday 'girlie' get-together, disguised as a housegroup, quickly became a lifeline to me. We met in Jan's magnificent house, with sofas that swallowed up its inhabitants and carpets that were ankle deep. Bible studies were conducted, not with stiff religiosity, but with shoes off and toes buried wriggling in the carpet; with nether regions snuggled deeply within the upholstery of the sofa and a glass of wine at hand. It was a time to explore God's Word as a woman – not just another 'person'. If you have ever struggled with the fact that God made you feminine, you will understand the need I had to learn to be just that: Feminine. It sounded strange, and something I never thought I would ever use to describe myself - and after two failed marriages, both of which ended with me being thrown away and replaced, God knew that.

"We've organised a night out for the group," Jennie announced one afternoon, " Bowling, followed by Pizza. Are you coming?"

I thought of the 75p in my purse, and the spare few pounds that I had after paying for supplies for Aaron and my share of the bills and food, and shook my head. There was no way that I was going to be able to afford £20 or £30 for a night out. Nothing more was said, then a week later Jennie cornered me at church.

"Do you want to come?" she asked, looking at me intently. I looked at the ground. I hated being so short of money, but I hated others knowing it, even more. I nodded.

"But I can't afford it," I explained, turning away.

Taking me by the shoulders, Jennie turned me back towards her.

"That's not what I asked," she replied gently, "I asked if you wanted to come."

Frustrated, I answered again, "Yes, but I can't afford it."

"I'll put your name down then," she continued, ignoring my protests, "and we'll see you at 7pm on Thursday evening at my house. Your friends want you to come and we will pay for you." She hugged me and walked away, leaving me wondering what I had done to deserve such friends.

It was a fun-filled night as we shrieked with laughter in the bowling alley, watching our futile efforts meandering down the 'lane' and dropping into the side ruts - to completely miss the skittles, which continued to stand unhindered. Egging each other on, we finally managed a half decent score and I suddenly realised that I couldn't remember the last time I had laughed with such abandon. Pizza time was no different, and I am sure the waiter (posh pizza place!) was convinced we were all well oiled although no alcohol had been consumed all evening! It felt good, just having fun, although a little alien, and I realised that I had lived my life devoid of socialising with female friends far too long. It was good to relax and laugh in the company of other women and occasionally during the evening I would stop and look around me at these precious ladies and have to remind myself that I wasn't having a dream. I don't think any of them realised what an impact they made on my life that day, but by the end of the night I had made a promise to myself that I would never isolate myself from female company again. I began to spend more and more time reading my Bible and talking to God and, as more and more issues were unearthed, I found that He was gentle in every way as He dealt with my past. Gradually I began to change, emerging from my shell and discarding my masks, one at a time. One day I took stock, and realised that I was so far removed from the person who had stood in her bathroom many years before, crying out in desperation and self-loathing that I was unrecognisable, and I was so thankful.

Aaron, by now, was also changing. A year earlier he had lapsed into a thoughtful silence one Sunday evening, his little pink face upturned, as he lay in his bed.

"Mummy," he had finally asked

"Yes," I answered, anticipating the questions usually saved for bedtime that would require a complicated answer, and was therefore guaranteed to delay lights out for a minimum of 30 minutes. I couldn't have been more wrong.

"Jesus is your friend, isn't he?"

I nodded, wondering what was coming next.

"Would Jesus be my friend too?"

A huge lump arose in my throat, as I nodded and hugged him close. I gently shared God's good news with him and asked if he understood. He nodded, and then bowed his head to pray. So with tears running down my face, God gave me the privilege and honour of bringing my son to the point where he was born. Again. Only this time, it was eternal.

Now I realised it was time to move on with whatever plans God had for me and I began to seek God's face with regards to my future. I was aware that it was not God's best for me to be alone and certainly not for Aaron to have no male influence, so I began to pray about a husband – and father.

"Um.... Lord," I began. After all how does one ask Almighty God for a husband? I certainly didn't have a clue! In the end, I sat down with a pen and paper, but I found myself listing all the things I didn't want in a husband: I couldn't think of anything positive. Then it dawned on me – I really did not know what I wanted, and I wasn't going to be able to pray in faith if I didn't know what to ask for! Ok, I thought, I'll start from where I'm at and go from there. So I continued to make my list of what I did not want – and it was long. Extremely. Then, chewing the end of my pen, a habit I have never really grown out of despite ending up with a mouthful of foul-tasting liquid and a blue tongue on more than one occasion, I began to write down all the positive things I admire in a man. I feared it would be a really short list.

"Um, let me see," I muttered to myself, " Number one on the list is 'Saved'. Absolutely. Without a shadow of a doubt."

I had finally realised that if a marriage was to survive, it was absolutely essential for us to have that one thing in common. I had learned that the hard way. If Jesus was the core of my being how could I, in all honesty, be joined together with someone who didn't know him? The whole foundation of our union would be a sham. Who would I pray with when I was concerned about anything? Who could I get excited with as I thanked God for His goodness? How could I live with someone who did not have that precious experience of being born-again? How could we encourage each other as we shared our experiences if the one experience that mattered more than anything was not shared? This one had to be top priority.

"Number two," I mused, "oh yes – Solvent...and number three is Sober. Then there is Honest... and a sense of humour. Oh Lord, I would love someone who not only makes me laugh but makes me laugh out loud with delight. " Ah, they were coming thick and fast now and soon I had a longer list than the 'not wanted' list. I was quite surprised, but as I scanned down the list I began to feel apprehensive. Maybe I was being too picky – it looked like I would only be happy with Adam before the Fall! Then it dawned on me... that was because that is how it was meant to be, and I was suddenly filled with a sense of grief for the wholeness in our relationships that was lost at the beginning of man's history.

It was getting late so, after adding what sort of father I wanted for Aaron, I read my request out to God, feeling very presumptuous that I would ask God to single me out in such a way. Surely He had better things to do with His time, like populating Heaven, than to hunt out a 'perfect' man for me? Hmmm...

I folded up my piece of paper and slipped it into the cover of my Bible so I could read it another time and went to bed. It did not occupy my mind for quite a while after that, as if by writing it down it was a settled matter and not something to be anxious about, but occasionally I would extract it from its hiding place and read it, asking God silently to grant my request.

Meanwhile I was quite happy in my new life. My job at the Water Company was going well and I had made new friends in the new office. I discovered that I was popular because I had a unique sense of humour, which was very tongue in cheek ... and clean. For a while I sat on the same bank of desks with a couple of people who dealt with large accounts, (Supermarkets, Government Properties and the like). The manager of this department was also a Christian but a very serious one who rarely smiled. We got on relatively well and he even bestowed me with the occasional twitch of the mouth, although not quite a smile, at my humour. His assistant was a young blonde lady, Mel, who was his best friend ...to his face. She wanted his job and was ruthless in her pursuit of it, never missing an opportunity to undermine him and his authority, but blissfully unaware that she was the last person who would be given his job, were he to leave. Most of the time the rest of the office ignored her constant backstabbing, but eventually we all became weary of it.

One day Mel was typing a letter, asking him to spell every second word for her, and I could see it was beginning to crowd him, as he was trying to deal with a tricky account and had to keep breaking off his concentration to answer her. Although it was a well-known fact in the office that she couldn't spell, it was obvious to all of us that she had timed it on purpose so he would work the account out wrong – and give her more ammunition in her quest.

"Um, how do you spell Pharmaceutical?" she asked in the little girl voice she saved for when she was speaking to him, syrupy sweet but with the effect of nails grating down a blackboard. I watched him sigh and take a deep breath.

"I know it," I jumped in, smiling at him. He raised an eyebrow but let me continue.

Mel settled herself squarely in front of her computer and began to type as I spelt...

"F...A...R...M...E...R..."

There were a few quizzical looks from some of the other girls, but I daren't make eye contact with any of them.

"Uh huh" Mel sang, waiting for the next instalment.

"S...U...I...T..." I happily obliged, as she painstakingly typed away. By this time the office was deadly quiet and all eyes were on us.

"Yes?" Mel prompted. I gave her my best smile and said one word.

"Ickle!"

The office exploded as fourteen ladies of all ages laughed, howled, choked and cried simultaneously – and all the tension that had been building was suddenly dissolved. As the laughter subsided, Mel looked around in astonishment.

"Isn't that how you spell it then?" she asked, in all innocence. The resulting snorts and nose blowing that followed, from nameless people hidden behind books and piles of computer printouts, prompted another outburst. Her manager finally wiped his eyes dry (Yes! I had finally got him to laugh!), and in true humility, put his account aside and went to help her with her letter. Peace reigned for a few weeks afterwards and although she still did everything to undermine him, it always seemed half-hearted and lacked the venom of all her former attempts.

It was not long after this that the Water Company decided to export all the back-office work to India and we spent the next year training up groups of Indian gentlemen who chatted away to each other in their mother tongue, and to us in broken English. They were very friendly but they were met with a lot of hostility and viewed by many as the enemy, as the staff members training them were keenly aware that they were training themselves out of work. I got on extremely well with my 'trainee'. He collected paper money from all over the world and was very grateful when, at my request, my dad obligingly sent him a Guernsey One Pound Note (yes, they do still have them!) for his collection. The Call Centre was expanded, ready for the influx of ex back-office staff that would be returning, but to many it was an insult to offer them a position there, as it was the starting point into the company and most of them had, like me, had to undergo interviews and upgrades in order to move out to new departments. Moving back there was like a demotion and none of us were looking forward to the return. Things were looking grim.

To cheer myself up I saved up and booked a holiday in Devon for Aaron, Mum and myself. Mum and I sat at the computer and found a quaint sounding place in the South Hams called Hope Cove, a tiny fishing hamlet, tucked into the coastline just an hour south east of Plymouth. The moment we arrived there for our week's break I knew I was going to love it. We breathed clean air and walked over cliff paths, we swam in blue sea and lay on golden sand; we had no computer, no mobile phone signal and no landline in the rented cottage, no outside contact at all – and it was bliss. On the second day I took a bus ride into the nearest town, Kingsbridge, where I bought lots of fresh local produce at the farmer's market, while Mum and Aaron relaxed on the beach. (Well, no nine-year-old boy would pass up a day playing on the beach to go shopping, would they?) I found a lovely little Christian Bookshop and had the time of my life, just mooching and exploring. It was an independent shop, not part of the large chain that operated in my hometown and it was wonderful to see a range of different goodies for sale. I was more excited, however, when I spotted a fridge magnet displaying a picture of some green hills and a quote from Psalm 27 vs. 14:

"Wait for the Lord; be strong and take heart and wait for the Lord." which is what God had been speaking to me about every time I brought the subject of a husband into my prayer time. So I bought it and, once home I displayed it in my bedroom, where I could read it when I had times of doubt. After all I had been praying for some time now and it sometimes felt like God had gone to sleep.

"I can't believe the difference in you!" exclaimed Mum as the week wore on. I knew what she meant. I had suffered with hay fever for years and often felt very lethargic, sometimes to the point of not being able to go to work. However, since we had arrived at Hope Cove, I had been a different person. I had no symptoms of hay fever whatsoever, and I had so much energy, I was practically bouncing.

"I think the problem is where we live, near that pharmaceutical factory. I reckon the fallout from the chimney affects you." she continued, "Let's move here."

I was overjoyed, as I had really fallen in love with the South Hams with all its picturesque villages and cottages. Once back home she contacted an estate agent and before the day was out, her house was on the market.

It sold in three days.

Panic stations! We hadn't even begun to look at houses, but we began now – in earnest. However, no suitable properties were coming available in Devon and after a couple of months we began to wonder whether we should move there. Eventually Mum came to the conclusion that the moving part was right, but maybe Devon was not the place to move to as it was so far away from the rest of the family (my sister was now in London). So, after consulting a map, she decided on going east instead, somewhere between Eastbourne and Kent.

It was October before we found a house that looked perfect for our needs, complete with a study room for Aaron's education. It was situated in Eastbourne and with high hopes we bundled into the car and began our hour journey with songs on our lips. However, after we hit the border of Eastbourne we began to feel that things were not as 'right' as we first thought. As we drove into the estate from the main road, it seemed as though the hordes of Hell had descended and were lining the pavements, waving as we passed. The atmosphere became darker and darker the closer we got to the address on our glossy estate agent's paper and the feeling that we had just driven into 'gangland' 'drugzone' and 'hoodie-city' would not be shaken, as the houses crowded in closer and closer together. We pulled up outside a run-down neglected building and stared in disbelief, looking from our 'glossy' picture to the reality and back again. Before we had time to turn tail and drive back the way we had come the estate agent arrived and ushered us into the interior of this 'hovel', which was even worse than the outside had portrayed. We viewed the house as quickly as we could, trying not to comment on the gaudy bedroom décor which had a distinct air of 'business' about it, or the oddity of a mantelpiece bolted to the wall at the bottom of the stairs for no apparent reason! The whole house had a disjointed, unloved, thoroughly unwelcome feel to it and as we made our excuses and backed out of the door we began to laugh with disbelief that we had just wasted an afternoon driving for ninety minutes to view this abomination. We couldn't get back into the car fast enough and, after mum had given the estate agent a piece of her mind about false advertising, we left - in a hurry.

Standing on Pevensey beach an hour later, eating chips in silence as we mulled over our lucky escape, my mobile phone rang. As I answered it my sister gushed,

"Well how was the house?"

Stunned silence followed as I described how our morning had been spent.

"It's funny," she eventually mentioned, "but I was looking around the internet the other day and found a house that sounds exactly what you want, but I didn't keep it on my computer because you sounded so sure about this one."

Lots of clicking sounded down the phone as she typed her way back into the website.

"Listen to this," she announced, "Private seller. 3 bedrooms. House has just been renovated, ready to move in." and she went on to describe what I can only say was the most perfect house anyone could want.

"Tell mum what you just told me." I said when she had finished, handing the phone to mum, who had been staring out to sea, looking very dejected.

Within the month, she had viewed the house, which was everything it had been described as, and more. On top of a hill, just outside the main town, it had a breathtaking view of the Kent border, where (as she was going to discover) she could watch the snowstorms approaching! It had been on the market for a year and the current owners were amazed that nobody had even requested a second viewing, let alone made an offer on the property. For Mum, however, no other house would do, and the sale of both houses was set in motion, with a moving date set for March 2007

Chapter 19
THE PROMISED LAND

"What do you mean, you're leaving?"

Shock showed on the face of my supervisor as the news sank in. The date of the move was now official and I was free to hand my notice in at work, but it wasn't going well. I took a deep breath and launched into the reasons of the whys and wherefores, watching her face change as she realised the implications of what I was saying.

"But...but...but..." she spluttered, "I was relying on you."

I nodded sympathetically, whilst trying to stop the small smile that was threatening to reveal my true feelings. The past year had been tough. As well as moving the work abroad, the Water Company had also decided to introduce a new computer billing system, which involved a huge amount of training, and I hated it, as I was having to spend half my time learning the new system and then working the rest of the time on the old, familiar one. This, coupled with teaching someone else to take over my job, had brought my morale down to an all time low - along with my colleagues'. Unfortunately, the knock on effect of this was that I began to intensely dislike working for this company, finding the computer training so intense that I (and many of my colleagues) was signed off work by my GP for 'stress' on more than one occasion.

However, I somehow passed the final exam with flying colours, (?) with a top score beaten only by my supervisor, who liked to delegate jobs which she was paid to do, prompting her to earmark me for extra training in her place so I could help her by doing some of the mundane jobs she didn't like. And now I was going to leave a week after the new system went 'live' ... and she hadn't been fully trained. Oops...

My last week flew by. It was deemed a waste of time to register me on the new system for only one week, so the powers that be decided that I would remain on the old one during the 'change-over' period, which meant that I was not connected to the new telephone system and unable to be used as extra cover for the call centre, something that was standard procedure, especially on Mondays. This was wonderful news for me as I found it so frustrating to sit at my desk watching the paperwork pile up, while answering calls from the call centre all day. I was the envy of the office that week. By now, though, life at home was extremely exciting. Boxes, both packed and empty, were everywhere in the house, the attic had been cleared, the garage sorted and the post redirected. I had emailed my new friend Kay whom I had met on an internet support forum for Christian home-educators while she and her family were missionaries in India, and found out that they were not only back in the UK, but living just down the road from where the new house was. They were members of a good church and invited us all to go with them once we had settled in, and I couldn't wait. Aaron, however, was in a constant state of hype, one minute excited and the next scared, as everything was new to him, having never moved house before, and he was unsure how to react.

But March 1st finally came, and with it the removal lorries. Aaron watched the removal men run up and down our stairs in wonderment, as they carried filing cabinets (full) and clothes rails exploding with clothes with ease. Finally they had pity on him and he was allowed to 'help'. He was in his element! When they stopped for a tea break, he joined them in the lorry with his juice and chatted with them, reminding them to watch their language and pointing out the 'No Smoking' sign stuck to the van dashboard. The guy about to light up pushed his cigarette back into the packet with a sigh! When Aaron asked if he could travel to the new house in the van with the guys, Mum and I took one look at their faces and laughed.

"No, " I said, "You're not allowed to go with them. They're working"

Never mind the fact that I was not in the habit of allowing my son to be driven 60 miles by complete strangers!

We said farewell to our friends who lived opposite, jumped into our cars and set out on our next adventure. My Proton had limped sadly into oblivion about a year previously and now I had a Seat, a compact four-seater with the boot space the size of a cardboard shoebox. I somehow managed to pack Aaron, the fish tank, the goldfish and myself cosily into this dependable little car and we set off happily east, towards our new horizons. However, as we were passing Brighton, my 'dependable' little car began to splutter and lose power whenever we went uphill – a problem when trying to drive over the South Downs! Worried that we weren't going to make it all the way past Eastbourne, I pulled into a lay-by and did the only thing I could do. I prayed. And we made it - just. Finally we limped and spluttered up the last hill and as we pulled up outside the house I breathed a sigh of relief, offering up a silent prayer of thanks to God for lending me His angels to push the car!

Three days later, we had just finished unpacking when Mum called up the stairs

"Alison, it's snowing!"

My bedroom looked out over the Kent / East Sussex border, an amazing view at any time of the year and one which I never grew tired of. I rushed over to the window and drew a deep breath at the scene that met my eyes and lightened my heart. Against a backdrop of steely blue sky and gently rolling hills I could see thousands of huge flakes swirling as they rushed across the beautiful valley – straight at us. What a beautiful sight it was to behold and as I didn't yet have a job, I could go out in it if I wanted – or not, as the case may be. I thought of wrapping up warm and going out for walks in the day, and snuggling down on the settee with a hot chocolate at night with great contentment: then I thought of my car, which was now in the garage down the road having the distributor cap replaced (no wonder it wouldn't go up the hills!) and decided I was in no hurry to go and collect it – especially as I would have to navigate a sharp steep 90° bend to get it home. No, it could wait until the snow had gone!

But it wasn't all good news: it's funny how a new setting can seriously upset an established routine, and this is what I found now that we had moved. Before leaving our old house home schooling had been the top priority. Aaron had been interested in anything and everything and I was having trouble keeping up with him, but during the last few weeks or so I had been so busy with packing and leaving work and then unpacking that the schooling had been neglected, and issues and problems began to surface. I began to find that he was spending more and more time on his Playstation (a Christmas gift) and less and less concentration was available for school. Every day was a battle to motivate him and more often than not, I was the one who lost and he began to fall further and further behind. Added to that, of course, was the fact that I was now job-hunting, which ate into schooling time even more.

"There's a job going in the supermarket up the road, in the office." I was informed one morning in November as I came downstairs for breakfast. Inwardly I groaned. Please, not a supermarket. I had been looking for work for some time and had applied for jobs as a personal secretary, as church secretary, as anything BUT a supermarket worker. Why? Because my last job in Guernsey had been in a supermarket (Guernsey sized, of course) and although my colleagues were lovely, the job itself was dirty, tiring and, at times, backbreaking – and I had vowed never to go back to that, not even in the office. But eventually I telephoned, and to my horror, was granted an interview. Thankfully, however, I was not offered the job but as I turned to leave the building, smiling gently, I heard those words I dreaded.

"But we have another job coming up in the cashier's office, I'll put your name down for that one." Groan.

A week later the postman brought tidings of great sorrow. I

had another interview. Again I dressed the part and took myself back to the HR department, but once again was not successful in securing the job. I was starting to get a trifle annoyed with God. I had told Him that I didn't want to work in a supermarket, so why was He getting me all these interviews? And why was I upset at not getting the job that I didn't want? Finally I received another letter requesting my presence at an interview for the position of shelf-filler. What a comedown! I definitely did NOT want this job, but one look at mum's face sent me back out for the dreaded interview. This time, however, I wore casual clothes and didn't bother with make-up, so sure was I that it was a waste of my time and that I wouldn't be offered the job, and as I sat looking out of the window at the end of my interview, I began to think about which jobs to apply for next.

"When can you start?" The voice jolted me back to reality as I realised with sinking heart that I had just acquired the one job I knew I was going to hate. Mum greeted my return home and subsequent news, very enthusiastically, but I was in a state of shock and all I could see ahead was misery.

Outside of work, I absolutely loved living in the new town. We were only a short walk from a beautiful Country Park, a wild windswept three-mile long area of gorse, woods, hills, glens, cliffs and rabbits, and in the winter – mud - lots of mud. The views of the sea from the cliff tops were spectacular and Aaron and I began to take walks there, watching the sheep and the West Highland Cattle and talking to the dogs and their owners out for exercise. Further afield, we found a Farmers Market in a nearby village and a farm that sold Guernsey milk, cream and yoghurt, unpasturised. And we began attending the church that my friend Kay had invited us to. Our first visit had been on the day the Pastor spoke about a recent missions trip.

"Today I want to talk about the conference I have just returned from in Europe", boomed the larger than life man at the front of the church, his Glaswegian accent softened slightly by his smile.

This was indeed the Pastor, and I settled into my chair, ready to be bored with details of numbers, statistics and things that had no relevance for me at all.

I was pleasantly surprised when he began to describe, in detail, the miracles that God had performed during this week long blessing that he had been a part of. I was enthralled.

"... I heard a clicking sound and watched as the lady's legs began to straighten, and then realised that the clicking sound was that of her bones being put back into place. It wasn't anything I had been doing – I had just prayed..."

Wow, I thought, I am coming to this church! I had been to so many churches that preached a compromised message that I had begun to despair of finding one that preached the Gospel. When Kay and her husband had invited me to their church, a Foursquare Gospel Church, which met in a village hall, I must admit I was a little reluctant but I found that I loved it, as did Aaron. Mum never really felt at home there and ended up driving 50 miles (each way) every week to attend my sister's church in London for a few years. I was actually quite relieved at this, as Mum was very involved in many aspects of my life and it was good to have time apart.

There was not many in the congregation, but as I prefer a small church to one of a hundred or so, I did not mind at all! I joined a house-group, where just a few of us would gather for Bible study and fellowship, and gradually good friendships were forged. The village hall, however, had a down side. Most Saturday evenings it was booked for wedding receptions, and many Sunday mornings were spent cleaning up the aftermath before we could start the meetings, so after a couple of months the Pastor found us a new meeting place. One of the schools in the town had a built-in theatre and they very kindly decided to allow us to use it on Sundays. What they failed to mention, obviously thinking it wouldn't be an issue, was that the heating system in that part of the school did not actually work. Half a dozen people rattling around for two hours in an unheated theatre in the middle of winter was not fun, especially for the couple of older members of the congregation, although the sight of the worship leader attempting to play his guitar wearing gloves and trying to sing with his scarf wrapped around his face did lighten the tone of the meetings somewhat!

During this time, God began to take me in a new direction, and birthed in my spirit a desire to do something that, left to myself, I would never have tackled.

"I'd like to do your Bible Theology course," I admitted to the Pastor one Sunday, "But I don't know if I would be able to."

I had been feeling the pull of the Holy Spirit every time I had looked over the leaflet that was displayed week by week on the notice board, but I wasn't feeling too convinced. After all, isn't theology boring? And for people who like to argue their point? Belligerently.

"Of course you could do it," he smiled back, "You would have to be a raving heretic to fail it! You just need to develop a 'can do' attitude."

So, filled with trepidation... uh faith, I signed up for The Timothy Course, a year-long Biblical Study Course by Reverend Kenneth Baird. (B.A. DipTh. DipCPC. MIC. CCC.), designed for leaders or potential leaders within the church. Hmmmm... where was this going to lead, I wondered? To help me prepare, I began to meet at the Pastor's house once a week, along with another lady who wasn't a Christian but was searching for answers, for a small course called The Master Plan by Beth Barone. The time spent there was very precious: I was encouraged to face issues that I had with my identity, my abilities and my past, with all it's failures and mistakes – and the other lady accepted Jesus as her Lord and Saviour. There are many gems that I was exposed to in that time, that continue to shape me to this day... and yes, I began to develop a 'can do' attitude.

The year sped on. Home schooling was still a battle but my

job wasn't as bad as I had thought. I liked my colleagues, and spent more time on the checkouts than on the shop floor – a development that was definitely in my favour. I often thought about when my 'husband' would turn up and dreamed of moving out from under Mum's wing, so I could be my own person again. It is very difficult, once you have owned your own house, to move back into your parent's home again and not resume the old "mother/daughter" hierarchy, and it is especially difficult when a child is added to the equation – am I a mother in this house, or a daughter? My mixed emotions only sought to confuse me and often caused contention within the home. I began to pray again, in earnest, about a husband and finally I cried out to God.

" How much longer do I have to wait, Lord?" I sighed, one sunny August day "It has been nearly eight years, and Aaron is growing up with no male influence. I don't ask just for me, Lord, although the fact that I don't want to stay on my own does have a lot to do with it!"

Very quietly, I heard Him say to my heart, as He does when I listen properly

"By this time next year you will have met the man that I have for you…"

It is amazing how just a dozen or so words spoken and heard in faith can have such an impact on one's life. Everywhere I went for the next six months I looked for "him." I didn't find him. Not at work, not at church, in fact not anywhere that I was going and I began to feel frustrated, but eventually I decided that if God was bringing us together, then He didn't need my help, and relaxed to the point that I was no longer searching, but living my life – otherwise known as "letting go and letting God".

Our first Christmas in the new house was an exciting time and as mum and I rushed around putting up decorations and yelling at Aaron who, at ten years old, instead of helping like he used to, was convinced that he could do everything better than us and kept getting in the way, I found myself wondering about someone who I had not heard from for years: Peter, the family friend from Guernsey. Years after he had prayed with me at Pastor Fransch's house, he had worked with my father, but then emigrated to the Middle East around the same time that Aaron had been born and we had lost touch. Occasionally Mum or I would sense something from God and knew we needed to pray, which we did, although we never knew why or for what purpose. My sister and her husband were invited to spend Christmas with us that year and so it was a full house when we awoke on Christmas Day. After we had breakfasted and opened some presents it was time to call Dad. My sister and I shared the telephone handset and as he answered we shouted,

"Happy Christmas Dad!" in unison, making him chuckle. We exchanged all the usual pleasantries, enquiring after health and thanking each other for our presents and then as an afterthought, I added,

"Do you ever hear from Pete Sehmi, Dad?"

"No, I think he's dead" came the unexpected reply. I was stunned.

"What makes you say that?" I queried.

"Well, someone was trying to trace him a while back and they lost the trail: it was like he had dropped off the face of the planet, so they reckoned he must be dead."

'Nah,' I thought, logic kicking in. God wouldn't have Mum and me praying for someone who was dead! Well, maybe he needed those prayers more than we knew.

A couple of days later we were all sitting at the table eating breakfast when we heard the letterbox clunk.

"Postman!"

Aaron leapt from the breakfast table, and skidded along the hall tiles in his socks. He grabbed whatever was hanging out of the letterbox and then slid back into the kitchen where we were all eating breakfast, like a whirlwind on ice. It was the day after Boxing Day, and I was surprised that we would have post already. Maybe it was a late present? Mum took the small padded envelope, frowning as she struggled to read the unfamiliar handwriting that addressed the package to her, as it was almost obscured by the Post Office redirection notice. As she held it up to open it, my sister read the sender's name on the back and her jaw dropped open.

"Mum...mum...mum..." was all she could say, her mouth full of toast, whilst pointing frantically and gesturing to Mum to turn the envelope over. As she complied, we all saw the name and great was the rejoicing around that table. It was from Peter in the Middle East! Excitedly mum tore open the envelope and a CD dropped out, with a small letter. Silence descended on the room as she read it aloud. Not only was our dear friend alive and well, he had been travelling around a lot, which explained the mystery of why he couldn't be found. He had also included a temporary telephone number in case we received the letter before he went on his travels again, so it was unanimously agreed that we would call and wish him a Merry Christmas as a surprise.

Excitedly Mum dialled the number and we all gathered around the phone, waiting for him to pick up. Finally, there was a click and a very familiar voice tentatively answered.

"Hello?"

"Merry Christmas!" we all yelled together. The shock was evident in his voice as he returned the greeting, as the last thing he had expected to hear when he answered the phone was his long lost friends wishing him God's blessings and sharing their news with him. It was so good to catch up with him and hear all about his travels and he was amazed when we admitted that we had been praying for him – and yes, he agreed, those prayers were definitely needed. And as we drew the call to a close, I knew there was something else I needed to do.

I called my father.

"Guess what?" I crowed, "He's not dead...!"

Chapter 20
LIBERTY AND THEOLOGY

By now, after much praying and seeking God, our church had found a new home in the town centre above an estate agents' office. We felt very spoilt, with plush carpets, double-glazing and heating – and a three-year lease: no more moving around for a while. What a joy, especially when the winter began to close in! The main room was split 60/40 by a glass wall, so the smaller part was used for the Sunday School and crèche during the service, and as a coffee room afterwards. It was great as the children could see their parents during the morning; although the downside was that they had to be very quiet so we could hear the Pastor preach! But the best distraction in my opinion was the doorstops. Installed behind every door was a large spring, enabling the door to bounce back when opened instead of banging on the wooden skirting boards. One of the babies had just learned to crawl, and he was a little livewire. The first week, the preaching went like this:

"If you'd like to turn to the book of Revelation, chapter t...."

Boing! Boing! Boingoing! Boingoingoing!

"... Chapter two, and we'll start reading at verse si..."

Boing! Boing! Boingoing! Boingoingoing!

All heads followed the noise to find this little boy had escaped from his parents' side and was thoroughly enjoying himself whacking the doorstop from side to side. As he was gently and firmly removed from the main room and taken into the Sunday School room, he began to howl. Sermon then put on hold for ten minutes while his parents tried to placate him. He finally subsided into snuffles and hiccups and the preaching resumed.

"We'll start at verse s..."

Boing! Boing! Boingoing! Boingoingoing!

The Pastor chuckled at the horrified faces of the parents

through the glass wall. Obviously there was a doorstop in that room too!

"We'll just carry on, " he announced smiling. "Let the wee lad have his fun!"

And so we did just that.

However, the church did not have the monopoly on moving to a new home, as new situations and opportunities also began to present themselves to me in my personal life. After Christmas my sister and her husband had invited Mum to see in the New Year with them in London. I was glad to be able to spend some quality time alone with Aaron and we decided, for fun, that we would go camping over the New Year - but with a difference. Dad's Christmas presents to us had been two very warm sleeping bags, bought after we had gone camping with him in the summer with only a duvet – on the night the temperature had plummeted to 5°C, causing us to vow never to go camping again, so we decided to try them out in the comfort of our lounge. We made a meandering 'stream' out of blue paper, and sticks out of brown paper (which we piled up in a heap) and cut out yellow and red flames and threw them on top. Then we had a (real) fry-up and laid down in our sleeping bags next to the stream in our little make-believe world. Unfortunately, we giggled too much and became too hot very quickly so the sleeping bags had to be discarded. But we stayed up to see the New Year in, and as we prayed at the onset of 2008, I heard the Lord speak gently to my heart,

"This will be your last Christmas in this house."

Time stood still for a few moments, but I kept quiet and tucked it right to the back of my subconscious, just in case I had heard wrong.

A few short days later I was walking through the local park with Kay, chatting while her two children and Aaron rode bikes, stalked us in the bushes and got wet and muddy. The subject turned innocently to home life and I was horrified to find myself suddenly weeping in despair. I had been feeling increasingly stifled living under my mother's shadow, and desperately needed to be in my own home; my own person. But although I had been seeking God and I knew that He had heard me, I couldn't see how my dream could be achieved. I had begun to view the situation as hopeless, and as this lovely lady held me in a sisterly embrace, I poured out my heart and let my tears fall.

"I think it's time you spoke to the Pastor," Kay decided, rubbing my back as I hiccupped on her shoulder and sniffled into a rapidly disintegrating paper hanky.

"You can't carry on like this. I'll come with you for support, if you like."

I nodded in agreement, although I couldn't see what difference it would make.

An appointment was made for me while Mum was still at my sister's, so I wouldn't have to explain why I was visiting him, and the next day found me sitting in front of his open fire, drinking a hot coffee and letting everything out, while his bearded collie wiped his wet whiskers all over my feet and his spaniel sat with his head on my knee, gazing up at my face like he understood and sympathised. At his invitation, I took a deep breath and launched into my problem.

"...and I can't see a way out..." I finished, and sighed. It had been hard to admit how I felt: helpless, frustrated and a failure, but as I brought it all out into the open I was suddenly aware that I had needed to face up to those feelings in order to deal with them. The room hushed as I struggled to come to terms with this revelation.

"So," the Pastor spoke unexpectedly into the silence, "What do you want to do about it?"

I looked at him, incredulous. Hadn't he been listening? There was nothing I could do about it. To begin with I had no money, so how could I possibly do anything?

"Well," I stuttered, as he waited expectantly for an answer, "I want to move out and get my own place with Aaron." My voice trailed off as the futility of my dream hit and my heart sank.

"But..." I began to add, but he held up his hand to silence me.

"Then let me help you. The church has an emergency fund for such times as these." he smiled, and began to lay his plan out before me.

Within a week I was registered at a few letting agencies and viewing properties. I viewed flats with purple walls, green carpets and mould; I viewed flats with ill-fitting windows and nothing in the kitchen but a sink; I viewed flats with broken doors and strange smells – and I realised this may take a while! Then I had a brilliant idea. One so fantastic that it took my breath away. PRAY. Revelation! So Aaron and I sat down together and made a request list to bring before God. Number one: I actually did not want a flat, I wanted a house... two bedrooms...with cream walls... a small garden...double glazing...and central heating.... a fitted kitchen...and a proper shower. Aaron wanted somewhere to ride his bike...friends nearby...a big bedroom... and a shower that was attached to the taps. Hmmm, we may have to compromise on some things, I thought to myself. I also realised that I was subconsciously only looking at the cheapest properties on the market and saw I was limiting God. So with all this in mind, I began to pray and allow God to move. Mum, by now, was back from London after staying nearly three weeks. I told her my plans, not wanting secrets between us, but unfortunately it just served to bring an uncomfortable atmosphere into the home, with tensions rising whenever the subject was broached. I was a little surprised, as I had spoken of the desire to have my own home again for many years now, until I realised that Mum probably thought it was all just talk and wishing, like planning what I'd spend my £1million Lottery winnings on – even though I don't actually play the lottery.

February arrived, and with it the commencement of the Timothy Course. Leaving Aaron with Mum for the day I made my way to the arranged meeting place filled with an excited expectation. However, as I settled down with the other half-dozen students for the day-long teaching session, old feelings began to surface.

"What if I can't do this?" I worried. I felt out of my depth. What was I thinking of, pretending to be a theologian? The accusations were coming thick and fast and I began to believe that I had made a mistake: I was an impostor who had no place being there. I prayed and pushed the thoughts out of my head. It was a battle, but one that I knew I couldn't afford to lose. If I allowed the thoughts to remain I would not do this course, but more than that, I would have set a precedent that would ensure that, once again, I would amount to nothing. God spoke gently to my heart, telling me that I had nothing to fear, and when I finally relaxed the day passed pleasantly. I made new friends (as some of the half dozen students were from Foursquare churches in London) and I found myself thoroughly enjoying the teaching. In fact, by lunchtime I was engrossed in all that was being explained, challenged and questioned, and looking forward to the remainder of the year's course.

"Exams in by the middle of March, please" the Pastor announced, handing out the essay choice list at the end of the day. I nodded then drew in my breath as I glanced down at the options. They all looked equally impossible. Was he serious? A 1500-word essay? I hadn't written essays since my school days and even then I had never attempted one this size. Well, I told myself, at least I had six weeks in which to write it. My head was full of scriptures and essays and information as I returned home, and I knew that I would have no peace until I had given the whole situation over to God. So after I had sent Aaron off to bed, I sat at my computer with the list of subjects and my notes from the day and prayed. Hard.

"Well Lord," I began, " You wanted me to do this course, and I am doing it, but would you please help me to do my exams.

Please show me which would be the best option to go for. In Jesus' Name, Amen." And I went to bed.

I continued to pray about my new home and scour the local papers, and then one Saturday morning I glanced at the 'Private Landlord' section and an advert jumped out at me.

"Two bedroom house, small garden. Available now." The rent was manageable, so I called the telephone number and was pleasantly surprised when the man who answered said that he could meet me there in half an hour. Frantically, I grabbed my map book, told Mum I was off to view a house and, with Aaron excitedly chattering next to me in the car, set off. The property was in a small close of 17 houses, arranged in a horseshoe around a large grassy area with a pathway around and diagonally across. Aaron looked at me, his eyes shining and I could see his mind thinking '…somewhere to ride my bike…'

The close overlooked the Country Park, only five minutes drive down the hill from Mum. It was closer to the town centre, church and work than her house, although it was still on the outskirts of the town, and as we pulled into the parking space, I was aware how quiet it was. 'Hmm, so far so good' I thought, getting out of the car as a young man walked toward me, hand outstretched, and introduced himself.

"It's this one," he smiled as he directed me to the last house in the horseshoe – with a small secluded garden full of flowering shrubs and a little path.

"Oh my goodness," I breathed, as he opened the front door to reveal…cream walls. Aaron asked if he could stay outside while I viewed the house, as two children his age that were visiting their grandparents next door had invited him to join their game. I could see him mentally ticking off another point in his prayer list. '…friends…', and nodded my agreement. The guided tour of the house was extraordinary as one-by-one each item on my list (and Aaron's) was ticked off until there was nothing left to see except the bathroom, and as I stepped through the doorway

I had to stop myself laughing out loud with delight. To my right, on the wall above the bath, was a proper plumbed-in shower. And over to my left, attached to the taps at the other end of the bath, was another one.

"I had this one installed for the last tenants," the young man enlightened me, pointing to the proper shower, as if this explained why he had left the other one there! But I knew already – this was my new home. A quick call to my Pastor sealed the deal and within minutes I was shaking hands with my new landlord. It was arranged that Aaron and I would move in on the last day of March, at the end of my annual holiday, which gave us about one month to organise ourselves. The reception at home was a little frosty but eventually Mum accepted the inevitable and began to get into the spirit of it all. God's hand was so evident in it all that even she could not dispute that this was God's timing. However, I was in a constant state of prayer over one issue - money. Living with mum for so long meant that I had no saucepans, no beds, no settee...absolutely nothing, only bookcases, a TV and clothes. Hmm, this would be interesting.

And God provided. Within two weeks I received a surprise tax rebate that had been stuck in the system for over a year which paid for towels, utensils, wash bin, dishes, pots, pans, crockery...etc: all the 'little' insignificant things that we take for granted but cost a lot when bought all at once. I was given the key a week early so I could put up curtains, move furniture in and clean – as long as I didn't sleep there as I wasn't officially the tenant until my lease began. Every available moment was spent at the house, once homeschooling had been done for the day, and Mum spent many an afternoon with me scrubbing and cleaning until we had my new little home spick and span, while Aaron made friends with all the children that lived in the close. Unfortunately this usually meant that I had a stream of kids screaming and shouting while they ran around inside our empty house, creating havoc, because it was raining outside! But eventually moving day arrived and with it came Kay and her husband and other friends from the church, who collected a free settee for me and delivered it, made coffee and kept Aaron busy. Jennie drove the 60 miles to where we were and then drove to her parent's house 30 miles in the other direction to collect and bring a wardrobe, chest of drawers, futon and dining table to me. She also brought her parents so they could put the furniture together and by the time the sun had set Aaron and I were settled in, with no unpacking left to do. I even had my fridge magnet from Devon displayed proudly on the front of my fridge! I was so grateful to all my friends and I realised that God had given me something very special in the people who cared for me.

April emerged with the dawning of the new week, bringing a few days of snow and the second Timothy Course study day, and once again we assembled like school kids on the first day of term.

"Before I hand out your graded papers, I'd like to hear how you think you fared," began the Pastor, with a smile that left me in no doubt that he expected interaction from us.

There was a momentary silence, followed by a few stuttered mutterings.

"Um, well... I don't think I did too badly, but I don't know," volunteered one brave student. Encouraged by the Pastor's "uh huh", one by one we all murmured our agreement. All except one.

"Actually, I think I did really well" Sharon piped up, smiling confidently, her Australian accent bouncing the syllables around the room. "I was extremely pleased with what I did" "And," she added, "I thoroughly enjoyed myself!"

Her exuberance was typical of her personality and outlook on life, as if it was her mission and calling to always lighten the mood of each day, for the sole purpose of lifting another's spirits. However, on this particular occasion, silence reigned as the rest of us shifted uncomfortably, aware that we did not have any confidence in our collective efforts.

The Pastor sat smiling at us as we squirmed in our seats, awaiting judgement on our efforts at writing an essay. Most of us had not written essays for many years and we all felt differing levels of dread at hearing the outcome. I had chosen to discuss the various viewpoints regarding Holy Communion and although I had learned a lot during my research, I hadn't been entirely sure that I had grasped all the differing ideas, and who believed what. Finally, he rose and began to place our essays face down in front of us individually. I turned my paper over and was delighted to see a B++ in red proudly displayed in the top right hand corner. I looked up to find the Pastor smiling warmly at me with an "I knew you could do it" twinkle in his eye. The other students also had better grades than they expected, and they all visibly relaxed and smiled. All except one.

"F! I've got an 'F'!" Sharon's voice rose several decibels as she stared incredulously at her paper.

"Oh and I was SOOOO 'in yer face'!" she shrieked, laughing in spite of herself. She was infectious and before long we were all crying with laughter, as she mimicked how she had acted only moments before, with exaggerated movements and expressions. The day passed all too soon and culminated in another request for a 1500 word essay, which I determined to sit down and write as soon as possible - while the teaching was still fresh in my mind.

As spring began to burst forth in earnest, I looked at my garden which was also 'bursting forth', and realised that I had a lot of work to do. The shrubs were wild and unruly: the small lawn had encroached on the border and the Honeysuckle and Clematis had overtaken not only the fence, but the huge blue bush that formed one side of the gateway and was also heading for next door's shrubs as well. I began to spend half an hour a day tidying, cutting back and chopping, and eventually the border began to emerge from the lawn and the climbers became under control. There was also a very small back garden, with a cement pathway just outside the back door (perfect for Aaron's guinea pigs) and a whirly line for my washing. The grassy bit (it could never be called a 'lawn!) was shaped like a wonky triangle, and its high fence and even higher bushes afforded some privacy from the road. These were a little trickier to cut back into some sort of neat screen, as they were really high and the ground was uneven. Not owning a ladder meant that I had to balance on a chair in order to lop the branches into submission - but I managed, probably to the great amusement of the neighbours. Aaron insisted on getting involved and often came outside with me although on one occasion I took my eyes of him for just a second (which is all it took!) and turned around too late to stop him making a beeline for the fence.

"No, don't cut that bit!" I cried out in vain, as Aaron armed with a set of shears, decided to 'help' me by cutting a large stalk that was growing under the Clematis and Honeysuckle. Oh well, I mused, as I bent down under the bush to see the damage; I'll know which one he cut when it dies. I stood up and turned to see him heading for the fuchsia bush in the corner and leapt into action, grabbing the shears before he could decapitate my entire garden. He was going through a stage of 'do before listening' and was driving me to distraction.

"When is Peter coming over?" he asked me when we had come indoors for some lunch.

"Next week," I answered with a mixture or excitement and sadness, as my gaze fell on the CD that Peter had posted to Mum's house just four months ago at Christmas. Such a lot had happened since that day. The CD was one that he had produced of his own songs and it had quickly become a favourite of mine: I had listened to it quite a lot, although most of it was in a foreign language. Mum, however, never seemed to be able to get on with it, so when I moved she agreed that I could take it with me. I had a noticed an email address printed on the back of the CD cover and decided one day to try and contact him.

"Are you there?" I typed, signed it from me and hit the 'send' button. A few days later I received a return email and so began a spasmodic communication between two old friends in two very different countries, swapping news and sharing what God was doing in their lives. Now he was coming back to the UK for a family funeral and although I was excited that he was going to visit me and Mum in passing, I couldn't help wishing it could have been under happier circumstances. After all, how does one greet a long lost brother enthusiastically when he is in mourning? Oh well, it would just be great to see him after nearly eleven years, and maybe he will sense that in the midst everything.

The day of his visit dawned: an unseasonably warm day in May. The whole Town was out and about wearing short sleeves and sunglasses; I fact, the seafront looked like midsummer had hit – and in the centre of it all Mum, Aaron and I walked with Peter, attracting some odd glances. It wasn't so much the big heavy coat he was wearing that looked slightly out of place, but possibly the scarf, woolly hat, gloves and sunglasses... he was absolutely frozen. It had been a lot hotter in the Middle East and he had become acclimatised to the heat in the time he had been there. But it was still so good to see him. He had changed, as we all do, and had acquired a few grey hairs, but he was still Peter, with Peter's smile... Only he was no longer Peter.

The name he had been given at birth was Pritpal, but he had been known as Peter most of his life. Unbeknownst to Mum or me, he had reverted back to his proper name shortly before leaving Guernsey to move to the Middle East, but was now known by the much shorter version of "Pritt". It took a little getting used to, and I found myself calling him 'Pe...Pritt' on more than one occasion. We spent a precious day with this lovely man who had been such an influence in my early Christian walk, treating him to a fish and chip lunch at the seaside, which he shared with a few audacious seagulls that swooped constantly, missing our table (and fish!) by inches.

We rounded the day off in my recently tidied garden drinking tea and eating biscuits, after giving him the obligatory guided tour of the house. I was glad as it gave me an opportunity to study this friend who I had not seen for over a decade. Hmm, he was a little fuller than when I last saw him. Mind you, I thought, looking at myself, aren't we all! Then it dawned on me... actually, last time I had seen him was before my weight loss – and I wondered if he had noticed the change. Probably not, I decided. The more I studied, the more I saw and I realised that the greatest change in him was that he was much more serious than he used to be and no longer smiled or laughed quite as spontaneously as he used to do. This saddened me, as this had been his trademark in Guernsey and I wondered what trials he had endured to change him so much. Was it just because of the immediate situation, after all he was here for a funeral? But no, upon reflection I realised the Middle East can be a hard place and very unforgiving, and I determined that I would pray for him more often from now on.

After all, what are friends for?

Chapter 21
CHRISTMAS BLESSINGS

"I like Peter," Aaron announced later that evening, having obviously forgotten that his name was now Pritt. He had heard so much about him from stories I had shared about Guernsey that I think he had decided that he already liked him before they had even met.

"I wish he could be my new daddy," he continued, wistfully.

"Yes, that would be nice," I answered. I would like someone like him, I thought to myself, although I had more chance of marrying the King of Spain... or Timbuktu; and then continued to research my Timothy Course material on the Internet absentmindedly, not giving it a second thought. The next few months were a whirlwind of homeschooling, Timothy Course study days, research, praying, Bible study and examinations. I emailed Pritt every time I had another exam graded and shared my excitement with him, and he was very gracious and never said if I bored him! Personally, I was amazed at my grades, which ranged from B+ to A, and as I began to gain a little confidence in my abilities, I realised that I had found something that I was good at, and found enjoyable too, although it took over my life for a few weeks at a time.

Eventually the last Timothy Course Day came and went and all that was left to do was the concluding essay for the final exam. Deciding to work on it sooner rather than later, I found myself sat at my computer within a few days, Bible at the ready and enthusiasm to the fore. I stared at the essay question...no inspiration; I made a coffee... still no inspiration; I made a sandwich... food −1, inspiration − 0. I began to feel tremendously frustrated: this was my last essay for the course and I was struggling to get motivated, with thoughts and ideas defying me at every turn. However, I finally began and became totally lost in what I was doing.

"Hmmmmm" I stretched and yawned as I rubbed my eyes. I had been typing for a while now and was aware that my eyes were feeling a little strained. Aaron had gone to bed at 9:30 while I had been staring at the blank monitor, and I had just been about to close the computer down when, like a bolt from the blue, a flood of sentences, phrases and scriptures began to cascade into my mind. I just typed what came, thinking I would re-organise it later. Now my eyes were sore and as I glanced at the clock I was astonished to find that it was 3:30am. Well, that would explain why my eyes were feeling dry! Amazingly, the next morning when I re-read the essay, (after a few short hours sleep!) very little needed adjusting and the scriptures and quotes, which I had saved during my research, were just waiting to be slotted in at the appropriate places.

"Thank You, Lord, " I breathed, aware that something very special had taken place.

I was sad when the Timothy Course came to an end as I had learned so much about God, the Bible and myself, and had made new friends, one of which was Sharon – who is known as the 'Mad Australian Lady' in my house to this day. But, as in all of life, all good things do come to an end although when God is in the equation it usually means that something better is about to hit! And this time was no exception… for it was at this time that Pritt, to my delight, returned to live in the UK. He had been mentioning in his emails that he felt his time away was coming to an end and I was overjoyed to find that he was now living only 50 miles away in London, working in a Christian Drug and Alcohol Rehabilitation Centre. The six weeks countdown to Christmas had begun when I had an inspired thought.

"Would you like to come and visit over Christmas?" I emailed, " I have an air-bed, if you want to stay a few days – or you could just come for the day if you prefer."

The affirmative answer was not long in coming, although he wasn't sure if he could be spared at Christmas time when the residents of the centre were at their most vulnerable, so I pencilled the visit in my diary… and waited. Sure enough, a couple of weeks before Christmas the email came with the news we had both suspected: he was needed for Christmas – but he could come for New Year, if that was okay? It was more than okay, and I began to stock up on food and plan which local sights I could take him to see – somewhere where eleven-year-old Aaron wouldn't be bored out of his socks.

The first Christmas in our little house was an amazing time, and we saw even more of God's provision. Our landlord had told us that there was some stuff left in the attic by the previous tenants, and that we were free to throw it all away unless there was something we wanted, in which case we were free to keep it. We found boxes of Christmas decorations (something I did not have!) and a piano stool, and I realised how much I missed having a piano as I still wrote songs, and it was much easier to work out chords and melodies on an instrument than to guess. My previous piano had been left with Mum so I brought the stool down from the attic, re-covered it and prayed that one day I would have a piano of my own to go with it. As usual on Christmas morning, I had to awaken Aaron so he could open his stocking: I must have the only child in the world who does not wake at 3am and begin Christmas day loudly with high spirits, cheerfulness and enthusiasm, driving everyone else to distraction – he sleeps! And I am eternally grateful. After meeting and greeting all our friends at church, and thanking God for the best gift of all - Jesus, we spent the day: just the two of us, relaxing and enjoying the festivities. On Boxing Day Kay and I began a tradition that we have held to ever since; one year she and her family (and visiting guests) come over to us, and the next year it is reversed, with a return hospitality meal scheduled somewhere before the New Year.

When we arrived home at the end of Boxing Day I looked at Aaron and was suddenly overwhelmed by the immense blessings that God had showered on us. I beckoned Aaron over, putting my arm around his shoulders and giving him a hug.

"Let's pray."

As we stood before our Christmas tree with its lights twinkling and thanked our Creator for all He had done two thousand years ago and, more recently this last year, I stopped, suddenly reminded of those words I had heard twelve months earlier, 'This will be your last Christmas in this house...' and knew that I had heard the voice of God. I began to think of prayers that had been sent heavenward in the many days since then, prayers about heart's desires, husbands and fathers, and wondered what the New Year would have in store for us.

"Thank you for this first Christmas with just the two of us." I finally continued, and then I looked sideways at Aaron and grinned.

" But Lord," I added, "please let it be the last one."

"Amen" came the firm reply from beside me.

New Year's Eve finally arrived, and as I waited for Pritt to call me with the time his train was due to arrive, I glanced at the small gift under the tree with his name on it, and smiled to myself. Knowing that he was a fan of Keith Green, a Christian musical genius, I had visited the local Christian bookshop with the intent of buying him a double album (volume one) of Keith's greatest hits. To my surprise, I found the bookshop in the throes of a 'closing down' sale with everything at half price, so I bought myself volume two, as it had all my favourite Keith Green songs on it. Returning home a little sad that the bookshop was closing but feeling pleased with my bargains, I wrapped Pritt's CD and placed it under the tree. I fished the second CD out of the bag and began plugging the stereo into the wall socket, looking forward to playing volume two, as it had been a long time since I had sat down and listened to Keith Green, and his songs had always impacted me in such a positive way.

"Give Pritt both CDs," flashed through my mind.

Unperturbed, I continued to switch on my stereo and took the CD out of its case.

"Give Pritt both CDs." There it was again. Placing the CD in the player, I hesitated as my finger hovered over the 'play' button.

"Give Pritt both CDs." It was stronger now and I was in no doubt that this was not a request.

"But this one has all my favourites on it," I argued with myself. The silence that followed was tangible as I become conscious that I was, in fact, not arguing with myself, but with Someone much more significant. Sending a silent 'sorry' to the Lord, I proceeded to painstakingly unwrap the gift that I had so meticulously wrapped only five minutes earlier, and before long the new, improved version was nestled proudly under the tree.

"Brrring Brrring!"

I jumped as the phone rang, jolting me back to reality.

"Hi...leaving...last stop...before...about five minutes..." Pritt's voice faded in and out as the mobile signal crackled and died as the train entered a tunnel. Panic hit as I realised that he was about to arrive at the station, as the preceding station was literally two minutes away. Calling to Aaron and grabbing my coat, I clutched my car keys and opened the front door, to find two of the neighbours' children running up the path intent on asking Aaron to go and play. I nodded my head at his enquiring look and he bounded off enthusiastically, leaving me to gather my wits and drive sedately down to the station alone. Fast. The station was crowded, but I finally saw Pritt and waved excitedly as he walked towards me, backpack on his shoulder, guitar case in his hand ... and an Asian-looking woman and two small children at his side. Wait! Stop just a moment...double take. Yes, she is definitely with him. Oh my goodness; he's married with two kids and never told me! How thoughtless! Where am I going to put them all? I wondered, mentally visualising my small house with its small rooms being filled to capacity with four extra people - all on one double airbed, with one double duvet, which is all I had. What fun!

"Alison!" he exclaimed, leaning forward to hug me as his face lit up in a smile. I returned his hug and turned to face his companion, ready to introduce myself, and hoping that my shock at her presence hadn't shown in my face, as I am useless at hiding my true thoughts or feelings.

"Alison," he laughed, "this is my niece, Sharon."

"Very nice to meet you" I greeted her warmly, as we shook hands. Inwardly, however, my thoughts were racing. The problem had just been upgraded to a crisis.

'But it doesn't solve my dilemma of where to put you all,' I thought desperately, 'in fact, it just made the predicament worse, because now you can't even share the airbed!'

"And this is Pablo, her husband." He continued, as a man previously unnoticed by me stepped up and offered me his hand. He looked vaguely familiar, but I was too worried to think anything of it. This situation was becoming seriously awkward.

O Lord, what am I going to do? I prayed, where am I going to put all these people?

Blissfully unaware of my internal struggles, Pritt began to explain that Sharon and her family lived in the town and were on their way home. Slowly I breathed out a huge sigh of relief that was probably felt six miles away and wondered if God was laughing yet. We arranged to visit them sometime over the New Year, finding out in the process that they lived in the road adjacent to mine. Pablo was describing where in the road their house was situated, when I suddenly had a feeling of déjà vu. I had heard these directions before. And then it struck me why he had seemed familiar. When Aaron and I had just moved into our house, I realised I needed a video player and found an unwanted one on an Internet based local recycling site called 'Freecycle'. I had called the number and spoken to a man called Pablo who had given me directions to the house, informing me that he would be leaving in fifteen minutes to meet his wife, Sharon, from work. I had left immediately and within ten minutes I was back home and the VCR was installed in my lounge. Wow, I mused, it's a small world!

But now there was more to this story: Pritt had previously mentioned to me in an email that he had a niece who he had never met. He would love to meet her, he had said, but all he had was an old photo and the knowledge that she lived in my town ... somewhere. On the day he was coming to visit us, he had missed his planned train and had had to wait an hour before he could catch the next one. During the journey down while reading the free "Metro" paper, his guitar on the seat beside him, he became aware that a young woman who had walked past a couple of times was walking past him again. She had already been past a couple of times on her own, but now she was appearing with children in tow and heading for the WC. Pritt thought it a little odd, but kept his head down in his paper. Eventually, as she came past yet again, this young woman poked her head around his paper and asked,

"Are you Peter?"

"Yes," he nodded, " Do I know you?"

"I'm your niece." She smiled. "You look just like my Dad and he said that you always carry your guitar with you wherever you go, so I thought I'd stop and introduce myself."

Pritt stayed for three days and during that time, we saw the hand of God move in so many ways. We visited Sharon, as planned, and she went on to become a good friend of mine, while her son became a firm friend of Aaron's. Still reeling from the excitement of finding her, Pritt also admitted that he would like to contact one person who was connected with the Rehabilitation Programme that Pritt was involved with at the Rehab Centre. He had a name but no other information, and although we tried the phone book and the Internet, we could not locate him or find any way of contacting him. Finally I had an idea.

"There's a café in the town that's run by one of the churches for the homeless and the addicts" I informed Pritt, looking at the piece of paper with a single name written on it. "Maybe someone there will know who he is? Why don't we pop down there and see if they have any idea how to contact him?"

Pritt seemed pleased with the idea and so later that day we made our way down to the café. While I ordered coffees for us, and a Coke for Aaron, he approached the gentleman behind the counter and asked him if he knew where we could find this particular person.

"Yes," he answered, smiling, "That's me."

Isn't God amazing?

Over the three days, we talked of Guernsey and the Middle East. We also talked of God and His miracles, and Pritt had plenty of those to talk about. Aaron even managed to get him to play on his playstation with him, although the unfair advantage of Pritt having never played on one before meant that Aaron beat him hollow! We exchanged Christmas gifts and I glowed with pleasure at the look on his face when he saw the Keith Green CDs, and then squirmed as I told him the story of how he ended up with two instead of one, which he found rather amusing.

The years rolled back and I found myself walking arm in arm with him in total ease wherever we went, and chattering away to him about everything and nothing, while he relaxed and began to smile again. I was aware that this was a time for Pritt to unwind and share his heart, which he did, and it was a hard parting when he boarded his homeward bound train. I hadn't realised how much I had missed my brother and friend, but before he went I made him promise to come back for my Timothy Course Graduation Ceremony, which was set for some time in February.

Chapter 22
RUTH

"Oh Lord," I prayed one afternoon, late in January, "What's happening?"

Aaron was playing outside with his friends and I was lying on my bed, staring up at the ceiling, feeling very emotionally perplexed. It had been gradual, but the feelings that had emerged for Pritt over the last few weeks had grown and were now present in my every thought. My mind wandered back to that first 'shopping list' prayer regarding my future husband and I realised with a start that Pritt had all the qualities I had asked for. He even had the ones I had not asked for: not officially, anyway. Like the time that I had stood at the entrance to the close where I lived, and looked wistfully over at the Country Park and thought 'Lord, I would much rather marry someone I already know; someone with no skeletons in the closet and with friends that I already know; someone I am already comfortable with; someone who would encourage me and push me to be my best. Oh, and if he was musical, it would be wonderful...'

Suddenly I sat up as the futility of it all hit me. I had never expected to feel like this about Pritt, of all people, and I was convinced that it was going to ruin our friendship. And I got cross...with God.

"Two Augusts ago, Lord, I was so sure you said that I would meet the man that you had chosen for me within the year!" I ranted, getting madder by the minute, " and I looked and looked, but he never came! And now I am feeling this way about Pritt and I am so confused. I am obviously never going to get things right."

My breath was coming in gasps now, as tears of disappointment coursed down my face. I had tried so hard not to let it bother me that I must have heard wrong that day, but like a dam breaking, once the frustration over my failure finally pushed its way through, there was no stopping it. I threw myself face down on my bed and wept as though my heart would break. I did not know how I was going to cope with these feelings that were so deep. As my tears subsided into sniffles, I sat up, numb and empty and almost missed the small quiet voice that spoke gently to my heart.

"When did Pritt first come back to the UK…originally?"

"May." I answered absentmindedly. Then as the significance of that date between the two Augusts grew in intensity, my mouth dropped open.

"Oh." I whispered in hushed awe.

I made a decision that day, which was probably the wisest I had ever made. I resolved to let God do everything that was needed to bring what I felt was His plan together – without my help. I was determined that I wasn't going to tell anybody, not even Aaron and most importantly, I was not going to tell Pritt. If God was bringing us together I realised that His timing was the only perfect one, and I did not want to miss out by running ahead, or by dragging my feet, or saying something out of turn that could set us off on a tangent. No, this had to be God, or nothing.

"Oh no!" I suddenly wailed, "I've invited him down for the Graduation in two weeks' time. How am I going to manage to act normal?" It was easy on email, but face-to-face?

The Timothy Course Graduation on Saturday 7th February 2009 brought all my friends together in one place, including the entire congregation of my church. There had been snow a couple of days before so my sister and her husband never made it out of their road, let alone out of London, but my cousin came, as did Jennie, Mum and, of course, Pritt. I should have been presented with an "Oscar" for my performance that day. I managed to keep a respectable distance from Pritt without making it look like I was ignoring him, when all I wanted to do was to stand as close as I could and breathe him in! A couple of times I caught him watching me with an expression on his face that I couldn't fathom, and it disturbed me.

"What?" I asked, as I turned and found him studying me intently for the third time that afternoon. "Have I got a smudge on my nose, or something?"

He shook his head, smiling dismissively, but I was unnerved and found myself glancing sideways at him often, unable to shake the feeling that I was being scrutinized.

The large Baptist Church in the Town Centre had lent us their building to hold the ceremony in and as we all assembled in-between the columns and under the balcony later that afternoon, I was aware of all the support that was evident in the faces of those I loved, and it was humbling.

"Wow," I breathed, as I surveyed the high ceilings painted crisp white and soft Wedgwood blue, "What a beautiful place for a wedding." It was true. It was a very striking building and one that was very warm and inviting, but as the words left my mouth I became very conscious of what I had just said in all innocence, and very quietly shut up, glancing round to satisfy myself that no-one had heard me. I was relieved when the ceremony finally got underway, as it gave me something else to concentrate on. The celebration began with a wonderful time of worship, and it was lovely to put all my thoughts and questions, worries and fears out of my head and just concentrate on my Saviour God: and as I felt myself being drawn into His presence I began to lose myself in him, and it was special. As the time of worship drew to a close, the Pastor stood and began to explain about the Timothy Course: what it was, how long it took, and how 'YOU' could also enrol.

Finally he could put off the inevitable no longer.

"And now, the bit we've all been waiting for!" he announced, smiling down at our apprehensive faces. One by one the graduates were called up to the platform, presented with their certificate, photographed and then led to the lectern for their acceptance speech. I was last and really nervous by the time my name was called.

"And last, but by no means least, we have Alison," he smiled broadly, "and she is an excellent example of what can be achieved when one adopts a 'can do' attitude. Come on up, Ali"

I could feel my face burning as I stepped up onto the platform to receive my certificate, and I daren't look at anyone in case my emotions got the better of me. Then I glanced at Pritt, sitting in the audience, and saw that look on his face again... and nearly forgot my speech.

"Well, it was really good to see you, and I pray you have a safe journey home"

It was now late Sunday evening and we were assembled at the station, waiting for Pritt's train to arrive. He had stayed the weekend, again on my airbed in the lounge, and we had spent that morning at Church where he had met all my friends, and the afternoon enjoying the sunshine sitting on a bench overlooking the Country Park while Aaron played football. Pritt had commented on how quiet it was compared to London and wistfully mentioned in passing that he'd love to live somewhere like this, somewhere that reminded him of the Guernsey cliffs, with yellow gorse bushes and beautiful scenery. As daylight faded, Mum had arrived and as we made our way to the train station I had found myself wondering how, and indeed if, God was going to bring everything together – and how long it would take. I felt pleased with myself as I had managed to hide my affection, had not said anything, or acted strange, and I was confident that Pritt did not know anything of how I was feeling.

I relaxed and smiled at him, oblivious to the comings and goings of the other travellers.

"God Bless you," I continued, "And come back to visit us soon."

I leaned forward to give him a hug, then stepped back

allowing Mum and Aaron to do the same. The tannoy announced loudly in muffled tones that the approaching train was bound for London and Pritt began to make his way through the unmanned barriers to the platform, and then stopped and turned to face me.

"Thank you for inviting me down, it has been a lovely time," he said quietly, "It was good to see you graduate. You did well."

"Thank you for coming," I countered, leaving Aaron and Mum in the foyer and walking him to the train. Giving him another hug, I wished him a safe trip again as he boarded the train and stood back to wait for the doors to close. Suddenly he looked at me intently, as if there was an internal struggle going on somewhere within him.

"Alison," he spoke, thoughtfully "Would you do me a favour?"

"Yes," I answered, wondering what was coming next. I didn't have to wait long.

"Would you read the Book of Ruth for me and pray about it?"

I opened my mouth to answer, but at that moment the doors closed with a swish and the train departed, leaving me standing astonished and speechless on the empty platform, waving slowly as it rounded the corner and disappeared from sight.

Chapter 23
FRIENDS IN LOW PLACES

The Book of Ruth? There was nothing in the Book of Ruth but a love story about Ruth and Boaz! Surely he couldn't have meant...? Maybe there was another message in there and I had missed it. Maybe...

My heart leapt and I found myself smiling all the way home in the car.

"What's up with you, mummy?" Aaron asked, looking at me strangely,

"Oh nothing" I smiled, making a concerted effort to look nonchalant and failing miserably. Mum dropped us home and after Aaron had retired to bed, I took my Bible out of the bookcase and turned to the Book of Ruth, in the Old Testament. Trying to keep calm and collected, I read the book from beginning to end...and found Ruth and Boaz, Ruth and Boaz and nothing but Ruth and Boaz. If you are unfamiliar with the story, I shall explain. Ruth was a young widow from Moab who, through tough circumstances, came to live in Israel with her mother-in-law, Naomi. Being young, but destitute, she ended up 'gleaning' (collecting the grain dropped by the harvesters) in the fields of a rich man called Boaz to provide food for them both. He, in turn, was impressed by her integrity and love for Naomi and, with a little help from Naomi and God, found himself falling in love. They were married and had a son, who became the grandfather of King David... and that, in a nutshell, is the book of Ruth. I read and re-read the book until my eyelids drooped and my head throbbed, but I still couldn't find anything else that Pritt may have been referring to, so I finally went to bed.

I awoke the next morning wondering if I had dreamed it all, as it seemed so surreal, but as I walked into the lounge I found the Bible, still open at Ruth, and had to concede...it had really happened. I spent the day with my head in the clouds; I had no idea what Aaron was doing in his schoolwork – he could have been swinging on the chandeliers (if I'd had any!) and I wouldn't have noticed. Finally, by lunchtime I realised that I couldn't continue like this and so I sat down to send Pritt a text from my mobile.

"Are you asking what I think you're asking? Cause if you're not I am going to feel really stupid." I took a deep breath, sent it and waited for an answer…and waited …and waited. I was like a 'cat on hot bricks' all day until I could finally stand the suspense no longer.

Aaron was due to be at church for a 7:30pm youth band practice, so that evening instead of staying in the room and watching as I usually did, I wandered in with him and then while he was bashing away on the drums I rushed upstairs to the solitude of the kitchen area, mobile in hand and dialled Pritt's number.

"Hello?"

"Hello, did you get my text?" I blurted, not even saying who I was.

"Yes, yes I did." Then silence.

"And?" I could feel the tension in my neck growing.

"And what?"

I could have screamed. Didn't he know how wound up I had been all day? So I took a deep breath, tried to keep my voice calm and repeated the question I had texted him.

"Well, are you asking what I think you're asking? Cause if you're not I am going to feel really stupid."

The silence this time was deafening and seemed to last a lifetime, and I held my breath, hoping against hope that I hadn't just read something into a situation that wasn't there.

"Yes…I suppose I am" came back the slightly cautious answer.

I let my breath out with a 'whoosh' and flopped into one of the chairs. By the end of the call we had decided to take things very slowly and check with God every step of the way, as both of us had bad experiences under our belts and neither of us wanted to repeat them. We realised it was going to cost us a lot of money to talk via mobile, so we agreed to text and email for now and see where we went from there…and we decided to tell no one…not Mum, Dad, Aaron, or even friends, until there was something to tell. Either God was doing this – or it wasn't going to happen.

"Come on Aaron, hurry up, we've a long way to go."

I heard the usual non-committal "humph" signifying that I had been heard as Aaron finally emerged from the house, dragging his heels and grumbling.

"I wanted to stay here and play with my friends," he complained as I hurried him towards the car, obviously unaware that probably the last thing I would expect his friends' parents to do is child-mind for an entire day. I started the car engine, and then turned to face him.

"Well, it's not an option, and you'll enjoy yourself once we're there" I insisted firmly, as he buckled his seat belt. I had been looking forward to this day for a few weeks and nothing; absolutely nothing was going to spoil it for me.

We were on our way to London for lunch. Not just any part of London, but the road parallel to where Pritt was living in London. And not just lunch with anyone, Oh no. Lunch with none less than Pastor Fransch and his wife from Guernsey, who were now living in London and pastoring the church that Pritt had begun attending.

"What! You mean Willie Fransch is your Pastor again?" I had asked incredulously, choking on my coffee, when Pritt had mentioned it in passing, while on his Graduation visit.

"Yes," he had nodded, "and he hasn't changed a bit!"

He rummaged around for his mobile.

"I've got his number here somewhere" he added, "Ah, here it is, are you ready?" And he proceeded to read the number out to me.

Later on I had called Pastor Fransch, who had been most surprised, but extremely pleased, to hear from me and he had invited Aaron and I to lunch, adding that he would invite 'Peter' too as he only lived around the corner. I smiled at Pritt being called 'Peter' as I had finally got used to calling him by his real name and felt that the name 'Peter' no longer belonged to him, but to someone else. Obviously Pastor Fransch was just as absentminded as ever though and to him Pritt would always be Peter. I looked at the pretty bouquet of flowers that I had proudly placed on the back seat and smiled as I thought of the pleasure they were going to give Celia, Will's wife. As we pulled out of the close, I recalled the day when Pritt had prayed with me in Pastor Fransch's lounge all those years ago and before long my mind had taken me back further, to the time when I had left home to live with my dubious boyfriend when I was sixteen; and I realised how far I had come since those days.

I thought of the house that I had lived in, just around the corner from the Manse, which had been split into flats and rented to some of Guernsey's 'undesirables'. Being the naïve person I was at the time, I never really saw the potential danger that I was in whilst living there: all I saw was the funny side: like the time Sam, who rented the room down the hall, had rushed into our lounge without knocking, as usual.

"Look who's out there?" he had laughed, pointing towards the window. Obediently, we took a peek and saw the well-known Head of the C.I.D sitting in an equally well-known unmarked police car at the entrance to the road opposite, with his sergeant, obviously watching our house. It was a regular occurrence, but one that we never failed to make the most of.

"Keep watching." Sam whispered and disappeared, re-emerging in our lounge moments later dressed head to toe in black and looking like a cat burglar.

"I'll give them something get excited about!" One quick smile and he was gone. We heard the front door close and strained to see what he was doing without moving the curtain, as that would give us away. Looking up and down the road, left and right, Sam flattened himself against the front of the house and snuck, like a shadow, past the house next door, following the contour of the building as it rounded the corner in the adjacent road. I looked quickly to see what the police were doing and found, to my delight, that the scene resembled something out of a Laurel and Hardy show.

They had watched, incredulous, as Sam had made his way to the corner, then as he disappeared they realised they were going to lose him and panicked. By the time they had sorted themselves out and started the car, our lounge door had opened once more, and we had turned to find Sam gleefully rushing to the window, pushing the curtain aside and waving, yes waving to the poor men who, looking totally bewildered, stared back. As they realised they had been outwitted, their expressions changed and we watched as a torrent of angry words poured forth out of the driver's mouth, making me wish I could lip-read, but although we could hear nothing, the meaning was crystal clear. They drove off with a squeal of tyres down the hill towards the police station, while we laughed until our sides ached.

"But how did you get back in?" I asked Sam, as he obviously had not used the front door.

"Oh that was easy," he remarked, " once I was in the next road I just jumped over the neighbour's fences, into our back garden and in through the back door. Don't know what I would have done if the door had been locked though!"

I turned onto the motorway and glanced at Aaron who, having inherited my bookworm traits, had his nose entrenched firmly in The Chronicles of Narnia (C.S. Lewis) and sighed. Although I had allowed myself a little chuckle over those memories, I knew that life had been hard at that time, and I had tasted a bitter experience in leaving home. Oh, the foolishness of youth, when we think we are invincible and beyond the law. I was so glad that I had seen the folly of my ways...eventually. It wouldn't do to share these stories with Aaron, I thought, although he would find them funny, as they didn't exactly give the impression that crime was a bad thing, or that the police were to be respected. I started as I heard the roar of an engine and an Audi overtook me in a blur of blue paint and tyres.

"Boy, he was going well over the limit" I grumbled to myself, then smiled grimly as I realised that I sounded like my grandparents! But that Audi had brought back more memories of Sam and his misdemeanours and, as we were only half way to London, I took the opportunity of reminiscing a little more...

"I'm just going to the Police Station to drop some cigarettes off for Sam and Colin," I called out as I shut the front door behind me and made my way across the busy intersection. Turning left down the hill, I wondered how they had got caught. There had been a spate of car thefts recently in the island, and the locals were in an uproar. Nearly every night between two and four cars, usually Mercedes, BMWs, and even a Bentley or two, were being stolen, taken for a joyride and dumped somewhere, usually on the beach via the slipway or cliff top. Nobody knew for sure who the culprits were but we had our suspicions, as Colin, who lived on the top floor, and Sam were usually out on the same nights, returning very late and silently dispersing to their respective rooms. That is, until one day when they failed to arrive and we waited for the phone call that would result in me being sent to drop the supply of cigarettes down to them. Legally the Police could hold them for seventy-two hours without being charged; but that was a long time without a smoke, and I was the obvious choice to send on such a mission, as everybody else in the house had a criminal record and the thought of voluntarily walking into the Police Station brought them out in a cold sweat!

I marched into the Station, but my nerve wavered under the stern gaze of the officer behind the desk. Although I behaved like I didn't care what people thought of me, I cringed inwardly at the possibility that I was being 'tarred with the same brush' as my acquaintances and I knew that I had been brought up better than that. But, rebellion of the heart takes us to all sorts of places where we would never in our saner moments ever dream of going, and this was no exception. Announcing who the cigarettes were for, I handed them over and turned to leave.

"Before you go, young lady," the voice came from behind the desk, full of authority, and I froze rooted to the spot. "We'd like to ask you some questions". It was not a request.

A policewoman appeared from nowhere and opened a heavy door, indicating that I should go through it. I was terrified, but followed her into a small room, furnished with two chairs and a table. Moments later a male officer entered and sat at the table, beckoning me to also sit, while the policewoman positioned herself by the door. The half an hour I was in that room was the longest thirty minutes of my life, as they asked me what I knew about the car thefts. Thankfully I knew nothing and so I was not lying when I stated that I did not know who had done it, and eventually I was allowed to leave. I practically ran out of the building, determined that I was never ever going to put myself in that position again. Then I realised with a start that if I continued to maintain my current friendships, that was precisely the life that was staring me in the face, and it would be a long road, downhill all the way.

Seventy-two hours went by, and we waited for the front door to click open, signifying the return of the prodigals, Sam and Colin, but it was to be another two hours before they appeared, tired and dishevelled in our lounge doorway.

"Why were you so long?" I asked.

Sam threw a disgusted look Colin's way.

"Ask him - 'Brains of Britain'" he sat down on the settee and put his head in his hands.

"It wasn't my fault," Colin began, "How was I to know?"

"Just shut up, " Sam interrupted crossly. We all exchanged looks. This wasn't sounding too good.

Finally, over a hot cup of coffee it all came out: after months of stealing cars, racing them, wrecking them and dumping them, and managing to evade the police, they had become overconfident. Colin's father was the proud owner of a really nice 'top of the range' Audi, which he kept under lock and key in his garage and Colin had decided this particular night that he wanted to take it for a 'spin'. The plan was to break in, take the car and then return it unscathed, putting it back in the garage and having a laugh on the way home...and 'Daddy' would never know. But they hadn't taken into consideration the possibility of 'Daddy' phoning the police as he heard his prized possession being driven away from the house. An island-wide car chase ensued, resulting in Colin and Sam managing to lose the police long enough to return the car and escape. However... the police were pretty sure that they knew who had stolen the car – and so was 'Daddy', and warrants were issued for the arrest of Sam and Colin.

"Don't tell them anything." Sam had whispered to Colin on the way to the station. "They don't know it was us for sure and they can't do us if they can't get a confession. Just give your name, but say nothing else, got it?"

Colin had nodded, but Sam was worried, as Colin was well known as someone who spoke before he thought, and usually opened his mouth only to put his foot straight in it. They were kept isolated in the station and questioned separately, but both Colin and Sam kept very quiet, and at the end of the seventy-two hours the police had nothing to work with and begrudgingly released them. Elated, they were about to leave the station when one of the officers called them over.

"I'm going your way," he explained, "I'll give you a lift to the top of the road if you like."

Both boys grinned. This would be a feather in their caps: not only could the police not pin the car thefts on them, but also they were now actually offering to drive them home in style. Unable to resist milking the situation for all it was worth, they readily agreed and jumped into the back of the police car, making themselves comfortable, all the while smirking smugly to each other. The officer buckled up, started the engine and began the journey up the steep hill, slowing down as he approached the junction. As the car pulled out onto the main road, it seemed to struggle a little with the gradient of the steep incline and almost stalled.

"This Mondeo's rubbish" announced Colin cheerfully from the back seat, "It's got no guts...not like the Audi!"

Silence...

The officer turned slowly in his seat, a huge smile of triumph on his face, and turned the car around back towards the station. Poetic justice for two lads who loved to exasperate the police, I think!

Actually, in our immaturity we all enjoyed winding up the local police force, although most of the time, they took it in good humour and many years later I can say that there are a few 'Bobbies' in Guernsey who I count as my friends. Mind you, back then in the early 1980s the police seemed a lot more relaxed than they are now. For instance, I had a friend who was good at fixing electronic machines and when my VCR broke, David, another friend of mine walked to his house with it in a box, probably so it wouldn't look like he had stolen it, ... and was stopped by the police as he was returning with the empty box just before midnight.

"What have you got in the box, son?"

"Nothing"

"Open the box, and show me what's in there"

"I told you, officer, there's nothing in there"

The officer took the box out of David's hand, placed it on the pavement and proceeded to open it - to find it empty, just as he had been told. He stood up, dumbfounded, and stared at David.

"See, " David shrugged, "I told you it was empty"

"But why," queried the confused law man, "are you walking up the road with an empty box at this time of night?"

"Well," came back the answer, quick as a flash," It was such a nice evening that I came out for some fresh air, and thought I'd take some back home for the missus!"

The officer had to laugh. They shook hands and went their separate ways, but I bet my friend David was the topic of conversation at the station for many weeks after!

Back in the present, the road sign looming up indicated that the next junction was my exit, so I pulled back into the nearside lane ready to turn off. By now Aaron was sleeping peacefully, lulled into slumber by the gentle swaying of the car and the droning of the engine and I realised afresh how much I loved him. He had been showing a few signs of jealousy since the Graduation ceremony, as he began to realise that Mum's friend was becoming an important part of her life and I understood that he would have a lot of adjusting to do if this relationship with Pritt was going where I hoped. But I was confidant that God was in control and that his plan would unfold in due course. Indicating left, I exited the motorway, praying quietly for God's wisdom and patience for the days to come.

Chapter 24
RUN A STRAIGHT RACE

"Wake up! We're here."

I nudged Aaron and he sat upright, rubbing his eyes as we pulled into the road where Pastor Fransch lived. I found the house and reversed the car into the parking spot outside as the heavens opened and the rain started pouring.

"Quickly!" I hurried Aaron out of the car, ran round to the passenger door to lock it (the driver's side lock had never worked) and turned to run to the Manse, my coat over my head, when I heard a strange mechanical sound and turned back to see both of my front windows opening…fully.

I looked at Aaron who shrugged his shoulders and looked back at me. I retraced my steps, still with my coat flapping about my head, and unlocked the car door…and the windows closed with a whirring sound. I locked it…windows opened; unlocked it… windows closed. Now I had a problem. I could either leave my car unlocked in the middle of London or with the windows wide open in the rain. Determined not to be beaten I tried everything and finally found a solution. If I opened the passenger door and put the lock down before I shut it, the windows stayed up when I locked it. However, I was to find out later that this only worked once and so for six months afterwards I had to play 'musical locks' as the electrical fault played havoc with my nerves. Finally I found a permanent solution: leave the key in the ignition once I had switched off the engine, open my door and lock it from the inside while it was open and swung in the breeze. (Yes, the driver's door that didn't lock!). Are you following this? Then take the key out of the ignition, alight from the car and shut the door …and then walk around to the passenger's side to actually lock the car up. I am sure the neighbours must have thought I was mad! And why did it remind me of the bathroom in the 'Dump' many years earlier?

By now, typically, the rain had stopped so I decided to text Pitt to let him know we had arrived. There was no answering text, which was unusual, so I called his mobile number and listened while it rang and rang... and then was picked up by his voicemail. I was confused, as we had made arrangements to meet and he knew I was coming. Suddenly, while I was mentally listing all the reasons why he hadn't answered his phone, there was a click and I heard his voice.

"I'll be there in five minutes" followed by another click as he rang off. Taken aback, I looked at my phone, then at Aaron, and waited.

True to his word, within five minutes I spotted him coming around the corner and made my way towards him. Aaron ran ahead of me and flung himself at Pritt for a bear hug. I hung back a little, as it was the first time we had seen each other since the Graduation and I was feeling shy, but Pritt reached out and hugged me and, with an apologetic smile, began to explain why I hadn't been able to contact him.

"I managed to lock myself out of my room late last night," he explained a little sheepishly "and I had to wait for the secretary to come into work this morning and unlock the office where the spare keys are."

"So where did you sleep?" Aaron wanted to know.

"In the Devotions Room, right up next to the radiator" came the reply.

"And your phone was...?"

"...in my room!" Pritt finished my sentence and we all laughed, linked arms and made our way down the hill towards the Manse.

Ring! Ring! Ring!

"Alright Aaron, you can stop ringing the bell now!" I whispered, as we saw a figure, distorted by the glass, moving slowly along the hallway towards us. The door opened and there stood Willie Fransch, his face wreathed in smiles, and we suddenly found ourselves enveloped in warm hugs amid exclamations of "It's been so long!"

"Come in, come in" he announced, leading the way into the kitchen where he proceeded to make us feel very welcome with his hospitality. I introduced Aaron, who said "Hi" and then promptly went off to play with Willie's granddaughter, who was also visiting along with her nine-month old baby sister. While sitting around the table, drinking coffee and sharing our news I took the opportunity to study our host. He really had not changed at all, except he had become a little greyer.

Originally from Zimbabwe, he had married Celia, a blonde haired, blue-eyed English lady, and together they had produced four lovely coffee-coloured children, the youngest of which was mother to the four year old who was now playing with Aaron. Willie spoke with great pride of his children and their accomplishments, as his son was now a Youth Pastor and two of the daughters were involved with Mission work: one with The Jesus Army and the other, Operation Mobilisation. Suddenly we heard the front door open and close with a bang and Celia emerged from the hallway, taking her coat off and apologising profusely for not being at home when we had arrived.

"I had to take someone for a hospital appointment at short notice," she explained amid smiles, more hugs and putting the kettle back on.

After lunch, not wanting to outstay our welcome, Pritt suggested showing Aaron and me around the Rehabilitation Centre. Willie and Celia offered to take Aaron to the park with them instead, as they were going to take the two girls for some fresh air.

"It will be good to let him run around for a bit," Celia noted, as he and his new friend came crashing into the room, came to a halt, looked at each other and rushed back out again.

"Thank you," I said, gratefully.

We arranged to meet them at the park in an hour and Pritt and I made our way to the 'Rehab', where I was given a guided tour and completely lost my bearings! It was a large building full of corridors, corners, steps and doors, with rooms even in the basement and an office. Originally two buildings, it had been modified into one, which is why I found it so confusing – everything had a double. I met a couple of the guys who were living at the Centre and undergoing the 'Programme' and I was glad that Aaron had gone to the park. I had never seen eyes so devoid of life before or sensed such an air of utter despair in a person as I did that day, and I realised that this Rehab Centre was probably their last chance to beat their addictions. I silently thanked God for the dedication of the Christians who ran it and whose mission was not just to help those in need to become free from dependency, but to also help them to find true Life... and to live it.

Pritt and I chatted as we walked arm in arm to the Park an hour later, but inwardly I was thoughtful, reflecting on what I had experienced that afternoon. My mind went back, once again, to my distant murky past and I realised that, had God not intervened in my life when He did, I could easily have ended up in a place like that, desperately trying to piece my life together.

"There, but for the Grace of God, go I." I whispered, finally understanding the implications of the well-known saying that I had quoted all my life. Pritt smiled at me and squeezed my arm gently.

"And I." He agreed, as we entered the park and made our way to where two adults and a buggy were positioned on the brow of a hill while two energetic kids romped in the giant sand pit.

We all walked together back to the Manse and said our farewells. I reached out and gave both Willie and Celia a hug, thanking them for their hospitality and promising to return soon, then did the same with Pritt, promising to call him once we had arrived home safely.

"Come on Aaron," I said finally, as I put my arm around his shoulder and ushered him to the car. It had been a long day, and we still had a two-hour drive ahead of us, which included a stopover time at Burger King as a treat!

"Time to go home."

March blew in cold and damp, heralding the preparations for the annual Hastings Half Marathon. Kay's husband, Salomon was competing, and Aaron and I had arranged to meet with her on the seafront with their children and support him with lots of cheers and shouts. When I mentioned this to Pritt in an email he announced, to my amazement, that he would have entered if he'd known but as it was too late maybe he could come down to watch, as he too was a long distance runner and had competed in both the Guernsey Marathon and Half Marathon. I was surprised, not just because in all the years that I had known him I had been unaware that he was a runner, but also that I had lived in Guernsey all my life and never knew that a Marathon, half or full, was run there!

"If you came down for the Half Marathon," I agreed, only too delighted to have any reason at all to see him, "it would give you an excuse to be here and then you could talk to Mum, like you said you wanted to."

By now our relationship had grown considerably and, although still in the embryonic stages, we felt secure enough to see that it was time to speak with Mum about where we were and where we felt God was taking us. Pritt was old-fashioned in that he wanted to be the one to tell Mum what God had been doing, which I liked, and we agreed that until he had spoken to her we would not publicly show affection for each other, out of respect.

"But you won't be able to stay with me if you come." I added.

"Yes, I know" he agreed, "It would be inappropriate now."

As Kay was my closest friend I confided in her what had

transpired in February and she and her husband, amidst huge smiles and promises of lots of prayer, agreed that they would be willing to have Pritt stay with them overnight. To my amazement, she didn't seem at all surprised by my news.

"You know," she smiled at me over her coffee cup, " I had a feeling something was going on when he came down for the Timothy Course Graduation."

"No, nothing was going on then." I countered, shaking my head "Why do you say that?" I cast my mind back to that weekend of nerves and internal wrestling, and caught myself inwardly groaning at the realisation that I couldn't have hidden my feelings as well as I had thought.

"Well, I looked out of the church window as you and Pritt came out of the car-park on the Sunday, arm in arm, and there was something about the way the two of you were talking and the way you looked at each other, that made me wonder 'hmm, what's going on there?'"

I was amazed. 'The way we had looked at each other?' Surely that meant that he had been looking at me the same way I had looking at him? How come I hadn't seen it? Suddenly the times I had caught him watching me over the course of that weekend flashed before my eyes and I recognised the look she meant. Oh boy, did that mean that Mum also knew?

The month grew steadily colder and windier as the day of the Half Marathon approached but finally the Saturday I had been waiting for arrived, bringing Pritt on the lunchtime train. The run wasn't until the Sunday, so that gave us a day to relax and spend time together, with Aaron. After dropping Pritt's luggage off at Kay's house, we decided to pay an impromptu visit on Sharon and her family. As she opened the door, her face lit up and she ushered us all inside, calling out to someone to come and meet her visitors, and scolding me for not warning her that Pritt was coming down. Wondering to whom it was she was calling, we followed her into the lounge and came face to face with her mother and stepfather. Pritt was overjoyed, as he hadn't seen Sharon's mum for a number of years, and they sat and swapped news, while Sharon and I made coffee and Aaron went off to find her son. Pritt had a habit of taking his guitar with him everywhere he went, a habit that I hope he never breaks, and before long he was singing some Cat Stevens numbers, and taking requests. Coffee made, Sharon and I came into the lounge and handed out the mugs, humming along with Pritt as we did so.

"So," began Sharon, finally sitting down with her coffee and looking directly at Pritt, as he finished singing a Beatles hit. "What I want to know is: why did you become a Christian? I mean, none of the family have actively continued in the Sikh faith, but you are the only one who has become a Christian. How did that happen? What made you decide?"

Pritt smiled and relaxed and as the room lapsed into a hushed kind of silence, he began to share his testimony. I sat, just as enthralled as everyone else, as most of it was new to me, and as I heard about his journey into life I found myself viewing him with a renewed respect and admiration; here was a man who was not ashamed to speak of his past and the amazing changes that God had brought about in his life. He spoke of his mistakes, his faith in Jesus, and his belief that Jesus would return for him and the rest of the believers one day. There was a thoughtful silence in the room as he drew to a close, and I prayed silently that the words that had been spoken would not be cast aside but that God would birth something in their hearts from that day onward.

The afternoon drew on and we chatted and drank coffee as Pritt sang many old favourites including some Elvis songs and folk songs from Ralph McTell. We even had a bit of Led Zeppelin to contend with, which was a novelty on an acoustic guitar!

"Have you eaten?" Sharon's stepfather suddenly asked out of the blue. I glanced at my watch and was horrified to find that it was five-thirty pm; we had been there all afternoon.

"We need to get home" I turned to Pritt, "it's tea-time."

He nodded and began to pack up his guitar.

"We're going to Cosmos if you'd care to join us – our treat," the stepfather continued, smiling, "I'll just see if they can book three more into the party." And he strode out of the room to call the restaurant. I looked helplessly at Pritt, who shrugged his shoulders and made a face at me, making me giggle. I saw Sharon look from me to Pritt and back again, but didn't react – we were still not at liberty to tell anyone, not until we had spoken to Mum.

Cosmos is a large buffet-style Chinese restaurant on the seafront, that operates on a 'pay £10 for three courses and eat as much as you like" basis. The meal was booked for six-thirty so we had just enough time to rush home and get changed, before driving down to the town centre and meeting up at the restaurant. Aaron was in seventh heaven; he had never been to a restaurant in the evening before and thought this too wonderful for words. His eyes lit up when he saw the starter bar, and the main course bar, but when he spotted the 'puddings and sweets' and the chocolate fountain, his mouth dropped open and I could see his mind ticking over as he planned his strategy. Two tiny helpings of starter and main course later, he made his way over to the sweet counter and took up the biggest plate he could find. In true 'typical boy left alone with food' fashion; he began piling spoonfuls of trifle, profiteroles, cakes and tarts onto the plate, then continued over to the chocolate fountain, where he topped the mountain with marshmallows and warm, runny chocolate. I had been oblivious as I was talking to Sharon, but I happened to look up as he returned to the table, his 'sweet' course resembling Kilimanjaro swimming in melted chocolate, and my initial response was to rebuke him for his gluttony. Judging by the comments and the giggles from our hosts, however, everyone else found the situation amusing and I decided to reserve my irritation for later.

I didn't have to wait long for the effects of Aaron's gluttony to show. His stomach was unaccustomed to being bombarded with mountains of sugar and chocolate, and he began to complain of feeling unwell while his face changed from one degree of a greenish sheen to another.

"I did that, the first time I came here" Sharon's son cheerfully acknowledged, "And boy, was I sick!"

Thanking him for his helpful (?) comments and our hosts for a wonderful evening, we excused ourselves and left and after dropping Pritt off at Kay and Salomon's house we continued on our way home.

"I feel sick" Aaron groaned, his face ashen, as I parked the car.

"Good" I countered, still furious with him. We spent the remainder of the evening waiting to see if the results of Aaron's folly would end up on my lounge carpet. Thankfully it didn't, and when I finally went to bed, it was to dream of all the promise of tomorrow.

Sunday morning finally arrived and the weather was overcast and a little breezy – but not as cold as it had been, much to my relief. We decided to walk down to the seafront to watch the Half Marathon, as it was only twenty minutes on foot, and the brisk walk would keep us warm.

"There they are!" Aaron shouted, as we spotted Kay, Pritt and Kay's two children standing in a little huddle, backs to the wind, about half a mile from the finish line. We waved and Pritt and I smiled at each other as we made our way towards them.

"So glad you made it," Kay was saying as she gave me a hug. Wild horses wouldn't have kept me away, I thought, as I returned the gentle squeeze. It was lovely to embrace Pritt again, although I had to keep a respectful distance, and I realised suddenly how strange it all was. During the five weeks that we had been a 'couple', we had only communicated via email, phone or text: and although we had spent time together at Pastor Willie's house, we had been still very much in the frame of mind that it was very early days and that nothing was yet definite by any stretch of the imagination. However, by now we were in a position to state that we were officially an 'item' and so, in essence, our first 'date' had been last night at a table with seven other people who were unaware of our situation, and yet I felt so close to him as though being by his side was where I belonged.

"Nannie!" Aaron spotted my mum making her way across the road and leapt into action, flinging himself into her arms as he always did, and almost knocking her off balance. I had invited Mum to meet up with us, but as the date had drawn nearer I had begun to wonder if she would back out. After all, standing for a couple of hours on a freezing seafront wasn't something she would normally do, given a choice!

"How's Salomon doing?" I asked Kay, who had been keeping in touch with her husband by mobile phone. He had been a little concerned as he had only recently recovered from a particularly nasty flu virus and hadn't managed to train as much as he would have liked.

"He's a little slower than he had hoped, but he's doing okay," she answered. Salomon had been running Marathons since his youth, including an 'ultra marathon' called the 'Two Oceans' in Cape Town, South Africa, an endurance race of 35 miles as opposed to the normal 26, and Kay had not missed any of his races in their twelve year marriage, always standing somewhere en route and cheering him on, apart from when she had also ran - and today was going to be no different.

We heard the first cheers of the onlookers before we saw the lead runner, a small wiry Kenyan who hadn't even broken into a sweat. He was alone at the front and looked as though he was out on a Sunday jog, but was totally focussed, his legs moving like piston engines. I had never really watched someone run long distance, and found myself staring at him with awe as I noted the determination on his face and the graceful way he moved; he reminded me of a racehorse. We cheered him on and encouraged him, as did the entire crowd, with whistles and clapping hands. One by one the front-runners passed us by, each receiving cheers and applause and gradually the gaps between runners began to close until there were groups of people passing together. Eventually the road resembled a seething mass of humanity as hundreds of runners packed tightly close together ran past us as one body, their heads bobbing independently like raindrops bouncing off a path. We craned our necks, keeping a look out for Salomon. After all it would be awful to wait for two hours and miss him!

"There he is!" shouted one of the children, running up from the beach where they had all been playing. We shouted his name and gave him the thumbs up, as he ran past us waving. We watched until he became a speck in the distance and blurred into the landscape of bodies, then Kay called her children.

"By the time we've walked to the finish line, he'll have had time to clock in and have a rest." she explained, her face shining with pride. "Thanks for coming. He really appreciated it, and so did I."

Later we found out that Salomon had completed the Half Marathon in two hours, thirteen minutes and twenty-three seconds, finishing number 2661 out of over 5000 runners. No wonder Kay was so proud of him!

We invited Mum back to our house for lunch after the Half Marathon and while I was busy making coffee, I saw that she was alone in the lounge. I was feeling nervous about Pritt speaking to her, and the anxiety was building the longer I had to wait. Reaching for the milk, I glanced at the fridge magnet that I had bought in Devon and I felt God speak to my heart. Only last week he had once again confirmed his plan for my life with Pritt during my 'quiet time' and I had begun to keep a journal, as almost daily God had been speaking into my situation from the Bible and I had realised that I needed to keep a record. On this particular day I had been reading Psalm 27, and when I reached verse 13, which spoke of having confidence that I will see God's goodness in my lifetime, I felt the nudge of the Holy Spirit. Verse14 however, stopped me in my tracks.

"Wait for the Lord; be strong and let your heart take courage; yes wait for the Lord"

I couldn't get the scripture out of my head, and as I had gone into the kitchen to make a coffee, my eyes had rested on the fridge magnet with that exact verse on it– and my mouth had dropped open. Although I had read it many times there was something that I had never noticed. Below the picture was the Bible verse, but above the picture the same verse was displayed in Hebrew, which is what Pritt had studied during his time in the Middle East.

"You're amazing," I breathed to God.

"But" I added, "I don't want to be reading things into the situation that aren't there. It could be a coincidence." However, a few days later mum had sent me a text saying she had been praying for Pritt and that she had a verse for him. Would I pass it on? I agreed and then stared dumbfounded as the next text came.

"Psalm 27 verses 13 and 14" and then I danced like a whirling dervish around the kitchen, whooping like a Red Indian while Aaron stood in the doorway and shook his head.

"Go on," I whispered to Pritt "Now's your chance to talk to her."

"Okay, I'll speak to her now," Pritt agreed, smiling warmly at me. He stepped into the lounge and I heard a murmur of voices as he began telling her the events that had transpired since the Timothy Course Graduation. She was silent for a few moments and I felt my stomach tie itself in knots. 'What if she doesn't approve?' I thought to myself, 'Then what?' I steeled myself and made my way slowly into the room to stand beside Pritt, steaming coffees in each hand. One look at her face as I handed her coffee to her confirmed my worst fears. She was not amused. And I felt myself retreating inwardly as I immediately began to question my feelings, my choice of partner and my belief that this was God's plan for my life... again.

Suddenly I woke as if from a dream and I knew why God had called me to write my journal: Mum had influenced my thoughts, feelings and actions for most of my life, and as a result I had felt unable to trust my own judgement and even my faith, if she disagreed with any of it, but God was changing that now. All at once I was aware that I was an adult, capable of making my own decisions, with my own personal walk with God, my own thoughts, my own feelings and the ability to make good choices.

I began to sense an awakening of a determination that I was going to walk God's way, and nobody else's, even if that meant being misunderstood, and I stood straighter, relaxed and linked my arm through Pritt's. It was difficult not to be intimidated by the silence that continued, and the atmosphere that penetrated the room, but I firmly believed that God was bringing Pritt and I together and as long as I knew that, I could stand and face anything... even this.

Chapter 25
AND GOD WAS IN THE WHIRLWIND

I was ecstatic.

It was the end of March and finally the official question I had been waiting for had been asked thrusting us into the throes of planning our wedding. Mum had distanced herself from us, believing that we were rushing into a marriage that neither of us were ready for, but although I couldn't believe how quickly everything was happening, I also couldn't deny the hand of God on every decision that was made. I had called Dad in Guernsey, who was extremely pleased for us both, and I could hear the relief in his voice that Aaron would finally have a male role model. He promised to make it over for the wedding if he could and offered us the self-contained flat that he had built over his garage for our honeymoon – perfect for newlyweds…and Aaron.

When I visited my Pastor and shared what God had been doing he had smiled and given his blessing, adding that it had come as no surprise to him, and arranged a pre-wedding counselling session for us both. Pritt came down by train twice during the next two months and we sat discussing issues and expectations candidly. Being straightforward, Pastor Kenn spoke of the fact that neither of us were young teenagers embarking on untested ground, but two mature adults (mature??) who knew what marriage was about and what to expect, having both been there before.

"In fact," he concluded, " I would say to you not to leave too much time between your engagement and marriage, as the pressure to compromise your conviction to honour God and remain separate until marriage will increase as the day draws nearer. But at the same time, don't rush things. God's timing is always perfect." He paused for effect.

"In a nutshell, I would say ' hurry slowly'"

"When would you like to get married?" Pritt asked me a short while later over the phone. Our mobile provider had recently very kindly introduced a deal between phones using their services whereby all texts were totally free and all phone calls were free for fifteen minutes, leading to some hilarious moments as we called each other back every quarter of an hour and timed each call to the millisecond! This had been a godsend for us and meant that we could finally talk to each other, real in-depth conversations that needed to be said and shared and we began to spend every waking moment on the phone. It was lovely to finally be able to communicate freely, although bantering by text can be a little risky as it is so easy to misunderstand what the other person is saying when you can't hear or see their smile, but we managed and I even managed to perfect the art of cooking with a phone under my chin!

"This year would be nice," I answered, mentally working out how long it would take to organise and pay for.

"Hmm yes, I was thinking of June" he answered. Time stood still. Wow, I thought, he's really keen – but three months? Can we physically book, organise, and pay for a wedding in this day and age in just twelve weeks, maximum? I checked my calendar and noted the Saturdays in June; they were the 6th, 13th, 20th and 27th. The next morning I awoke, with a certainty that the 27th was the date that God was laying on my heart, so I wrote it in my journal and waited. When Pritt called that evening, he told me that the 27th was the date that he felt at peace with. Amazed, I shared how I also felt and so we decided to aim for that date and pray.

After a weekend of seeking God regarding the wedding date, Monday dawned with a sense of urgency to begin moving forward in our plans. I called the Registry Office to inquire about the dates, and found that the 13th and 20th were already booked up, so that only left the 6th or the 27th. I called my Pastor, who couldn't make the 6th but was free on the 27th. Then I called Dad, who confirmed he was also free on the 27th and could come over with the campervan, and Kay (who had offered to organise the catering for us), who confirmed in amazement that she had booked the week of the 20th to 27th off work already, but hadn't known why. Excited, I phoned Pritt, apologising for interrupting the Devotional Time at the Rehabilitation Centre, and quickly explained the situation.

"So do we go for the 27th?" I asked, adding, "because if so, I will need to book it today… like now."

Pritt agreed and, after promising to call him back with an update after Devotions, I rang off and dialled the Registrar's number. The receptionist checked the 27th again and advised me that although the entire day had been free when I had called earlier, there were now only two slots available, 11am or 3pm. Quickly I provisionally booked the 11am slot and arranged to drop into the office later that afternoon to confirm the arrangements and pay. Phew! Now I knew why there had been such an urgent nudge from the Holy Spirit! I rang Pastor Kenn, who obligingly booked us into his diary and suggested that, as we couldn't hold the church ceremony in our little 'office' church in the town, maybe the Pastor of the Baptist Church that we held the Timothy Course Graduation in would lend us his building for the day. He offered to speak to the Pastor, and as he hung up I was filled with such a wonderment as I thought back to what I had said as I had walked into that church the last time. Self fulfilled prophecy? Maybe.

After lunch Aaron and I drove to the Registry Office.

"Do you have your I.D. with you, and the paperwork we requested over the telephone?" questioned the Registrar solemnly, as we sat in her office. I nodded and pulled my driving license and other documents out of my handbag, handing them over for her to inspect.

"I'll take some other details from you now." She said, still unsmiling, as she pulled a wad of papers towards her and picked up her pen. As we finished the last form I leaned back in my chair and relaxed, but she reached out and took another few pieces of paper from the pile on her desk.

"And now I need some details about your fiancé."

"Oh. Okay" I smiled. It was the first time I had heard him called my fiancé and I liked it.

Still with the same serious expression, the Registrar began the interrogation... ahem... questions.

"What is his full name?"

I told her.

"And how is that spelt?"

Blank look.

"Oh. Um, well I don't actually know. I mean, I've known him as Peter for about 25 years and now he's known as Pritt." I was aware that I was beginning to babble and turned to Aaron for help. "Does Pritpal have one or two 'T's?"

Aaron shrugged and I began to feel a little embarrassed. What must she be thinking? This is legal paperwork we are filling out and I don't know how to spell my future husband's name!

"We'll go for two "T's" I couldn't look at her.

"What is his date of birth?"

Easy.

"And his full address?"

Time was sucked into a vacuum. What was his address?

"Ha ha, I don't actually know." I laughed nervously, aware that I must be sounding like some mad lunatic who was obviously marrying someone dodgy, maybe an illegal immigrant, "I mean, I've been there a couple of times...it's in London...I can picture the house...I could take you there..."

I trailed off and an awkward silence descended on the office. Aaron started to giggle.

"It's a Rehab" I blurted, desperate to show I did know something about where Pritt lived, then, as I saw the expression on the poor lady's face, I quickly added, "He's staff!"

That did it, and I spent the next few moments frantically

trying in vain to contain my amusement of the situation. I daren't look at Aaron, as I knew that if I caught his eye I would explode into uncontrollable laughter. Instead I looked across the table at the Registrar as I struggled to regain my composure and caught a smile hovering round her mouth. I took a deep breath.

"I think its number 150, but I'm not sure of the post code. I think it's…" and I recited the post code that was in my head.

"Right," she said briskly, gathering up her paperwork and standing up. I took this as a cue and followed suit, extending my hand towards her.

"Just a little word of warning," she said, a twinkle in her eye, " When he goes to the Registry Office in London, they will ask him the same questions…" and with that she shook my hand and walked out of the office. Once out of the building, Aaron and I laughed until we cried, and then I had a sudden thought. I rummaged for my mobile phone and began texting…

'My middle name is spelt 'J.A.N.E'… my date of birth is… my full address is…and my post code is …"

The next few weeks flew by in a blur. Kay and Salomon offered to design the Wedding Invites and came up with a simple design of two wedding rings entwined under our names, with 'A Celebration of God's Goodness' printed underneath, and a matching 'Order of Service'. Kay also suggested that, as we did not need anything materially for wedding presents, maybe we should ask our guests to think about how much they would have spent on a present, and donate the money instead to the catering fund, something that was embraced by all we asked.

As the days passed, each confirmation we received only succeeded in convincing Pritt and myself that God was in this, and everything was going according to His plan. We were astounded at the way one thing after another was planned, organised, paid for and confirmed and likened it to a train journey, where we were passengers watching everything happening around us and enjoying the scenery, while God drove the train from one station to another- at high speed.

"It feels like we are having an 'arranged' marriage," Pritt mentioned one day over the phone. I was speechless, as that same thought had flashed through my mind that very morning.

One of the ladies in the church had offered, as a present, to make our Wedding Cake; one of the men had offered to be my chauffer on the day; Kay and Salomon's two children had agreed to be my bridesmaid and pageboy, along with Aaron, and the outfits had been bought; my bouquet of pale pink silk roses, matching bridesmaid's posy and buttonholes had been ordered and delivered; Salomon had agreed to be Best Man and Dad had confirmed that he was definitely coming and had agreed to give me away, adding that I was non-returnable! The Baptist Church was confirmed as the Wedding Celebration Venue, and I was excited to find that we were also given the use of the kitchen and church hall for the reception, all for free. I found a beautiful elegant summer dress, in turquoise Indian print, with delicate shiny beads and a matching chiffon scarf to wear to the Registry Office… and I bought my wedding dress.

It was a stunning strapless dress with a fitted bodice and long flowing skirt, delicately designed with a few sequins, with a lace-up back. I decided against a veil and opted instead for a simple tiara, and pale pink jewellery to complete the outfit. The day the dress was delivered to my door I rushed upstairs with the box and opened it slowly, taking my time as I ran my fingers over the beads and sequins and gently fingered the satin. I couldn't believe how beautiful it was: the wedding dress I had always wanted, and finally I could resist it no longer. As a small child I loved dressing up as a princess with charity shop bargains and feather boas, not to mention sparkly shoes that were many sizes too big, and I would parade around with my back straight and my head held high, convinced I was a beautiful princess. As I grew up I left those childish things behind, but I never forgot how it felt to be the most beautiful lady in the world, even if had only been make-believe: and now, standing before my full-length mirror in my white wedding gown, all those feelings came flooding over me and I was back in my fantasy-world, only this time it was real. A noise at my bedroom door brought me back to the real world.

"Mummy, you look beautiful"

I turned to find Aaron standing in the bedroom doorway, looking overwhelmed.

"You look like a Princess" he whispered, awestruck. I nodded.

"I feel like one," I agreed, and as he came towards me with tears in his eyes, I hugged him. Hard.

Finally the big day before the 'Big' day came. Salomon had signed up to run in the London Marathon and again Aaron and I had arranged to go with Pritt to watch with Kay and the children. We had booked a room in a guesthouse, a stone's throw from where Pritt was living so we didn't have to drive up on the actual day of the Marathon, but there was another reason for this visit... Pritt had bought my ring and we were finally getting officially engaged.

"So how do we do this?" Pritt had asked over the phone, one evening.

"Well, first you have to go and find a really expensive ring," I joked.

"Mmm hmm"

"No, seriously, "I laughed, "I can either look for one here, or we could look for one together. Or..." I added hopefully, "You could buy one and surprise me."

"I think that's what I'll do," he agreed thoughtfully, to my joy.

A week later, he called me one morning and there was a lot of traffic noise in the background.

"Where are you?" I asked

"Hunting for a ring," came the reply, "but I can't decide which one to go for."

"Why? Have you found more than one?"

"I've found three that I like," he explained, "so now I have to go back to all three shops, which are in three different parts of London, to make my mind up!"

Lord, please don't let him buy a solitaire diamond ring, I had prayed silently. I have fingers that do not suit delicate little rings and, to be honest, I wanted something a little unusual for my engagement ring. So I had prayed that He would show Pritt which ring was the right one, and left it with Him.

Now we were here in London, and I was wondering if Pritt was going to be romantic and get down on one knee. Aaron and I booked into the guesthouse and wandered up the road to the Rehab Unit. The residents knew us by now, as we had visited a few times, and came over to chat to us.

"Do you fancy a walk to the Park?" Pritt asked me over a cup of coffee, just as Aaron's eyes spied a chess set on the bookshelf. I nodded.

"Can we have a game of chess?" Aaron asked, oblivious to what Pritt had just said.

I was about to refuse when the owner of the Rehab came to the rescue.

"It's alright," he smiled," you go on to the park, and I'll have a game of chess with Aaron." He looked at me kindly, "I'll explain things as we go and teach him a few moves and things"

"Thank you" I replied, as Pritt took my hand to lead me out of the room.

We walked slowly to the park and sat on the bench, where Pritt proceeded to take a small box out of his pocket and hand it to me…and I held my breath. I lifted the lid and breathed out slowly. Inside was the most exquisite ring I had ever seen. It was shaped like a flower with six round petals, each with a diamond in it, and the centre was raised with another diamond in it. I had never seen a ring like it. It fitted beautifully and really suited my finger: I couldn't have picked a better one if I had tried and

God had answered my prayer. I swallowed the lump that had appeared in my throat from nowhere and flung my arms around Pritt's neck.

"Thank you," I cried, "Its perfect."

"I'm glad you like it," his relief was obvious, "I went back to all three shops three times until I knew for sure which one I wanted for you."

"I love you." I said, quietly.

"I love you too." came his reply.

"I love you more," I smiled.

Pritt stayed silent and thoughtful.

"I can live with that!" he quipped finally. Laughing at his cheekiness, we linked arms and strolled back to the rehab where, to our surprise, we found the owner in shock.

"He beat me!" he shook his head, as I laughed at the triumphant look on Aaron's face. Well, I hadn't had the heart to tell him that I had taught Aaron to play chess a couple of years ago and he had just spent the last two weeks working out a strategy for a three-move checkmate that he had been desperate to try out on someone!

The next day, after watching the Marathon with Kay and the children, Pritt took Aaron and me to the Natural History Museum where we gazed, open-mouthed at the sheer size of the huge dinosaurs and the whales, and marvelled at the Tyrannosaurus Rex, which moved so realistically, although it was all done with clever technology. On our way back to the Underground, we were walking through a tunnel, when I heard a busker and stopped. He was playing one of my favourite pieces on the guitar, and I felt compelled to stand and listen in silence, my eyes closed. As he finished, I dropped some change into his guitar case and thanked him.

"I don't normally give money to buskers," I explained to Pritt, who was watching me, bemused, "But that is my all-time favourite and he played it so beautifully."

"Will you pay me too, if I play it for you?" Pritt asked with a smile.

"Why?" I answered, "Do you know it then?" I had only really heard him play songs in church, or more recently, Cat Stevens, the Moody Blues or Elvis.

"Yes," he replied, "It's called 'Romance for Guitar'"

"Well, I won't pay you for playing it," I retorted, "But," I added with a twinkle in my eye, "I'll kiss you every time you play it for me!"

"It's a deal!"

And so later on, before Aaron and I drove back down to the coast, Pritt got on one knee (a little late, but still...) and played my favourite tune – in the car park of the Rehab Centre, with half the residents listening out of their windows, and was paid with a kiss! Who says romance is dead?

We now only had seven weeks to wait for our wedding and I was fast becoming aware of how much I had changed. Gone was the person who was scared to make decisions. Gone too, was the person who was terrified of getting lost. Coming from an island of 24 square miles, where every road will either take you to the coast, or to a road that you recognise, I had found it difficult to adjust to roads in the UK. If I took a wrong turning would I end up in Wales? Scotland? Land's-End? And what if I ran out of petrol and didn't know where the next filling station was? In Guernsey, not only did I know where each filling station was, I knew the name of the person who manned the pumps!

Yes, it had been a daunting time, moving to England, but now I was happy to grab a map and drive up to London – and back in the dark, where everything looks different. In fact I had been so many times now, that I no longer needed the maps. Gone was the person who worried about trivial things and who believed everything was a big deal, and in her place was someone who was fast becoming her own true self, and learning to trust her own judgements. God had done amazing things within my heart and mind, and I hardly knew myself anymore – but I liked what I saw.

And finally, gone was the person who allowed others the control over her emotions and the right to dictate her life. Sadly, my mother and sister, each with their own reasons, had decided that this marriage was not right for me and had announced their intention to be absent from the wedding. I was shocked at first and shared parts of my journal with them, hoping they would see God's hand in all that had been happening. But they were unable to move forward from their pre-conceived notions and eventually I had to let go graciously and pray that God would open their hearts in due course.

Although I was sad with their decisions I found, to my surprise, that for the first time in my life I was able to stand by my convictions without any feelings of resentment or defiance. This was a miracle of Red Sea proportions, for I knew how badly I had handled my past because of these vary same emotions. God had truly changed my heart and I was so thankful, because I knew somehow that this new direction my life was taking was going to be the next instalment in God's plan for me – my very own great adventure story.

Chapter 26
A FAIR SWAP

"He who finds a wife finds what is good and receives favour from the Lord." (Proverbs 18vs. 22)

June began very unpredictable, but as the month wore on the weather began to settle, The temperatures rose into the thirties, the beaches became crowded and the seaside town where I lived was permanently in a holiday mood. The 27th dawned bright and a little breezy, which was extremely welcome on this day where the cloudless sky was a bright blue, the sun was a deep yellow and the ground shimmered in the sweltering heat. Even the sea was a giant immovable looking-glass, which stretched to the horizon and back. At the water's edge the tiny ripples crept onto the sand, a far cry from the usual roar of surf and pounding waves crashing onto the shore: a perfect day for a wedding. Yes, my 'Big Day' had arrived at last and all my prayers were being answered... right down to the weather!

I glanced at the clock hanging on the lounge wall. Ten o'clock.

"A whole hour before I need to be at the Registry Office," I sighed. I made yet another coffee that I knew I would not drink and wandered from room to room in my bathrobe, unable to settle. Finally I drifted upstairs and spent some time praying, while Aaron kept himself amused on his Playstation, and I began to relax.

"You are getting married today," I told my reflection in the mirror half an hour later while zipping up my new pretty Indian print dress bought especially for the morning ceremony at the Registry Office and smoothing down the skirt with my hands, waiting for the reality of it all to sink in. I was still in too much of a daze to show my excitement yet and I had not wanted to get ready too early in case I spilt my coffee, or creased my dress while I fidgeted; after all, I didn't want to turn up looking like I had been dragged through a hedge backwards! I made my way back downstairs rousing Aaron from his game as I did so.

"Ok Aaron, let's go" I ruffled his hair as I walked past and he smiled up at me. He looked very handsome decked out in smart new clothes for the occasion but, like myself, he was saving the best for the Church service. It felt strange, driving myself to the Registry Office with my son... almost surreal, and I was silent for most of the way, lost in thought, but as we pulled into the car park the excitement hit with a 'whoosh!' and by the time we entered the building I was practically dancing and my smile couldn't have been any bigger. Pritt was already there, waiting, and he took my hand firmly as we walked together into the 'Wedding Room' where we were greeted by the Registrar (yes, the same one who I had seen only a couple of months earlier). As we made our vows to each other, I was keenly aware that she was studying us and I wondered if she was remembering our last meeting. Finally those immortal words were uttered:

"You may now kiss the bride."

The Registrar smiled as she led us to the table to sign our Marriage Certificate. I had no idea how long we had been there, as the entire time had passed in a blur; Kay and Salomon had acted as our witnesses, while the three children had sat quietly, but I had been unaware of anything but my new husband. As we were pronounced 'husband and wife' I looked into his eyes shining with so much love for me that it took my breath away and I felt such a welling up within me that I couldn't contain it.

"I love you" I smiled through my tears. He held me tight and said nothing. He didn't need to. As we were about to leave the Registrar took me aside.

"It was a joy to marry you two," she confided, " It was so obvious that you really love each other. To be honest, sometimes I look at some couples coming in here to get married and wonder 'why?' I sincerely wish you both all the best." And with a twinkle in her eye and a spring in her step she turned and disappeared into her office, leaving me a little nonplussed. I was glad that we had made her day, and I thanked God for the witness that we had been to her, especially after the fiasco the last time I had seen her.

But for now, it was time to go our separate ways for the last time, Pritt to Kay and Salomon's house and me and Aaron back home so I could get changed. Dad had come over the night before with the Campervan, and was staying at a campsite only ten minutes walk from where we lived. He arrived at our house minutes after we did and there was lots of hugging and kissing for a while, as he held me tight. He didn't say much, being the 'strong silent type', but I knew that he was so proud of me and I struggled to contain the tears that welled up. I gave him his buttonhole and he smiled when I showed him the wedding ribbon I had bought for the car. It was pale pink and had 'Pritt and Alison' on it, along with the date of our wedding all in a lovely fancy script.

"Papa", suddenly came a little voice, "Would you play on my playstation with me?"

Sensing a slight hesitation on Dad's part Aaron continued, "We could play a racing game if you like... Burnout 3."

I laughed to see the change in Dad as the thought of speed made up his mind for him. 'He's in for a shock, though,' I thought, 'because he'll be prepared for a track race, and Burnout 3 is on the roads... with traffic'. It was the only game of Aaron's that I had managed to beat him on occasionally, and that was only because I was determined to come in first and I was prepared to do whatever it took to win, including reverting back to my 'unsaved' days when I was a danger to myself and all other road users...and driving like a lunatic! I made Dad a coffee and left them sat side by side on the settee, controllers in hand, laughing quietly to myself as Dad bounced his way around the circuit like a pinball. Aaron was in his element: in the lead and in control – as usual!

I checked my watch. (Waiting is an art I am still learning.)

'Jennie should be here soon,' I mused, beginning to feel a little in limbo. She was coming over to help me dress, and had also stepped in to be my chauffer after the gentleman who had originally offered had managed to write his car off a week before the wedding. I thought back to the day I had called to ask her assistance.

"Yes I'd love to, me lovely," she had agreed instantly, "But I wish you'd asked me sooner."

"Why?" I enquired.

"Well, someone drove into our car" she began. I groaned, envisioning walking to the church in my wedding dress.

"So the garage has given us a courtesy car while they fix ours...a Jag." She continued. Wow! That's good news! I thought...

"So what's the problem?" I wanted to know.

"Well I didn't like it, so I gave it back yesterday and they gave me a different car."

I nearly cried. Well, I thought, as long as it's not a Reliant Robin or a Smart car, I'll be all right. I took deep breath.

"So what have you got, now?" I asked with great trepidation.

"A Range Rover..."

The doorbell rang and there was Jennie with a huge smile and open arms, ready for a hug. As usual, Aaron flung his PS2 controller down and launched himself into the space between us and managed to squeeze his hug in first. Armed with coffee, we disappeared upstairs, leaving Aaron and Dad back racing on the Playstation, and half an hour later we descended like a royal entourage (a small one!) and I was presented to my father, who looked suitably impressed and choked up.

"Time to go!" I sang, as we filed out of the house and made our way to the brand new Range Rover, now proudly displaying its wedding ribbon courtesy of my father. Gone were my wedding nerves and jitters; gone was the feeling of being in a dream;

all that was coursing through me now was excitement. You see, in doing the 'legal bit' at the Registry Office, all the pressure that one feels on the day was taken care of. The emotions that accompany a wedding had all surfaced one after the other that morning leaving me with nothing but sheer elation. Pritt and I were already married in the eyes of the Law, but as far as we were concerned we were not married before God until we had been blessed in the Church Service and I was aware that it was going to be a time of celebration, not solemnity.

We arrived at the church in good time – what was the point of making Pritt wait in suspense? We were already man and wife and I couldn't wait to see his face when he saw my beautiful wedding dress, as all he had known about it was that it was white and that I had pale pink accessories to match the flowers and his buttonhole. My bridesmaid, wearing a layered pale pink dress was waiting for me at the door, looking every inch a princess and next to her stood my two pageboys Aaron and his friend (her brother) who were wearing matching outfits of white shirts, powder blue waistcoats with matching cravats ... and school trousers. This they had thought rather a novelty, as being home-educated they never wore school uniform and had laughed and danced hilariously in the shop whilst trying them on, while Kay and I pretended not to know them.

The ceremony went without a hitch. Pastor Kenn had joked previously that as we would already be married by the time we arrived at the church, when he asked if anyone knew of any reason why we couldn't be joined in Holy Matrimony he wouldn't pause but just carry on talking, as it was going to be simply a formality.

"And," he had smiled, "If anyone does stand up at that point we will just usher them out of the building!"

I had almost chuckled with delight at the look on Pritt's face as he turned to see me walk down the aisle on the arm of my father, and I was very proud of Aaron as he and his friend, impeccably behaved, held our wedding rings for us. We said our vows before God under a 'Talit' canopy (Prayer Shawl) to signify that we were under the covering of God's blessing, which was held above our heads by four very able volunteers: Dad, Pastor Willie Fransch, Salomon and one of Pritt's brothers. Aaron proudly read a passage of Scripture and looked so adorable that all the mums became rather misty-eyed, but there wasn't a dry eye in the church when my new husband took centre stage, picked up his guitar and sang Cliff Richard's "You, Me and Jesus" to me. Pritt never went anywhere without his guitar, a habit he still has, and I had joked on more than one occasion that I could visualise me saying,

"I now take thee, Pritt and thy guitar to be my lawful wedded husband…"

It's just slightly worrying how close I came to it!

Pritt was amazed to find his entire family had travelled from many places to be at his wedding and he silently thanked God for making his day even more special. He had only invited one brother, who lived in London, thinking that the other siblings would not be able to come at such short notice, as they were scattered countrywide and abroad. But two weeks before the wedding he had received a phone call.

"They are all coming." His brother informed him.

"Who is?" Pritt asked

"The family."

Pritt looked at me, shocked. He hadn't seen most of them for nearly twenty years and they were quite a large family.

"All of them?"

"Yes, I phoned them all and they are coming."

And so apart from one sister living in America who was unwell and could not make it over, they descended on our little seaside town from Scotland, Kent, Cambridgeshire, America and Turkey, some with their children; and I got to meet them all in one fell swoop. I loved them all instantly and felt very 'approved of', which was a blessing. They were all very different in some ways, with diverse accents, depending on where they lived – something I marvel at to this day – and personalities, but a common thread which ran through them was creativity. This family was full of singers, artists, actors, songwriters, musicians, poets, scientists, teachers and designers and they all had a desire to succeed in everything they did with an almost stubborn refusal to give up. I laughed when I realised what God had done. I had married into a family of 'can-do attitudes'!

I had looked round as I entered the church and had spotted Sharon and Pablo, who had recently moved to London, with their children, and my cousin who had travelled from West Sussex with her family. But it wasn't until we emerged after the ceremony into the bright sunshine for the photographs, that I really saw just how many people had come and by the end of the day I was overwhelmed by the sheer dedication of our friends and family who wanted to be part of our special day. Half the congregation from Pastor Willie's church in London had come; the entire local Foursquare Church was there, along with some of my fellow Timothy Course Graduates and half of the Close where I lived. We even had a guest from Pritt's (and Pastor Willie's) previous church in Guernsey, who we had both known from our 'Pilgrims' days. He had been visiting another friend in London who had also known us from 'Pilgrims', and they came together. It was a blast from the past, seeing the two of them together again and it honestly felt more like a reunion at times than a wedding!

"Look at that huge pile of strawberries" I exclaimed, my eyes wide as I viewed the two rows of tables groaning under the weight of a sumptuous banquet, topped off by a massive display of hundreds of strawberries. The photographs done, we had filed into the lower hall of the church for the Reception to find that Kay and her helpers had surpassed themselves organising the buffet, while the abundance of food reminded me that God was indeed taking care of every detail of our day.

"I think I picked about a hundred of them." Pritt whispered in my ear. As he had been staying with Kay and Salomon before the wedding he had been taken with them on their outing to a local 'pick-your-own' farm and set to work gathering the strawberries, just like the kids, only he didn't eat as many on the way round!

"I really enjoyed it," he admitted, taking my hand under the table and drawing me close. The variety of food was astounding, with cheese and crackers, fresh ham and salad, fruit, crisps and pizza...and the mountain of strawberries, and a gentle hum descended on the room as we gave thanks and tucked in.

Chink! Chink! Chink!

All private chat was interrupted as Salomon stood to his feet and tapped the side of his glass. I winced, waiting for the glass to break. Toasts were made, speeches were said and key people thanked, and then my Dad also stood to his feet. My father is a man of deep thoughts and few words and I held my breath, wondering what he was going to say. His previous wedding speeches had been quite short and what was usually expected at a wedding, but today I could see by the way he was holding himself that something different was on the agenda. He began by toasting Pritt and I and wishing us happiness for the future and then he reached into his pocket and pulled out a piece of paper and proceeded to read a poem that he had written especially for the occasion. It was simple and heartfelt, showing me that my father really approved of my choice of husband and I had trouble keeping my emotions in check, although one or two tears did escape.

We cut the cake and I giggled as I was reminded, as we posed for some photos, of something my friend Patricia had shared with me from her own wedding a few years earlier.

"When we cut the cake," she had laughed, " we were told to do an unusual pose, so I grabbed the knife and held it up behind him, blade down- like in a horror movie. It made a great photo!"

Finally it was time to leave our guests and make our way home as Mr and Mrs. I had been disappointed that the Rehab Centre had not been able to bring down some of the residents, as I knew they really wanted to come, but they relied on the Church minibus that Pastor Willie had used to bring his congregation down in and they been unable to secure alternative transport. Mind you, when I had seen them just three days earlier, after driving up for the final time to collect Pritt, I had honoured my promise that I would not leave them empty handed, and left them quite content.

"We're going to miss having Pritt around here," one of the guys had said to me on the visit before, while I was packing yet another suitcase and microphone stand into the back of my car.

"Well, you can't keep him" I had teased, "He's mine!"

We had laughed and then he had turned to go back to the house, when he stopped.

"I'm going to miss your flapjacks too." He added, a twinkle in his eye. I grinned, remembering the huge tin of homemade flapjacks I had come armed with on one visit, which had not lasted for more than five minutes, especially when this guy had found them.

"Tell you what," I suggested, "how about when I come back on Wednesday, I swap Pritt for another tin of my flapjacks?"

"Done!" he said, and ran into the house rubbing his hands together.

"But they'll be for everyone!" I called after him, aware that my stipulation had fallen on deaf ears and the others probably wouldn't even know flapjacks had entered their vicinity, let alone get to eat one! So four days later, when I had arrived to collect my most precious cargo yet – Pritt – I handed over my king's ransom – and then proceeded to inform everyone I saw that there were flapjacks in the kitchen, much to the delight of most of the residents and the disgust of just one.

'All in all,' I thought to myself, looking at my new husband as we left the reception and were driven back to our home in the Range Rover, 'It was a fair swap, and I got the better end of the bargain!'

Chapter 27
GUERNSEY WEETABIX

"Are we nearly there yet?

I glanced out of the campervan window at the sparsely vegetated landscape known as the New Forest and shook my head. The ferry port of Poole was quite a few miles away.

"Nope," I acknowledged, leaning back in my seat and smiling at Pritt. "We're about two thirds of the way there."

Aaron gave an audible sigh from the front passenger seat and turned to my Dad, who was driving.

"Can we have some music on, Papa?" he asked, reaching for the CD player before waiting for an answer. The campervan was suddenly filled with the Elvis Presley singing "Peace in the Valley" and Pritt and I smiled and began to sing along.

"Oh no, not Elvis," Aaron cried, but on it stayed, as he was outnumbered three to one. I saw Dad raise an eyebrow in his rear-view mirror as Aaron sat back in his seat, grumbling, and wondered what sort of time we were going to have in Guernsey. Yes, we were embarking on our honeymoon, and as Mum had decided that she wouldn't child–mind, and I wasn't going to inflict my best friend Kay with an adolescent boy for a week, (she'd already looked after him for our honeymoon night)... he was coming with us.

Dad had suggested that as he had come over for the wedding in the campervan, it would be cheaper for us to travel back with him on the ferry as car passengers, and then return as foot passengers a week later, ending the journey home by train. This had indeed worked out cheaper and so two days after our wedding, we found ourselves being chauffeured along the South Coast, listening to Elvis with a sulky twelve year old!

"But don't worry," Pritt had promised, "When Aaron gets married, we'll return the favour and accompany him on his honeymoon!" a comment which earned him a scathing look from the young man concerned and a stifled giggle from me!

"You have really got to try this!" Pritt said to Dad enthusiastically, as he motioned me to empty the bag I had just put under the table. We were finally on the ferry and we both grinned as we watched Dad's face while the contents of the bag were spread out over the table. Houmous, olive oil, crackers, a spoon, paper plates and a home-made herb mixture made mainly from Hyssop, which we called 'Houmous Heaven' were taken, one by one, from the bag and proudly displayed. Dad looked intrigued.

"This is something I loved to eat in the Middle East," Pritt explained, as he spread the houmous onto the plate and began to make a large 'well' in the centre. He picked up the bottle of olive oil and began to pour some into the well. Dad's eyes grew larger as he watched the well being filled to the brim and I could almost read the thoughts running around in his head and screaming 'Oh my goodness, that is an oil slick!'

I caught Pritt's eye and he chuckled. He was used to this reaction – it happened every time!

"It doesn't taste at all oily." I enlightened Dad as Pritt sprinkled the Houmous Heaven generously all over the houmous, creating what looked like a dark green lid on a flat wet cement volcano. Looking rather unconvinced, Dad picked up a cracker and tentatively scraped at the edge of the plate.

"No, no" admonished Pritt, mixing the houmous, oil and Houmous Heaven together into a greenish looking splodge in the plate, "You have to mix it and take a dollop!"

Looking even less convinced Dad scooped a miniscule amount onto his cracker and popped it into his mouth. We waited.

"Mmmmmm" was all we heard for the next ten minutes, as his scoops grew larger, and the houmous rapidly disappeared. Pritt and I smiled at each other...we had another convert.

Settling back in my seat to enjoy the trip I felt Pritt's hand reach for mine and sighed contentedly as my fingers became wrapped up in his. Aaron had been given permission to wander around the ship and had disappeared, probably to find some food. It seemed I had only just closed my eyes when I felt myself being gently shaken.

"We're here." Pritt pointed out of the window at the pretty island rising out of the sea. The water sparkled like a thousand silver pennies on blue silk and the familiar outline of the hills to the south, the Town Church spire, the Victoria Tower and the Elizabeth College brought a lump to my throat: I was home. Aaron finally returned, munching something that smelt remotely like burger, as the tannoy announcement sent us scuttling down the stairs towards the hold, ready to sit in our vehicle and choke on the exhaust fumes of seventy-plus cars starting their engines immediately after the next announcement, which specifically requested them not to.

As we disembarked, however, I was shocked by the changes that had happened since I had last been to the island. Gone was the Royal Hotel, which admittedly had been rather an eyesore after fire had gutted it, and in its place was a huge glass modern monstrosity of banks and offices.

"They could have kept in keeping with the rest of the seafront" I complained, "Especially when there are so many quaint buildings here."

Disgruntled, I sat back in my seat as we headed towards the North end of the island and I found myself staring idly out of the window at the scenery. My eyes swept from left to right, looking for the familiar Bougourd Brothers Garage and the Fruit Export Garden Centre that dominated the main stretch on the seafront between St Peter Port and St Sampsons. They weren't there. Startled, I sat bolt upright and stared. No, none of it was there... just more modern offices and a supermarket that looked like it had come from the film set of Back To The Future 2. I was gutted. What had happened to my pretty little island?

"Well, it looks to me as if they have built it in keeping with the rest of the seafront." My husband said drily, his eyes daring me to laugh. Thankfully, as we drove inland, I was relieved to see that only the seafront had been changed: Guernsey was still Guernsey.

Our honeymoon suite was perfect. Dad had built the self-contained flat around and over his garage and it was upside-down. The lounge, with wide windows that gave a panoramic view of the lowlands of the North, along with Alderney and a glimpse of France, was built on top of the garage, while the bedroom, bathroom and kitchen nestled snugly against the garage wall. Aaron was to sleep upstairs in the lounge, and Dad had cordoned off a corner of the room to make it feel more like a bedroom.

"Let's go out for a walk," suggested Pritt, after we had unpacked. Glancing out of the window at the rooftops bathing in the afternoon sunshine, the fields full of lush green grass and the sea shining beyond I readily agreed, ignoring the look of despair Aaron was throwing my way.

Guernsey roads are very narrow with most footpaths only wide enough for one person to walk on at a time, and usually on one side of the road only. This made a romantic walk very difficult, as we had to walk in single file holding hands or risk one of us being run over or the other being squashed into a hedge or a wall. Aaron decided to walk ahead of us. Not the cleverest idea he had ever had as he had no idea where we were going and we spent much of our time calling him back so we could take shortcuts through winding leafy lanes, past quaint Guernsey granite cottages where the familiar strong smelling, brightly coloured mesembryanthemums that grew on the hedges made me inhale deeply in wonder.

"Wow, Lord," I breathed. I had forgotten how beautiful Guernsey really was and I suddenly knew that I had been very privileged to grow up here.

Watching Aaron march on ahead, oblivious to the beauty around him, I began to pray. I knew he was having a hard time with all the changes and my constant prayer was that he would be able to see how necessary they were. I was not so naïve as to be unaware of tensions between Aaron and Pritt, as I knew Aaron saw himself as the man of the house and head of the home, despite my admonishing to the contrary, and now his self-worth was being threatened. My heart went out to him as I could see his struggles, but I was also aware that this was something that he had to get straight in his own head before he could move on. I prayed that it would not take long, but knowing my stubborn son as I did, I did not hold out much hope of a swift paradigm shift, short of an intervening miracle of Red Sea proportions.

We spent a couple of hours at Sausmerez Park, with it's wide open spaces, duck pond, play area, tea room and museum and then as the clouds began to gather, we headed for home intent on beating the rain. We didn't make it...and arrived back at the flat looking like drowned rats. Later that evening, when the rain had washed the sky clean and the garden was smelling new and perfumed, Dad and his girlfriend, Rose, invited us up to the house for a barbeque, something that quickly became a daily habit and Pritt brought his guitar and sang some Beatles and Elvis numbers. This quickly established itself as the entertainment at the barbeques and became part of the evening ritual, as did the Houmous and Houmous Heaven, which was eaten with Pizza, Barbequed Chicken, chips and anything else that could be dipped in any way!

The weather became more changeable as the week progressed but that didn't dampen our spirits. We decided we would like to spring a surprise visit on George Torode, who had run Pilgies with Pritt many years ago, and now lived just around the corner from Dad. He had recently undergone heart surgery and we both felt that it was important that we see him. Neither of us knew just how important. Aaron had heard so much about him that he was intrigued about meeting this larger than life character that had made such an impact on both Pritt's life and mine in the past. We had no idea when he would be in so we decided to ask the 'oracle'... Dad.

"Do you know if George is home during the day?" I asked him the next morning, after he had popped in for a coffee. Aaron was, as usual, wrapped around him like a Boa Constrictor and I realised by the look on my father's face that this was probably the real reason for the visit.

"Yes, I think he is when he's not working at Guernsey Radio, although he often has hospital appointments. Why?"

As I explained I could see Dad thinking hard. Suddenly he smiled, picked up the phone and dialled a number. We heard a muffled 'hello' as the phone was answered the other end and then my dad winked at us.

"Hello, Mon Vieux!" he cheerily greeted the recipient in the time-old Guernsey fashion. "What time are you in today, only I could do with popping round to see you?"

Pritt and I heard some unintelligible noises and looked at each other perplexed.

"Okay, see you at half twelve then. Cheerio!" Dad replaced the receiver and turned to us. "There you go," he announced, smiling broadly, "Now you have an appointment!"

Dad and George's friendship spanned way back to their teenage years. At Pilgies, George had often told the story of when, as a young teen, one of his favourite pastimes would be to hold onto the back of a mate's motorbike with his feet through the handles of two metal dustbin lids they raced down the central white line in St Julian's Avenue, a wide road which snakes down to the Harbour in the Town Centre. The resulting noise was deafening but the sparks, which flew in all directions, were in a class of their own and would have rivalled any Bonfire Night display. That was the fun bit ... but then he had to ditch the bin-lids, jump onto the back of the bike and take off before the police turned up! Sharing the story and laughing with Dad one day many years later, I was surprised when he remarked,

"Yes, I remember those days."

"Oh," said I, in all innocence, "Did you know about this then?"

"Oh yes," his eyes twinkled mischievously, "I was the 'mate' who rode the bike!"

"Do you think he knows?" I asked Pritt at twenty-five past twelve, as he, Aaron and I rounded the top of Dad's road like three little guinea pigs, all one behind the other on the narrow pavement. Pritt shook his head.

"No," he said confidently. I hoped he was right. Our friend who had come over from Guernsey to our wedding had been sworn to secrecy, only being allowed to tell George that Pritt had got married – but not to whom. Well, he could say it was to an 'Alison,' but not to which one…and we couldn't wait to see his face! As we turned off the footpath into his driveway, we saw a figure emerge from the garden shed at the corner of the front garden and the crunching of our feet on the gravel made him look up. He nodded in greeting and continued to walk to his front door, as Pritt and I stopped and stood hand in hand, grinning like two Cheshire Cats with Aaron beside us. We watched as George did a double take and turned slowly around as if he had only just barely registered - and didn't believe - what his eyes had just seen. His gaze swept from Pritt to me and back again as the realisation dawned on him who Pritt had married and we laughed with delight as his face lit up and he rushed to meet us, embracing us in bear hugs.

We introduced him to Aaron and he invited us in for a quick cup of tea.

"Only I've got an appointment at twelve-thirty," he explained regretfully.

We nodded innocently.

"Actually, it's with your Dad," he expounded, turning to me.

"Yes, we know," I enlightened him, "We were at his house when he called you. He wanted to make sure you were in when we came round to see you."

"You mean...?" he spluttered as we all grinned foolishly at him.

"Yep, we are your twelve thirty appointment!"

I think it needs to be recorded that it is probably the one and only time, in all the years that I have known George, that he was lost for words.

As we sat down to enjoy our coffee, while his wife filled Aaron up with cold drinks and biscuits, George rushed back out to his shed and returned looking triumphant with an old VCR 'video' cassette in his hand.

"I was just looking for this when you arrived." He shook his head, incredulous... looking at us and still amazed at what he was seeing.

"God knew you were coming!" he laughed. We were nonplussed. What did he have on that video? We didn't have too long to wait to find out as he inserted it into the video player and excitedly pressed 'play' on the remote control.

It was our turn to be speechless as we watched a typical Pilgies night emerge on the TV screen, and we were transported back in time to the night when, knowing that Pilgrims nightclub's days were numbered, George had brought a video recorder with him on a Friday night. We laughed at our 1980 hairstyles, shed a tear or two for old friends who had passed away, recalled old friendships long forgotten, and joined in with the singing. It was just like a Pilgies night and even Aaron joined in with "This little light of mine".

"Oh my goodness!" I wailed and hid my face in my hands as a close-up shot of two people came on screen. Without accompaniment of any description George and I had looked straight at the camera and begun to sing the Pilgies song I had written with my sister all those many years ago. I had completely forgotten that I had performed the duet with George on that night but now seeing it on the video, all the emotions and memories came to the surface and exploded in a burst of nostalgia that culminated in us all (Aaron included) singing along.

One year later, when George went home to Glory, Pritt and I looked back on our visit with thankful hearts. God knew it would be the last time we would see George in this life and He blessed us by making it such a special time that we would always remember. Incidentally, Guernsey Radio, in an unprecedented move, decided to broadcast George's entire funeral live to an island-wide audience. He had been a very funny, popular author and radio presenter, making no secret of his faith in Jesus – or apologies for that matter, and the whole island had been stunned to hear of his death.

It is amazing how God will always bring good out of every situation, and in this case it was the sight of two hundred and fifty plus people turning up at a church that seated fifty to say farewell to this man every Guernseyman felt he knew personally...the Mission Hall Minister preaching the Gospel, including an altar call, for two and a half hours...and the radio station broadcasting God's word into practically every home of the sixty-five thousand plus population. I have often wondered since if George made more of an impact for the Kingdom of God in people's lives after his death than during his lifetime. Certainly many people were touched by the qualities of Jesus that he demonstrated in his daily life and I believe there will be many more who will seek God's face because of what they heard at his funeral. One day I will find out.

The week passed by remarkably fast. People recognised Pritt everywhere we went and "Are you back?" was the much asked question. I, on the other hand, was recognised by... nobody!

We went to St Peter Port, the main shopping centre: "Peter! Are you back?"

We went to my former church: " Peter! Are you back?"

We walked along the road: "Peter! Are you back?"

One day a taxi slowed down as it passed us and the window wound down. The driver leaned across the passenger seat. Surely it wasn't going to happen again, I thought, feeling slightly miffed.

"Peter!" she said, "I thought it was you! Are you back?" Aaargh!

Then it dawned on me. Pritt still looked the very recognisable person he had been when he had left the Island to go abroad. I, on the other hand, looked nothing like I used to. Oh well, I mused; I will just have to get used to being introduced to my old acquaintances as if I am a stranger!

The congregation at Spurgeon Baptist Church, where Pritt had attended before leaving for the Middle East, surprised us with an impromptu reception, with food, cards, hugs and well-wishes. We were amazed by their generosity and old friendships were renewed with mobile phone numbers and email addresses being exchanged. One lady, who had been at my former church with me and had attended the same home group for many years, was now going to Spurgeon, and after the initial "Peter! Are you back?" she turned to introduce herself to me.

"This is my wife, Alison" Pritt said, drawing me close.

She greeted me and gave me a hug. Then she frowned. She looked at me hard.

"Alison..." she thought out loud. I got excited. I nodded. Someone knows me! Oh, but wait...

"Alison..." she repeated, studying me. Again I nodded. "Yes" I confirmed.

"Alison..." she was looking perplexed now, as she searched my face. I couldn't help smiling at how ludicrous this was becoming. "Yeeees" I verified

"Alison..." Still she looked puzzled. Eventually, I saw the light dawn on her face as recognition finally kicked in.

"Alison!" she blurted triumphantly.

"Yes!" I blurted back, in relief. She looked at Pritt, then back to me. Back to Pritt and back to me.

"You… and… you…married…?" Incredulous now was her look, as she shook her head in wonderment.

"Yes!" we both said. And we laughed.

We dined out at St Pierre Park Hotel, the island's most exclusive hotel, for Sunday Lunch, while Dad and Rose took Aaron to the beach where they stuffed themselves with Pizza – Aaron's idea of heaven! We visited friends, churches, the old Pilgies site (for Aaron's benefit) and Aaron and Pritt went rock climbing at the Bathing Pools: I walked nonchalantly up the steps and waited for them at the top without breaking into a sweat – well, I had my street 'cred' to think about! We ate in, we ate out and we ate at Dad's barbeques. We ate late, we ate early, we ate lunch at teatime and tea at lunchtime…. and we ate breakfast. Ah…breakfast…

"Ah…ah…ATCHOO!" Pritt and I looked up in time to see Aaron, sat at the breakfast table with his Weetabix in a bowl in front of him. He had sneezed so violently that he had sounded like a horse blowing and had probably sprayed his germs across the island and the English Channel to Jersey. He stared at his breakfast for a couple of seconds and then he shrugged his shoulders, picked up his spoon and began to eat.

"Eeuw!" Pritt looked at me and screwed his nose up, "That's disgusting!"

Eager to move on and not dwell too much on what Aaron was possibly spooning into his mouth, I turned and began to prepare toast for the two of us, as neither of us could bring ourselves to eat Weetabix now. Later that morning, as we were preparing to go out there came another tremendous explosion from Aaron upstairs.

"Ah…ah…ah…ah…ATCHOO!" and the windows and doors rattled as the hurricane force sneeze bounced around the walls. Aaron was silent for a moment.

"Uh...Pritt," his voice finally floated down the stairs.

"Yes, Aaron," Pritt responded.

"Uh...could you get me a hanky please? I've just sneezed – (as if we didn't know) - and my hands are really wet and sticky now."

Pritt burst into peals of laughter and his shoulders began shaking.

"Well" he spluttered in between taking a breath, "Now you know what went into your Weetabix!..............."

Chapter 28
FOOTPRINTS IN THE SAND

All too soon it was time to board the ferry and return to Mainland Britain. It was hard. Pritt and I had reminisced so much that we felt we were back home and neither of us wanted to re-enter 'normal' life for a while yet. Aaron, although he didn't have the same ties to this beautiful corner of the British Empire as Pritt and I, still didn't want to leave his granddad, and so it was an emotional parting. The weather was glorious and the return ferry crossing was as calm as the outward journey. The return home via train was not so smooth as a couple of our trains were cancelled and so instead of a leisurely journey with two or three changes, we had to make our way across the South of England at a gallop: train-hopping with luggage (including the guitar), running across platforms, over bridges, and through underpasses and reaching each connecting train with seconds to spare, whilst trying to figure out which station we needed to change at next. We arrived home exhausted...and very late.

Over the next year or so, many things happened...some good and some not. Life at home was often tempestuous as Aaron struggled with the reality of having a father, and Home Education became a battle of wills as Pritt and I sought to address those issues that I had struggled with in relation to Aaron's schooling and attitude towards learning. Aaron still has his own issues to this day ...but this is my story, not his. Maybe when we have come out the other side of the present tunnel, I will write a sequel and God's hand will be seen plainly and miraculously in the healing and restoration that I believe He is working in all our lives.

Not long after we were married I was sitting at the keyboard, writing a new song, when Pritt came into the room.

"I like it" he announced, adding, "Why don't we record it?"

Shocked, I turned to stare at him. Record? My song?

"Do you still have all the songs that you've written?" he asked. I nodded.

"Well, have a look through them and see if any jump out at you. Maybe we can record an album." He carried on speaking but I heard nothing. I was still stunned. After many years, those songs borne out of "mountaintop" and "valley" experiences; from times of growing and times of yearning; from either sitting at Jesus feet in worship or returning to His arms in repentance; from declarations of His power and might to looking forward to His return: those songs were going to be shared and possibly, just possibly they might touch another in need of a word from God. I started to get excited.

As we began to work on the first song I realised that I had married an extremely talented musician. There is an anointing on my husband's musicianship that is tangible and I pray he remains humble enough to let it continue for God's glory. A year later, after many gruelling nights singing till I was hoarse and exhausted, but still continuing until we were both happy with what had been produced, my debut CD "The Wonder" was finished...or so I thought. Pritt had spent many hours, sometimes whole days, locked in the studio playing until each song became part of him and what had come forth from those sessions was truly amazing. I still listen to the CD and have to pinch myself. It really is us! But once all the tracks were down, the real work began in earnest for him, as he is also the sound engineer. Days and weeks melded into months as he mixed, re-mixed, tweaked and re-tweaked. We wanted a natural sound, with as little reverb and echo as possible, and this meant that sometimes I was called back to re-record a song. Wanting the best sound we could have, we had made a decision early on that we would not cut and splice bits into songs – if a mistake was made, it was back to the beginning and start again – a decision I bitterly regretted many times – but not when I heard the finished product!

One morning, as I was Home-Schooling Aaron, my mobile

informed me that I had been sent a text. During break, I checked it to find that it was from Sharon, Pritt's niece.

"Are you still looking for a piano?" she asked. I replied that I was.

"Well, my friend who lives just round the corner from you is moving and wants to give hers away. Give her a call, here's her number...."

Ten minutes later Pritt, Aaron and I were standing outside the house, knocking on the door. The door was opened and we were ushered into a really long dark hallway where an upright piano stood, half hidden in the corner, surrounded by moving boxes. We couldn't really see much of it in the gloomy light and it was terribly out of tune, as it hadn't been touched for years. I fell in love with it anyway, and after arranging for a local removal firm to collect it, went home to re-arrange my lounge and place my piano stool in the right place.

When the piano was delivered a couple of days later, I was astounded. The wood colouring on the piano matched my stool, and the design of the legs on both matched.

"Wow!" I breathed, "Thank You Lord!"

Now I knew that this was my new piano. We arranged for a tuner to come out who informed us that our 'new' piano was, in fact, 120 years old!

"But," he informed us, "It will never play at concert pitch. It is half a tone out, and that's a lot. If I tune it to concert pitch it may damage the piano ... and even if it didn't, it wouldn't keep true to pitch."

After he left, Pritt smiled at me and opened up the lid.

"Hmmm. We'll see." He said thoughtfully. Days later, I came home from work to find my piano in bits as Pritt and Aaron hoovered, scrubbed and polished it inside and out. The strings were rusty so they attacked them with a wire brush (which all the 'experts' tell you never to do) and the sound brightened up considerably. It was a start.

"Alison," Pritt announced a week later, "I've been looking at these strings and I reckon I could tune this piano to concert pitch. It doesn't look all that different to tuning the guitar- I just need a tuning fork. Do you mind if I have a go?"

I nodded, although I felt a little dubious. After all, the 'expert' said that it couldn't be done, and I didn't want my piano to be ruined... not after waiting for so long to get it. So the hunt began, and after many phone calls and visits to music shops we finally found a trade supplier (in Kent) who was happy to sell us a tuning fork, which incidentally looks nothing like a fork and suspiciously more like a spanner! A few days later, after a lovely drive through the pretty Kent countryside to collect it, we arrived back home and Pritt set to work. He tweaked and listened... tweaked a bit more and listened again. I watched, spellbound, as he used the guitar tuner to get one octave in tune and then tuned the rest of the piano by ear, using that one octave as the plumbline. It took him a while, but before too many weeks were gone, not only did I have a piano with a really rich sound... it was at concert pitch! And there it stayed.

I was in seventh heaven! Every available moment I was found sitting at the piano playing my songs, and writing new ones. Aaron began to learn to play as part of school and picked it up really easily, and when he or I weren't sat there, Pritt would manage to commandeer the piano stool and play some of his favourite Keith Green songs. Today I am still writing songs on this piano, which only needs the odd tweak to remain at concert pitch, and we are beginning to work on a second album in addition to the songs that Pritt writes and records in his own right. When I suggested to Aaron that maybe he could add his drumming skills to my new album, he rubbed his hands together like Fagin from "Oliver Twist" and said "Hmmm, Royalties!"

Kids!

Weekends began to change for me at this time, as we decided

to keep the Biblical Sabbath on a Saturday. Pritt had kept his Sabbath on Saturdays whilst he was in the Middle East and although he had continued to do so once he was back in the UK, it wasn't something that I had thought much about. He suggested that we keep it as a family and it quickly became my favourite part of the week as all our days began to point towards Friday night/Saturday morning. It felt a little strange at first, as it was alien to my previous way of life, and some of the preparation was done in another language, but it rapidly became very special to me, until I could not imagine a Friday night without praying for our families, preparing something special for tea, speaking blessings over each other and thanking God for His day of rest. When, as part of the Friday evening mealtime, Pritt held my hands and spoke Proverbs 31 over me, emotions welled up within me like nothing I had ever experienced before. Here was my husband, telling me in a very special way that he respected me, honoured me and that I blessed him by being his wife, and I felt extremely humbled by it all... and as the weeks went by I found that I was beginning to become more and more like the wife that Proverbs 31 described, for God's Word has power that is not of this world, and it will always accomplish that which it sets out to do.

Later on I found a recipe for 'Challah', the official Sabbath bread, and made it as a surprise, resulting in my husband having the biggest grin on his face all evening as he well and truly tucked in... which then resulted in me making it every week since! We decided that if we were to have a day of rest, then we were going to do it properly, and not do any shopping, or work of any kind, save cooking (and that was only if we felt like it!). The alarm clock was given the day off too and we began to spend our Saturday afternoons going for walks. The computer was switched off, as were the mobile phones (apart from Aaron's – have you ever tried to get a teenager to switch off their phone?) and peace descended on our home.

At the end of our first Sabbath, Pritt asked me how I felt about it now that I had experienced it.

"Wow!" I exclaimed. A raised eyebrow in response indicated he wanted a little more embellishment.

"I feel really rested, " I explained, "Probably because subconsciously I know that I have absolutely nothing that I need to do. No housework, no shopping, no phoning call centres to sort out bills and no banking! It can all wait until Monday. "

Even the car had a day off as we didn't have to go anywhere or do anything and it was liberating! It was such a blessing to just 'be' and contrary to what some may think, it wasn't at all legalistic, just good.

"The sad thing is though," I added, "That most people don't realise that this is how it should be, because they think it's a Jewish thing like I used to, and so they miss out. But it's not, it's a God thing, and it doesn't matter how busy I am during the week, because I know that come Friday night, the world gets switched off and I have twenty-four hours of total rest!"

"And do you know something else?" Pritt asked. I waited, expectantly.

"You can have your 'sabbath' on any other day of the week," he continued, "But it doesn't feel the same. When your Sabbath is on the seventh day of the week, somehow the food tastes different, and the feel of the day is different, and you don't just feel rested, you feel refreshed."

And all I could do was agree.

Changes mostly happen gradually but sometimes they burst into our lives with a jolt. I have had many of both kinds, but by far the most amazing thing that has happened in the past few years is that I have finally come to a place where I can stand and see the paths that God has brought me on, and how those experiences have not just changed me, but shaped me, moulded me, and released me.

One day my son will grow up and start out on an adventure of his own. My prayer is that he will learn his life lessons quickly and grow in wisdom to be the man of God that his Creator saw at the beginning of time, for before he was made in my womb God knew him. And I pray that he will love his wife with the same protective, encouraging, nurturing, all-or-nothing love that I experience from Pritt, truly loving her as Christ loves the Church and releasing her in all her potential to be the best that she can be.

I have learnt that I am valuable as a person, both to my husband and to God. After many years of searching for acceptance I have found that God accepts me as I am and helps me to improve, something that will never cease this side of Heaven. And I am enjoying the journey... no; I have given myself permission to enjoy the journey. Life does not have to make me a victim and I do not have to accept the limitations set for me by other people, whoever and whatever they are. God's plans for me are good, for He wants to give me hope and a future, so I choose His plans above all others, for I firmly believe that He will work all things for the good of all who trust in Him, and when the times get hard, He will carry me through.

This book may be at an end, but my journey still has far to go, for God's plans for me include my husband, my soul mate who is at my side constantly encouraging me to reach for the stars and reminding me that in Christ I can truly do all things. My heart has found a place of safety where I am free to give my love to another without fear, a place where I can love abundantly, for I know that he too follows the Creator's plans and that together, with Jesus at the centre, we have many more adventures awaiting us.

Someone once said:

"Until you know who you are you will always be a shadow of who others want you to be."

God in His mercy sought me and never gave up until He found me and now that I have found myself in Him, I can finally say that I truly am...

GLAD TO BE ME

Going Home

*Dreaming in a dream in which I saw two set of prints
along the shore
One was mine, the other yours: this is what I saw
Side by side, living, living in joy
And not being alone, and not being alone*

*Where were you when my trials came? One set of prints
is all I saw
'I'm alone!' I cried, 'You've left me on my own'
And my tears met the sea
By the seashore, by the seashore*

*In a little voice the answer came - deep inside, so near,
yet so far away
'The footprints in the sand you saw were Mine, and they
were Mine alone
I carried you with love; I carried you through
Through storm, through tempest I carried you through
To carry you home, to carry you home*

*In a little voice the answer came- deep inside, so near,
yet so far away
'The footprints in the sand you saw were Mine, as I carried
you through your trial time
I carried you with love; I carried you through
Through storm, through tempest I carried you through
To carry you home, to carry you home*

*To carry you home
To carry you home*

Lyrics and Music by Pritt Sehmi
©Copyright JMY Music 1985 All rights reserved. Used by permission
Inspired by 'Footprints' poem